Forgiv

Forgiveness in Perspective

Edited by
Christopher R. Allers and Marieke Smit

Amsterdam - New York, NY 2010

The paper on which this book is printed meets the requirements of "ISO 9706:1994, Information and documentation - Paper for documents - Requirements for permanence".

ISBN: 978-90-420-2995-8
E-Book ISBN: 978-90-420-2996-5
©Editions Rodopi B.V., Amsterdam - New York, NY 2010
Printed in the Netherlands

Table of Contents

Acknowledgments

This book is the result of Inter-Disciplinary.Net's 2nd Global Conference 'Forgiveness: Probing the Boundaries,' which took place in Salzburg, Austria in March 2009. The conference was organised by Rob Fisher, David White and Nancy Billias. We would like to thank them for their work. We would also like to thank all the participants of this conference, especially the authors who contributed to this book. Their work gives us a good look at the diversity of forgiveness. Also, we would like to thank our families.

Christopher R. Allers
Marieke Smit

Introduction

Putting Forgiveness in Perspective: Some First Words, No Last Word

Christopher R. Allers and Marieke Smit

In a world of great atrocities – war, terrorism, genocide, violence – and quotidian wrongdoings, the victimized people of the world long for a response to the evil and violence, pain and suffering, death and destruction meted out upon them. Some victims look to even the score, as it were, and respond by seeking revenge and restitution, vengeance and retribution, or other more or less tit-for-tat, eye-for-eye reactions aimed at balancing the scales of justice understood as equivalence. While others tread a different path – the path of forgiveness.[1] What is this path of forgiveness? How and why should we tread it? It seems that today everyone has something to say about forgiveness – it is a ware championed by many a peddler – and it is a word bandied about without much accountability, used and abused without a second thought. In the cacophony of claims made about forgiveness, we hope this book serves to aid in an effort to put forgiveness in perspective.

Forgiveness is a perplexing and enigmatic concept. However, by employing the copula 'is' and the word 'concept,' we may already be making things too easy for ourselves, stacking the deck in favour of a certain metaphysical definition of forgiveness that attempts to say what forgiveness 'is' (and by implication what it 'is not') and, furthermore, to reduce forgiveness to a concept (whatever that may mean). Nevertheless, there may be something to the statement 'forgiveness is a concept' (but we should remember that forgiveness is not just a concept). Take, for example, the concept 'blue' or 'beautiful.' Particular things may be blue (such as a blue crayon or the ocean) and beautiful (such as your partner or your children or the ceiling of the Sistine Chapel), but things are always blue or beautiful in different ways. Furthermore, there will always be future, indeterminate, and unknown ways of being blue and beautiful that we have not experienced yet. That is, these concepts exceed any particular determinations of them; they will always be determinable in different ways and cannot be exhausted. Nevertheless, they can only really be known in their determinations. While they cannot be exhausted by particular manifestations, they are also dependent on these manifestations in order to appear at all.[2]

The same is true of forgiveness. We may haggle over definitions, but we still call very disparate events 'forgiveness' – a mother forgiving a child after the child has done wrong, a Jew forgiving a German who was not even alive during the Holocaust, a representative of one nation-state forgiving the actions of another nation-state, a bank forgiving a loan, when someone forgives someone else after various conditions are met (such as asking for forgiveness or one apologizes, or one repents or one understands that what they did is wrong or one commits to never doing it again, among others) or even when one forgives when none of these conditions are met, etc.. This 'etc.' is important. There are many other ways to forgive and there will always be future, indeterminate, and unknown ways of forgiving. This 'etc.' signifies that there is no 'last word' on what counts as forgiveness, and we should not be satisfied with choosing one particular determination at the expense of all others, calling that determination 'forgiveness' *tout court*, and then proceeding to sit comfortably in our furniture, stretching our legs in self-satisfaction, self-assured that we are a 'forgiving person' and a shining beacon of virtue. Forgiveness exceeds any of its particular determinations and cannot be exhausted by them. Yet, forgiveness only ever arrives, only ever appears, we only ever experience it, in its determinations.

Keeping in mind this strange relationship between determinations and the indeterminate, the particular and the universal, the empirical and the rational, the conditional and the unconditional (or whatever other words you want to use to describe this strange relationship), we have collected here ten papers written by twelve authors from around the world and across the disciplinary spectrum including philosophers, practitioners, psychologists, literary theorists, prison chaplains, among others. That is, all the authors in this volume are coming at the topic of forgiveness *from* a perspective that does not simply bind and blind, but opens up the topic of forgiveness to them. The perspectives from which we approach forgiveness do not simply conceal, they also reveal. Yet, the authors are not just coming *from* a perspective, they are coming to forgiveness *with* a perspective, *by means of* a perspective. They need such a perspective, such an angle, in order to enter into a discussion on forgiveness – whether that perspective is a story within a story by Dostoevsky, the results of a survey one has conducted, one's role as a prison chaplain, various cultural examples, or the works of others. Again, coming to forgiveness with a perspective does not simply bind and blind, but gives access. The authors in this volume are coming *from* a perspective and *with* a perspective in order to put forgiveness *into* perspective. To 'put something in perspective' (or to 'put something into perspective') is an idiomatic expression that may not translate across language barriers, so a few descriptions may be in order. However, descriptions *simpliciter* are not our concern, so we will describe how we are using it in relation to forgiveness, what we mean by 'Forgiveness in Perspective' and what we mean when we say that these authors are putting forgiveness in perspective. First, the book offers ten different perspectives on forgiveness and, therefore, in this book you will find forgiveness in ten different perspectives. Secondly, all ten papers show the importance, significance, or relevance of the topic (this is one of the definitions of putting something 'in perspective') and they also help to make forgiveness more clear (another definition). However, and this would be the twist, none of the papers put forgiveness 'in perspective' in the sense of putting it in its 'correct place.' These papers are all perspectives on forgiveness that show the significance of forgiveness and make it more clear, but none of them grasp or encompass forgiveness as such, precisely because they are talking about forgiveness *from* a perspective and *with* a perspective (which is all we can ever do) makes it so they do not have forgiveness in perspective in the sense of putting forgiveness in its correct place.

All the papers collected here offer a perspective on forgiveness, put forgiveness in perspective, whether it be tracing what forgiveness 'is,' how this inheritance from the Abrahamic (Judeo-Christiano-Islamic) heritage is worked out in our secularizing societies, how forgiveness works in our quotidian experience, or a particular manifestation in a particular context such as marriage, prison, or after an abortion. We have attempted to divide these various perspectives into four parts which serve to group similar papers together – Part I: 'Forgiveness between Past and Future,' Part II: 'The Right to Forgive,' Part III: 'Forgiveness and the Judeo-Christian Tradition,' and Part IV: 'Narratives of Forgiveness.' The trajectory of the book is as follows.

Part I of this collection is entitled 'Forgiveness between Past and Future.' In this section the reader will find three essays that engage with the role and response of forgiveness between past atrocities and future possibilities – no easy task, to be sure. If one decides to forgive someone now, in this instant, what does this forgiveness have to do with the past? With the future? Is this forgiveness oriented to the past for the sake of the future? Or is it oriented to the past for the sake of the past? If forgiveness is 'between' past and future, does that mean it occurs in the present, that it can be 'present' or is it ever-receding, only leaving a trace? Or perhaps it never occurs in that instant between past and future but is a process that bridges the gap between the past and future, or a process that may begin now but will continue into the future. So, what is the role of forgiveness between the past, the no longer, and the future, the not-yet (and even the unforeseeable)?

In Chapter 1, 'Forgiveness: A Quiet Assault on the Malicious,' Steve Larocco discusses a forgiveness that operates as a response to what he calls 'vast memory-archives of injury.' Such forgiveness, for Larocco, is not only the opposite of revenge, which is another response to such memory-archives of injury, but also of the tit-for-tat equivalence of justice and the 'balancing responses' of punishment, reparation, and/or restitution. Rather, forgiveness, for Larocco, exceeds such reciprocal circles as a unilateral response to the malicious that serves to rework and resituate the stories we tell ourselves about the past offense in order to repair the ruptures the offense (and the stories we tell ourselves about it) has caused within the self, between the self and the offensive other, and across the social order.

In Chapter 2, 'Undoing What Has Been Done: Arendt and Levinas on Forgiveness,' Christopher R. Allers argues, with the help of Hannah Arendt and Emmanuel Levinas, that forgiveness is concerned with the past and, particularly, involves undoing the past misdeed in the sense of making it 'as if' it did not happen. But why is Allers discussing forgiving *what* was done, a deed *qua* misdeed, in the first place? Is this not condoning? Allers answers 'no' and argues that to forgive a person without forgiving what this person did is only forgiving this person up to a point, it is to already separate the doer and the deed and, therefore, it would be a forgiving of someone who is different and already 'better' than the one who did the deed. Such separation between doer and deed, according to Allers, does not happen prior to forgiveness. Rather, it is forgiveness that releases the offender from the offensive past, which affords the offender the possibility of beginning anew which, for Allers, connects such forgiveness to the future.

Inspired by victims of genocide (and, particularly, survivors of the Rwandan genocide) who claim to have forgiven their victimizers, Lynne Tirrell and Alisa Carse proffer what they call an 'emergent model' of forgiveness in Chapter 3 entitled 'Forgiving Grave Wrongs.' In this chapter, Tirrell and Carse begin by discussing what they call the 'classical model' of forgiveness in which a victim tenders forgiveness to a perpetrator as a result of a deliberate decision following a morally reparative transaction. From there, they offer what they call an 'emergent model' of forgiveness as an alternative to, but, admittedly, not necessarily a substitute for the so-called 'classical model.' This 'emergent model' is concerned with forgiving world-shattering wrongs in which forgiveness does not spring from a moment of decision but emerges from a process (in which no particular action is centrally aimed at forgiveness) that involves world-building and normative repair.

Part II, entitled 'The Right to Forgive,' focuses on who has the right, or authority, to forgive. Can so-called third parties forgive wrongs to which they are mere bystanders? Does one have any right to forgive when and where one is not the primary victim? In Chapter 4, 'Moral Bystanders and the Virtue of Forgiveness,' Linda Radzik draws on contemporary examples that have lead to the feeling of indignation in the general public over perceived wrongs to which they are mere bystanders. Such examples include the cases of Bill Clinton's affair and Eliot Spietzer patronization of a prostitute service as well as the use of racial epithets by Mel Gibson, Don Imus, Michael Richards, and George Allen. Radzik employs these examples in order to show that discussions of whether or not the general public *qua* third-party bystanders can forgive are not necessarily out of place. One can feel moral anger over perceived wrongs of which he or she is not the victim, but merely a bystander, and, furthermore, one can abjure such moral anger. If this is the case, Radzik asks, why is forgiveness a prerogative of the victim(s) alone? Radzik draws out the ways in which third-party forgiveness can help maintain and sustain the moral community as well as the limits of third-party forgiveness. Public indignation and, therefore, third-party forgiveness may, at times, be appropriate, but that does not give us license to jettison respect for privacy, respect for difference, and what Radzik calls 'the virtue of minding one's own business.'

Continuing with the question of third-party forgiveness, does a third party have the right or authority to forgive when that third party is God? If so, what happens to the victim's moral prerogative to forgive? If not, what happens to God's eschatological promises? In Chapter 5, 'If God Cannot Forgive, What Becomes of Harmony? The Strength of a Victim's Moral Prerogative Not to Forgive,' Regan Lance Reitsma pulls no punches and, most likely in fear and trembling, asks if God has the authority to forgive. Reitsma uses Dostoevsky's *Brothers Karamazov* in which Ivan claims that God cannot forgive wrongs to which God is a third party and, therefore, cannot insure the promise of 'a new heaven and a new earth' (Revelation 21) in which 'the wolf dwells with the lamb' (Isaiah 11) as a catalyst for his own argument. Reitsma puts his finger on an interesting paradox. Namely, in order to see God's promises come about, either God would have to disregard and pass over the victim's authoritative decision not to forgive – thus, transgressing the victim's moral prerogative (not) to forgive – or pressure the victim to forgive through various forms of strategic manoeuvrings, perhaps coercive or perhaps not. In his reflections on this dilemma, Reitsma makes some striking claims and suggestions that speak to various theological discussions, religious life and culture in general, as well as the ways of life and experiences of people with 'no religious affiliation' in our secularizing societies.

We just mentioned the word 'secularising,' and this – along with Reitsma's paper – leads us into Part III of this book entitled 'Forgiveness and the Judeo-Christian Tradition.' Forgiveness is a concept, a practice, and a claim made upon us that springs from the heritage of Abraham. While it may be true that *sungnômê* in Plato and Aristotle may amount to some sort of proto-forgiveness or at least judicial pardon, it neither played a significant role in their thought nor did is it as fecund as the forgiveness of the Judeo-Christian tradition (and *sungnômê* may simply have had the forgiveness of the Judeo-Christian tradition read back onto it). At any rate, as Vladimir Jankélévitch writes: 'Aristotle, himself, knew the gift; but only the Bible truly knew forgiveness.'[3] While forgiveness may have been previously 'neglected because of [its] allegedly exclusively religious nature,'[4] as Hannah Arendt would say, in our age of globalization and secularization (another religious concept), however, we see forgiveness everywhere, even between representatives of countries not primarily based on the Judeo-Christian tradition – such as Prime Minister Koizumi of Japan asking the Chinese people to forgive Japan's past aggressions. What, then, is the role of forgiveness in our globalizing and secularizing world? In the midst of the 'process of Christianisation with no need for the Christian Church,' to borrow a felicitous phrase from Jacques Derrida, what can the Judeo-Christian concept, practice, and claim of forgiveness say to us?[5]

In Chapter 6, 'From the Religious to the Political Apology: How the Religious Prehistory of Apology Makes Sense of Collective Responsibility,' Danielle Celermajer traces a thread from the contemporary phenomenon of political (e.g., representative, collective, and 'secular') apology back to its root in religious forms of apology – particularly, practices of apology in Judaism – in order to shed light on questions to which contemporary political apologies give rise. Celermajer begins with a discussion of a contemporary Australian example of the problems of political apology in light of modern understandings of moral individualism and the concomitant dilemma surrounding collective responsibility. While, as she shows, people have been able to make arguments for collective responsibility, they have yet to do the necessary legwork to connect collective responsibility and collective, political apology. While engaging various problems that might come up, Celermajer proposes that various forms of religious, collective apology may aid us in, and helpfully illuminate, our contemporary attempts at political apology.

In Chapter 7, 'In Search of Forgiveness: Men and Abortion, Managing Sin, Guilt and Shame in Post-Catholic Ireland,' Fergus Hogan offers an interpretation of the results of a previous study he conducted (with Harry Ferguson) entitled 'Men, Sexuality and Crisis Pregnancy: A Study of Men's Experience.' In this previous study, they interviewed 45 men on their sexual histories, knowledge of sex, contraception, sexual practices, and pregnancy services. In this chapter, Hogan traces the role religion, and particularly the Catholic Church, plays in the secularized, 'post-Catholic Ireland,' the role it continues to play in the Irish people's considerations of sin, guilt, shame, and forgiveness, and, particularly, the role that it plays in the lives of 8 men and their experiences with abortion. Hogan seeks to answer whether or not the search and process of forgiveness, which is a markedly religious word and concept, is still important in our secularizing, (post) modern times.

Part IV, 'Narratives of Forgiveness,' consists of three chapters geared toward the role of forgiveness in more quotidian, practical settings – namely, in marriage, prison, and community. In Chapter 8, 'Reconciling Irreconcilable Differences Through Forgiveness,' Carla Ross shares the findings of her study on the role of forgiveness in marital satisfaction. Ross suggests that married couples that report higher levels of marital satisfaction also report a higher propensity for forgiveness. In order to test this hypothesis, Ross examined three couples that have married, divorced, and subsequently remarried the same partner. The examination consisted of two surveys – the Enright Forgiveness Inventory and the Spanier Dyadic Adjustment Scale – as well as a series of written, open-ended questions, and aimed to determine the role forgiveness played in the original marriage, the divorce, their decision to remarry, and their second marriage. As her title suggests, forgiveness can lead to the reconciling of 'irreconcilable differences' that are generally cited as the grounds of divorce. Forgiveness, as Henri Nouwen claims (and Ross includes as the epigraph to her paper), 'is love practiced among people who love poorly.' Perhaps it can be added that it is practiced among people who are trying to love less poorly.

In Chapter 9, 'Prisoners and Forgiveness,' Marieke Smit, a prison chaplain, discusses the role of forgiveness and guilt in a prison environment, in the lives of convicted criminals, and in the process toward a successful re-entry into society. As a prison chaplain, Smit has organized and lead a series of group meetings about forgiveness with prisoners. In her essay, she describes the structure of these meetings as well as the changes these meetings have affected in the lives of the participants.

In Chapter 10, 'The Community Response To Violence: Do Rituals of Healing Support Forgiveness?,' Christina Tomacic-Niaros and Barbara Flood focus on the role of community in forgiveness and the role of forgiveness in communities. In light of mass media, they ask us to rethink our understanding of 'community' by employing such examples as the assassination of Harvey Milk, the shootings of Amish children at the Nickel Mines School in Pennsylvania and the shootings at Platte Canyon High School in Colorado, 9/11, and others. Furthermore, Flood and Tomacic-Niaros ask whether, within such a broader community, the various rituals of remembrance surrounding certain events undermine or promote forgiveness. This essay serves to present and review the various responses given by participants of 'The Annual Memorial for Victims of Homicide in Chicago' in a survey that Flood and Tomacic-Niaros designed and delivered in order to answer such a question among others.

These ten perspectives are offered to you, dear reader. We hope that you will allow your 'imagination to go visiting' and take these perspectives into account, thus, 'enlarging your mentality' and opening your understanding of forgiveness to other and future perspectives and determinations.[6] While these are the last words of the introduction, when it comes to forgiveness there is no last word.

Notes

[1] We are not seeking to set up a binary opposition between either responses of justice as equivalence, on the one hand, or forgiveness, on the other.

These responses are not the only ones available to victims. There are many others and many shades of gray between these two extreme responses (these responses are 'extreme' if we take a pure, unconditional forgiveness, characterised by an aneconomic, para-logic of superabundance and excess, on the one hand, and an unwavering tit-for-tat justice, characterized by an econo-logic of equivalence and exchange, on the other. If we take such extremes, extremes that would not be available to us, would not be 'possible' for us, would not be 'humanly possible,' but certainly no less provocative because of this, then perhaps all we would have are shades of gray between them. However, making an argument for such claims is beyond the scope of this introduction).

[2] I would like to thank Shannon Hoff (Professor of Social and Political Philosophy at the Institute for Christian Studies, Toronto) for this example.

[3] V Jankélévitch, *Forgiveness*, trans. A. Kelley, University of Chicago Press, Chicago and London, 2005, 128.

[4] H Arendt, *The Human Condition*, The University of Chicago Press, Chicago and London, 1958, 239.

[5] J Derrida, *On Cosmopolitanism and Forgiveness*, trans. by M Dooley and M Hughes, Routledge, London and New York, 2001, 31.

[6] H Arendt writes (amongst other places) of training your 'imagination to go visiting' and the notion of an 'enlarged mentality' or 'enlarged thought' in H Arendt, *Lectures on Kant's Political Philosophy*, ed. Ronald Beiner, The University of Chicago Press, Chicago, 1992, 43. With 'enlarged mentality,' Arendt is referring to what Immanuel Kant calls the 'expansion of the mind' in I Kant, *Critique of Judgment*, trans. Werner S. Pluhar, Hackett Publishing Company, 1987, cf. 112. With her notion of training one's 'imagination to go visiting,' Arendt asks us to compare (which is used ambiguously) this with Kant's discussion of 'visiting' in *Perpetual Peace* which can be found in his discussion of 'Third Definitive Article of Perpetual Peace: Cosmopolitan Right will be limited to Conditions of Universal Hospitality' (I Kant, 'Perpetual Peace,' Political Writings, ed. H.S. Reiss, trans. H.B. Nisbet, Cambridge University Press, Cambridge, 1991, 105ff). I think Kant's discussion of visiting in *The Metaphysics of Morals* would serve as a better analogy for Arendt's purposes. Kant writes:
However, visiting these coasts, and still more settling there to connect them with the mother country, provide the occasion for troubles and acts of violence in one place on our globe to be felt all over it. Yet this possible abuse cannot annul the right of citizens of the world to try to establish a community with all and, to this end, to visit all of the earth... (I Kant, *The Metaphysics of Morals*, trans. Mary Gregor, Cambridge University Press, Cambridge, 1996, 121).

Bibliography

Arendt, H., *The Human Condition*, The University of Chicago Press, Chicago and London, 1958.

——, *Lectures on Kant's Political Philosophy*, ed. Ronald Beiner, The University of Chicago Press, Chicago, 1992.

Derrida, J.. *On Cosmopolitanism and Forgiveness*, Trans. Mark Dooley and Michael Hughes, Routledge, London and New York, 2001.

Jankélévitch, V., *Forgiveness*, Trans. by A. Kelley, University of Chicago Press, Chicago and London, 2005.

Kant, I., The *Metaphysics of Morals*, trans. Mary Gregor, Cambridge University Press, Cambridge, 1996.

——, *Political Writings*, ed. H.S. Reiss, trans. H.B. Nisbet, Cambridge University Press, Cambridge, 1991.

PART I

Forgiveness between Past and Future

Forgiveness: A Quiet Assault on the Malicious

Steve Larocco

Abstract

Forgiveness is the self's quiet assault on the power of the malicious and the injurious. Its aim is to repair or mitigate the breaches and fractures the malicious and the injurious create within the self, between the self and other(s), and across the social order. It does this in two ways: publicly, as a ritualised speech-act, wherein forgiveness forges a special form of recognition, in which recognition of oneself as one who forgives stands in for and displaces various forms of non-recognition by the other(s); and privately, as a form of affective reattunement, in which a 'decathexis' of the breach wrought by the malicious releases the self from an imposed shame and facilitates the reassertion of a self which has affirmatively assimilated injury, a process necessary for its release. For forgiveness to be fully functional, it needs to operate both publicly and privately, both as a ritual speech-act and as a manifestation of affective reattunement. Publicly, it needs to operate as a ritual and not as a transaction, because forgiveness, unlike a transaction, can neither require nor demand reciprocity. As Paul Ricoeur might have said, forgiveness, as public ritual is a form of imputation, a way of holding the other accountable, yet it still must be able to function under conditions of non-reciprocity. Forgiveness always operates in the ineluctable possibility of its repudiation by the other. It functions as a ritual affirmation that itself refuses to recognize the other's power of negation; as ritualised speech-act, it imposes its own version of things on the other beyond the other's power of negation, something a transaction, enmeshed in the logic of exchange, cannot achieve. Public rituals of forgiveness, in spite of this structural non-reciprocity, hold the other accountable even in the act of releasement of that accountability, a releasement that, ephemerally, negates the ongoing force that the malicious or injurious purports to have. It does this in two ways: first, by verbally taking on and naming what is not one's own – the other's malevolence, indifference or harm – and releasing the self socially from the stigmatising traces of those capacities; and, second, by speaking into being a version of self and a form of social dignity that negates and survives the malicious. Privately, forgiveness involves affective reattunement, which begins with a decathexis of the breach in self-wrought by the malicious or the injurious. This entails an affective releasing of the psychic wound whose splitting force has generated a new, fractured identity-possibility for the self. While the breach may well be stigmatised psychically, in order for forgiveness to occur the self that has become simultaneously fractured and organized by an injurious breach must destigmatise that breach; that is, the self must withdraw investments in the identity possibilities constituted by psychic injury and the rectitude that transforms such injury into victimhood and identity formation. This involves the self's assimilation and release of the shame wrought by injury and malice. And this assimilation is itself a negation of the power of the malicious, a form of non-recognition that negates. Forgiveness, then, in its twofold structure – as public ritual and speech-act, and as affective reattunement – enables the self to generate an event and a condition of being that, at least ephemerally, negates much of the retroactive and ongoing force of the malicious and the injurious.

Key Words: Forgiveness, unilateral forgiveness, malice, memory, reactive moral sentiments, moral sentiments, justice, offence, bilateral forgiveness.

*****

We live in a world of malice and offence, one in which the boots and bullets of state violence, the desolations of genocide, the explosive blows of terrorism, the scourging and execrations of interpersonal hostility, and the pinches and belittlements of daily life generate and disperse vast memory-archives of injury. Each of us holds some tiny, singular portion of this archive. Memory is a compilation, or perhaps, better, an assembly of referential fragments, constructs and vignettes, and in a world marked by malice, many of those vignettes and fragments bear the traces of trauma and offence. One kind of response to memory's preservation of wrongs is retaliation and revenge, the transformation of one's archive of injury or slight (and the sense of shame or rage that derives from and is fuelled by that archive) into action. In this mode of response, one imagines that malice, when channelled as some form of reprisal, can expiate the psychic unrest and rancour created by the affect that arises in and binds itself to remembered offence –danger, indignation, contempt, scorn, resentment, dudgeon, spite, umbrage and so on.[1] These feelings take shape as reactive 'moral sentiments,' as feelings of malice legitimised by one's archived vignettes of victimization or injury at the hands of the other. In them, malice becomes a moral force, fuelled by the righteousness, however conjured, of archived wrongs.[2] This is one of Nietzsche's central insights in his comments on *ressentiment* in *The Genealogy of Morals*.

However, a second mode of response to the memory of an injurious past – and to the other or others connected to that past – is possible. This answer to offence relinquishes or, more self-assertively, abjures the possibility of certain kinds of reactive moral aggression towards the other. Such response conducts its own quiet assault on the malicious – and that is forgiveness. The aim of forgiveness is to alter the hold that the malicious has on affective life and the narratives, both public and in memory, which structure such life and which often legitimise reciprocal malice. Forgiveness accomplishes this transformation by attempting to alter and repair the breaches and fractures that the malicious and the injurious create within the subject's affect and sense of self, between the subject and the offensive other(s), and across the social order itself.

Forgiveness works to accomplish this alteration in three primary ways: first, publicly, as a performative and typically ritualised speech-act, as something *pronounced* that alters what is.[3]   In this performance of forgiveness, the subject takes a vignette from memory and, through the saying of forgiveness, publicly forges and enacts a new narrative possibility, one in which there is a clear imputation of fault to the offender and in which the subject recognizes herself as the one who forgives (and who has, significantly, thereby the *power* to forgive).[4]   In this ritualised act, one attempts to transform one's relation to the past as defined by the memory of offence or injury. It is an effort of transformative reclamation, an attempt to uncouple publicly the archive of memory from the affects consequent to offence and injury. Second, as an intersubjective possibility, forgiveness presents the other with the alluring possibility that s/he can be released from the stigma of culpability for wrongdoing, that while the narrative of guilt remains, the stigma that attaches to that story has been renounced. In this way, forgiveness makes it possible to amend the social status of the other acknowledged as at fault by supplementing the narrative of culpability with a narrative of release. It opens new story-possibilities and thereby transforms the old memory-vignette, reworking the weakness of the other defined by the stigma of fault by allowing a new, destigmatised narrative of renewal. This aspect of forgiveness focuses on what forgiveness can provide for the offender rather than for the offended. Third, forgiveness works to modify the offended's prior incorporation of offence or injury into narratives and representations of identity, emending the affect that fastens to a given memory-vignette of offence. Its aim is to institute what, in psychoanalytic language, might be called a 'decathexis' of the breach wrought in the subject by the memory of wrong; that is, forgiveness facilitates a withdrawal or release of the emotional turbulence, typically manifested as reactive moral sentiments, which are affixed to and fuelled by a particular narrative fragment or story of the past.

In this latter mode of functioning, as in public performance, forgiveness instantiates reclamation, however subtle, of power, and it is this possibility of empowerment that drives affective reattunement. Such reattunement entails the reorientation and redistribution of affect around a now-revised memory-vignette, narrative, or fragment. The breach in identity generated by an offence or injury typically produces a sense of damage, impairment, weakness or degradation, which registers affectively as feelings of shame. Such shame is one of the primary drivers of the reactive moral sentiments and brazes itself to the memory-vignettes of offence. The surface manifestation of this shame may be rage, spite or, all too typically, the barely acknowledged smoulder of resentment. Forgiveness exerts part of its force against the corrosive power of this shame, allowing a reassertion and affirmation of the moral *viability* by the victim of offence beyond the victim's often-impotent adhesion to feelings of moralized aggression. The victim, who through offence or injury receives a shaming assault of some kind on his or her identity formation and the self-narratives that support it, through forgiveness renews the standing of that identity as a potentially *nonreactive* moral agency, that is, as a moral agency that is not bound by the memory-vignettes of offence to *reactive* emotions, whether moral or not. Spite, contempt, rage, resentment and so on fall into the category of reactive emotions, and forgiveness aims to abjure or obliterate those sentiments. Through an act or acts of forgiveness, whether privately, where one affirms one's nonreactive moral standing for oneself, or publicly, where one performs that same standing for others, the victim of offence allows a reconstruction of who one is that is not affectively bound by memory-traces of what one was in the event of offence. To accomplish this affirmation of who and what one is, forgiveness instantiates revision of the self-narrative, both in terms of content and affective charge, in which the memory-vignette or fragment derived from the offence had found significance. This narrative revisioning, when realized, releases the forgiving subject from the binding power of the shame or resentment of having been offended or injured and facilitates the reconstruction and reassertion of a subjectivity that has affirmatively assimilated a rescripted and affectively modified version of the vignette of injury. Through this process of reconditioning memory, affect and their linkage in the narrative underpinnings of identity, forgiveness provides an alternative to the morality of malicious catharsis.

Forgiveness facilitates this forsaking of the malicious and reactive moral sentiments by creating a recursive, revisionary, forward-looking relation to the past. Reprisal and revenge are almost invariably conservative in relation to memory, potentially expiating hostile moral sentiments by converting them into action but not altering the *meaning* or *significance* of the vignettes and fragments to which they were bound, thereby keeping the offensive past as representation alive and accessible for the purpose of self and world-narration. In contrast, forgiveness aims specifically to *alter* the significance of the past by stopping the 'time of fault' to use the words of Julia Kristeva, a time bound up with narrative representations of offence.[5] Forgiveness's altering of the significance of the remembered past involves renouncing the vignette of offence as it is fused with hostile moral sentiment, but not renouncing the vignette itself; that is, forgiveness aims to alter the archive of fault, not by erasing the memory-vignette or the imputation of the guilty, but by unbinding the vignette from its submission to and complicity with the conservation of hostile moral affect.[6] Forgiveness as an event recomposes the archive of memory, facilitating self and social narratives that are no longer *bound* by any particular vignette of offence and the affect fused with it.

In addition and in a paradoxical way, forgiveness allows one to be freed from the implicit but operative claims of justice that attach to injuries and offence and which fuel reactive and often hostile moral sentiments. This release occurs because forgiveness frees one from justice's tacit logic of equivalence: that justice occurs when an offence meets with an equitable or balancing response, such as punishment, reparation or restitution.[7] Forgiveness, in contrast to justice, affirms an overt and acceptable *asymmetry* between offence and response. Such asymmetry operates beyond hostility and uses the act of relinquishing reactive moral affects as a sign of power, as a different mode of acting against the force of malice. This asymmetrical aspect of forgiveness works because forgiveness operates initially and primarily on the *representational field of injury* rather than on the intersubjective field of offender and offended. Instead of seeking to restore, in some fantasy form, the purported equity that preceded the injury (an impossibility when the injury, for example, is genocide), forgiveness relinquishes the very claim of restored equity that underlies justice. It assumes that the irreversibility of time forecloses at least some of the operative validity of rectification. While justice aims to restructure injury or offence as an interpersonal or social transaction to be counterbalanced through some form of compensation, forgiveness chooses instead to adhere to the asymmetry between self and other wrought by offence and to transform its significance. Consequently, whether public or private, an act of forgiveness is an assault on the representational substructure of malice rather than a transactive response to wrong or offence.[8]

Forgiveness possesses this power because its fundamental structure is unilateral. Much of the transformative power of forgiveness precedes and exceeds any response or gesture on the part of the imputed offender. To be sure, unilateral forgiveness is not the standard notion of what forgiveness is. The conventional version, represented in different ways in recent books by Trudy Govier and Charles Griswold, is that forgiveness, in its ideal form, is bilateral; that is, forgiveness occurs ideally only in the interaction between the offender and the offended and involves an apology by the offender, a release from culpability by the offended, and some form of reconciliation as the aim of the transaction. For Govier, forgiveness crucially involves a process of reframing 'the offender as someone capable of doing better in the future.'[9] Similarly, for Griswold, forgiveness ought to involve 'reciprocity between injurer and injured,'[10] and this entails the need to see 'the offender in a new light.'[11] For both, forgiveness ought to manifest acts of reciprocity and a transformation of the forgiver's representation of the offender. In this way, forgiveness remains allied, implicitly, with notions of justice. Forgiveness, in this model, entails a negotiated recalibration of equity between offender and offended and cannot occur without it.

The problem with this model of forgiveness is that it imagines forgiveness as a transaction or exchange between the parties, a transaction that paradoxically reaffirms the power that the offender possesses to offend and to shame (by not admitting culpability, by withholding apology, by not apologizing in the right way, and so on). It thereby *binds* the offended to the will of the offender, making the forgiver *dependent* on some manifestation of change in that other for forgiveness to occur. Potentially, this dependency on the other imprisons the offended in reactive moral sentiments such as resentment and rage, or in the debilitated, maimed sense of self that is shame. Here, a fantasy of exchange precludes affective repair or reconditioning. In a sense, the wish for a restorative transaction that parallels the implicit structure of justice trusses the offended to a potentially bootless nostalgia, one in which the desire to restore some version of what was prior to the offence (one's sense of self in relation to the other, one's sense of self as one once was – as innocent, as uninjured, as whole, etc.) entails one in a need to recover or reclaim something of the past. The transaction between the offender and the offended that bilateral forgiveness views as the essence of what forgiveness is entails the fantasy that *exchange* can allow a recovery of something of what was lost in the offence, that it allows a reconciliation of the present with the past, through a kind of reconciliation of accounts between offended and offender. In this bargaining, both offender and offended are drawn into the past, into the time of offence, and into what lay prior to it, the time of nostalgic desire. Bilateral forgiveness is driven, inevitably, by some form of this nostalgic desire, by some wish to hold the other accountable for what was in the past and what is no longer. The memory-vignette of offence, paradoxically, is the link between the offender, offended and this nostalgia of the past and thus can only partially be released, for the transaction can never quite restore what was – accounts can never be balanced in a way that will have conserved what was lost in the past. In a sense, exchange displaces this desire for recovery, but the problem is that it does so by binding the offended to the offender, while being unable to transcend the memory-vignette of offence that generates the nostalgia of desire and blocks the offended from satisfying it.

Bilateral forgiveness proves inadequate because forgiveness begins, in its fundamental structure, not in the dynamics of interpersonal negotiation around fault, not in exchange or transaction, but in the power to reconfigure memory (both individual and social), the vignettes and representational fragments that comprise it, and its affective charge or valence. This power, even in the matrix of sociality, is unilateral, or at least it begins in unilateral action. In the ritual of public forgiveness, the forgiver possesses the power of imputation and accusation; that is, by forgiving, paradoxically, the forgiver publicly renders the other as at fault, as an offender. In this way, the offended takes the past, and rather than endeavouring to transact a nostalgic escape, pulls that past into the present and, through a potentially shaming imputation against the offender, thrusts it into the future. The act of forgiving submits the imputed offender to an enacted representation of his or her fault. This is why, in certain situations, to forgive the other can be felt as itself an offence even as forgiving simultaneously offers a kind of release from or retraction of guilt.[12] For the other who will not accept fault or culpability for a given offence, forgiveness has the potential to change what otherwise might be an ambiguous or insignificant vignette in the archive of shared memory into a narrative of fault, legitimising an accusation. As a speech-act, forgiveness confers *fault* even as it releases *guilt*, and this conferral occurs even if the other rejects such an attribution. To be forgiven is to be interpolated or defined as at fault, and this gives a unilateral performative power to the forgiver, or, more precisely, to the act of forgiving. In this sense, forgiveness possesses a certain power of *offence*,[13] for by acting on the memory-vignette of violation, it allows a possibility of symbolic injury to the other. It is perhaps telling that Nietzsche worried about this power of forgiveness. The connection between unilateral forgiveness and the power of offence inherent in imputation also suggests that forgiveness is not simply on the side of restoring dignity as more humanist analyses often wish to argue.[14]

However, even though forgiveness can be understood as generating offence, as possessing a capacity for 'symbolic violence,' to use Pierre Bourdieu's term, that doesn't mean that it entails a sublimation of the reactive moral sentiments.[15] Unilateral forgiveness's primary aim is to release the other from guilt, and, through that act, to transform the affective charge of the memory-vignette that the offended holds of the situation of offence. The symbolic violence that forgiveness possesses as a potential has structural rather than intentional derivation. It is not an effect of rancorous emotion, at least not typically; rather, it is an after-effect of the necessity that forgiveness involves imputation. Forgiveness is always related to someone or something to be forgiven, and this structure necessitates that forgiveness entails imputation (which tonally is different and less symbolically violent than an accusation or a judgment). Consequently, the paradoxical aggression that attaches to the public release of the offender from guilt does not service a moral animus but rather provides, accidentally as it were, a transformation of the field of offence, in which the offender also becomes subject to the shame-potential of offence. He or she becomes, in the very act of being forgiven, the subject of symbolic violence.[16]

The notion of asymmetry is crucial to elucidating the complex structure of forgiveness. As a ritual speech-act, forgiveness must begin in unilateral possibility, because forgiveness, as I have argued, unlike a transaction, cannot effectively demand reciprocity.[17] The other, the one imputed guilty by the very act of forgiveness, always possesses the power to repudiate the act of forgiveness itself, to breach any possibilities of reciprocity, exchange or mutuality. And this power exists even when the other accedes to being forgiven, since forgiveness does not and cannot bind future behaviour. While the imputation of fault or offence will persist despite the retraction of the guilt in the act of forgiveness itself, that imputation has no necessary force on the behaviour of the offender. The offender can ignore, discount or disregard the imputation, or simply persist in offence. Nonetheless, as a speech-act, forgiveness in its structure *rejects* the power of negation inherent in the other's possible repudiation of the forgiver and/or of the act of forgiveness, functioning as an affirmation that refuses to recognize or be bound by the other's power of negation.[18] It assumes, consequently, an irrevocable asymmetry between offender and offended, and this acceptance of asymmetry, of an ongoing imbalance or inequity between offender and offended, provides a basis for its force, facilitating its own representation of particular memory-vignettes and life-narratives on the collective and private archive that is the past. To put it succinctly, rescripting precedes and obviates reconciliation, even if reconciliation remains desirable.

In contrast, as a bilateral transaction imprisoned in the logic of exchange, forgiveness has no power of its own against the negative capacities of the other, and thus remains impotent against the reservoir of maliciousness that the other holds in his or her ongoing capacity to negate. The dream of restored equity that underlies reconciliation – that the remorse of the offender, a public sign of shame and guilt, compensates the offended for the offence, injury and associated shame of the original breach – is a dream of a kind of symmetry with remorse matching and counterbalancing injury. The dream of reconciliation, however, assumes that the other's maliciousness has already been yielded or given up. It follows that such forgiveness has no effect on the maliciousness of the other, for that maliciousness has to have been already dissipated by remorse for forgiveness to begin. In bilateral forgiveness, oddly enough, forgiveness's first task is to confirm the transformation of the offender, to aid in the repentant offender's wish to escape guilt, and it does so by facilitating an imaginary equipoise between offender and offended, by accepting remorse as recompense or, at least, as a satisfaction for injury.

No such dream subtends unilateral forgiveness. As a ritualised speech-act, forgiveness imputes accountability *in the actuality of ineluctable asymmetry* between the aggrieved and his or her offender(s). It neither presupposes nor requires remorse, for by its conflation of imputation and release and the correlative emending of the affects attached to memory and representation, forgiveness negates much of the force that the malicious and injurious as modes of negation purport to have. It accomplishes this in two ways: first, by taking on and representing what is not one's own – the other's malevolence, negating indifference or act(s) of injury – and releasing the offended subject from the stigmatising traces of those capacities by *intervening* in the archive of memory. By actively and pre-emptively forgiving, the offended intercedes in the durative power of the offence by uncoupling the remnant of the other's malicious power in the representation of the offence from the offended's affectively charged memories, an uncoupling that facilitates an affective rescripting of the memory-vignette itself. Second, the act of forgiveness attaches to the forgiver a self-narration that has survived and negated the malicious itself (or at least certain aspects of it) and its manifestation in specific memory-vignettes. The person who forgives unilaterally is someone who has weathered malice's wounds and impingements on memory and taken up the asymmetry between offender and offended as a space of self-narration and affirmation. In its emendation of memory, narration and representation, forgiveness alters what is by its infringement on the archive of what was.

Forgiveness, of course, does not alter *all* memory, but in the act or process of forgiveness the 'I' asserts, whether tacitly or overtly, that 'I' have the power to alter *my* memory, my portion of the memory-archive of injury. In addition, through the asymmetrical assault on the other's power of negation, the 'I' claims the ability to revise the *collective* archive of memory as well. Crucially, such alteration does not involve forgetting; the vignette of offence itself remains largely intact and either retains or accentuates its force through imputation, as an attribution to the other of fault. What changes in forgiveness is that the vignette becomes part of an altered narrative of the life of the wronged and this modifies the vignette of offence itself by modifying its significance. This transformation enables affective reattunement by facilitating the 'decathexis' or release of the affect bound to a particular vignette. More precisely, forgiveness mobilizes for release the affect fused to the *breach in self-representations and self-narratives* wrought by that vignette. Whatever else injury and offence may be (violations of one's body, damage to one's family or group, defilement of one's beliefs), they are invariably assaults on aspects of self-representation – who am I and what have I become in relation to this wrong or harm?[19] What offences or injuries do is fragment preceding narrative and scripts of self-representation, rending self-narratives and self-representations in catastrophic or subtle ways, interrupting those aspects of self-construction with new narratives of offence. These new narratives fused to injury create and sustain the lacerations in prior, now damaged, self-narratives. The representations of self damaged by offence tend to draw and harbour an affective charge, shaping the ongoing process of self-representation involved in identity formation in relation to the breaches wrought by injury. The power of the reactive moral sentiments such as resentment and indignation to fashion and drive identity, at times against one's will, is an effect of this phenomenon, for those emotions typically are ancillary effects of the emergent shame created by damage to self-construction and identity. Forgiveness, by releasing the affect fused to these breaches in self-representations and self-narratives, undoes much of the ongoing power of the malicious (as both the negating power of the other and as the traces of that power lodged in self-representation). In particular, it combats the capacity of offences to fashion one's subjectivity by deforming and circumscribing the representational fabrication of identity.

What forgiveness does at this level is ablate the affective charge, the emotionally galvanized stigma, of the breach. As with public forgiveness, the essential power of such forgiveness is unilateral. By fashioning a new significance for the psychically stigmatising memory-vignette of offence, forgiveness allows the identity that has coalesced around damaged self-narratives and representations to restructure itself through the signifying event of forgiveness. One might say that forgiveness fosters a self-fashioning that surpasses the harrowing of identity formation and self-narration wrought by shame. In the wake of offence, forgiveness has the power to destigmatise the lacerated mnemonic representations of both self and event, which allows a relinquishing of the damaged identity possibilities that often come to form the basis for an identity forged as victim. At this level, forgiveness allows the subject constructed through offence to alter that very construction by besetting the hostile moral sentiments and shame that galvanize and preserve that identity formation. By driving the subject to withdraw investments in the rectitude and resentment that fastens to offence, forgiveness intervenes in the symbiosis between victimhood and identity. The subject, through forgiveness, can assimilate and metabolise the shame wrought by injury and malice, and it is typically shame, with anger, that fuels the hostile moral sentiments. This assimilation is itself a negation of the power of the malicious in its ability to pervade identity formation.

A final way in which forgiveness resists the malicious is by rejecting the urge to establish a mimetic relationship with it; that is, one temptation when one has been damaged in some way by offence is to emulate the malice that authored that offence. This imitation occurs when the offended reproduces and redirects malice either back at the offender, as in revenge, or displaces it through malicious behaviour to uninvolved others. The reactive moral sentiments, especially resentment, propagate and sustain themselves by establishing an ongoing mimetic relationship with the malice of the offender. The offender's malevolence is met and mirrored by one's own moralized malice. This mimesis allows the offended to redress the shame that accrues in the wake of being offended against or injured. It does so by binding shame with aggressive affects such as anger or resentment. This fusing of emotion coalesces the offended's identity around action-narratives of retaliation and recompense. The damage and breach in self-conception that generates shame needs repair, and the offended seeks to enact self-repair by mending that breach through a focalisation on an identity consolidated by moralized malice. In this venture, it is malice itself that rectifies and mends shame, and it does so by turning the affective turbulence generated by injury into convergent, aggressive moral sentiments. The offended surpasses the shame that undoes her by casting herself as the author of righteous malice.

Forgiveness refuses this lure of mimetic self-construction and empowerment, for in forgiveness even the act of imputation is driven by its simultaneous release. The offence or symbolic violence that imputation entails is both forged and suspended, foreclosing the offended from the identity-work of malice. In addition, forgiveness suspends the malice that often attends the finality of judgment. Whereas the moral sentiments simmer in the often malign and vindictive complicity between judgment and justice, forgiveness as a unilateral act disregards both. More precisely, it discounts the compensatory demands of justice and lets imputation stand in the place of judgment. The difference between imputation and judgment is that imputation is merely an ascription of fault; it provides a narration of fault from a subject-position, but does not claim to possess the finality of a verdict, as does judgment. By resisting judgment, forgiveness leaves the narratives and memory-vignettes of fault open-ended, emendable. Rather than allowing judgment to fuel and legitimise the reactive moral sentiments, forgiveness chooses to ally itself with imputation, which ascribes fault but leaves the *significance, meaning* and *affective charge* of that fault pliable. The shame set in place by offence is surpassed by the rescoring of memory and self-narratives, not by fusing it with moralised malice. In this sense, unilateral forgiveness refuses all collusion with the malicious. Instead, in its trust in imputation, the emendation of memory and self-narrative, and the necessity of releasing affect (rather than discharging it), forgiveness maintains its quiet assault on the malicious.

Forgiveness, then, is a subtle but crucial means of unilateral empowerment in the wake of wrong or malice. It authorizes an assault on the malicious both in others and in oneself. One of its powers is that it relinquishes or holds off the fantasy of binding the other in some form of balancing transaction, releasing the offended or injured from dependency on the response of the other. As both public speech-act and intervention in the subject's affective investments in psychic wounds, its power is in its ability to revise and resituate vignettes and representations of offence in the archives of memory and to surpass shame without resort to reactive moral sentiments (what I have sometimes called moralized malice). Its fundamental work is representational; what it *does*, even as a speech-act depends on its ability to alter the matrices of representation that situate and undergird the ongoing force of offence and injury. For the malicious to work, it not only has to locate itself in the social world; it also has to wreak its damage in the fields of representation. Forgiveness is a force against that work of the malicious; it is the fuse that releases the power of a future no longer simply fastened to the shame, broken representations, damaged stories and maligned identities of the past, a future that may overcome some of the socially desolating force of malice.

Notes

[1] Robert Solomon argues that 'Morality . . . is a caldron of sometimes violent as well as benign passions' R Solomon, *A Passion for Justice: Emotions and the Origins of the Social Contract*, Addison-Wesley, Reading MA, 1990, 200. Solomon's rhetoric may be exaggerated, but his sense that morality is driven, quite often, by sentiments that potentially stem from feelings of malice is largely correct. His attempt to suggest that resentment is at the core of justice, however, I find unpersuasive. See Solomon, 261-274. Jeffrie Murphy also argues for the moral value of 'appropriate' resentment J Murphy, 'Forgiveness, Self-Respect and the Value of Resentment.' *The Forgiveness Handbook*, ed. Everett L. Worthington, Jr., Routledge, New York, 2005, 35-36.

[2] Charles Griswold argues that 'one doesn't feel malicious when angry unless there is a moral component to the emotion' C Griswold, *Forgiveness: A Philosophical Investigation*, Cambridge, New York, 2007, 23.

[3] Jacques Derrida cautions against the possibility of creating a 'theatre of forgiveness.' J Derrida, *On Cosmopolitanism and Forgiveness*, trans. Mark Dooley and Michael Hughes, Routledge, New York, 2001, 28. Similarly, Paul Ricoeur worries about the 'sometimes monstrous failure of all efforts to institutionalize forgiveness' P Ricoeur, *Memory, History, Forgetting*, trans. Kathleen Blamey and David Pellauer, Chicago UP, Chicago, 2004, 488. Both concerns are valid, but don't speak to the potential force of forgiveness as a public speech-act apart from whatever political spectacles may surround or support it.

[4] Public forgiveness, of course, can be coerced, or performed because one can no longer bear the turbulence of maintaining a grievance, and therefore be an effect of a certain weakness, but that doesn't negate the social structuring of forgiveness in which the one who forgives is supposed to possess, in that ritual act, a reservoir of social power. It is some version of the forgiver's claim of injury or offense, some version of the forgiver's vignette that the ritual of forgiveness publically validates and legitimizes.

[5] A Rice and J Kristeva, 'Forgiveness: an Interview,' <u>PMLA</u> 117.2 (March 2002): 281.

[6] This leads to the traditional notion stemming from the work of Bishop Joseph Butler in the eighteenth century that forgiveness is the overcoming of

resentment, which becomes the label for conserved, hostile moral sentiment. See Griswold's account of this Griswold, 22-31.

[7] Such a notion of justice always bases equivalence on prevailing norms, and not on abstract notions of real equity in which all individuals would have truly equal status as individuals.

[8] Jacques Derrida argues that for forgiveness to really be forgiveness, is must be 'aneconomic,' granted to 'the guilty as guilty' Derrida, *On Cosmopolitanism and Forgiveness*, 34. P. D. Digeser, in contrast, argues that political forgiveness is inherently a kind of economic act, 'releasing what is owned, financially or morally' P D Digeser, *Political Forgiveness*, Cornell UP, Ithaca, 2001, 4; it is a kind of 'settling' of the accounts of the past. I would argue that this makes forgiveness part of justice, rather than a supplement beyond justice.

[9] T Govier, *Forgiveness and Revenge*, Routledge, New York 2002, 59.

[10] C Griswold, *Forgiveness: A Philosophical Investigation*, Cambridge, New York, 2007, xvi.

[11] Griswold, *Forgiveness*, 57. Paul Ricoeur also argues that forgiveness crucially is bilateral, for it allows the forgiven to be restored to 'the capacity for acting' and to become something other than his or her 'offences and faults' (Ricoeur, 493). Here, we hear echoes of the redemptive notion inherent in bilateral forgiveness, a sign of forgiveness's typical entailment with Judeo-Christian tradition.

[12] Ricoeur makes a similar observation when he refers to the 'dialectic of binding and unbinding posed by the problem of forgiveness' (Ricoeur, 496), though I'm not sure that 'dialectic' is the best way to characterize the contradictory trajectories of forgiveness, simultaneously towards imputation and change or release.

[13] Such power for forgiveness is not limited to what Derrida worries has become the 'theatrical space' of forgiveness, the public, orchestrated scenes in which ritual forgiveness of a political kind has often taken place (Derrida, 28-29). One doesn't need an audience for forgiveness to alter, unilaterally, tiny portions of the collective archive of memory. Structurally, it does this without the other.

[14] Ricoeur, for example, asserts that forgiveness is a 'consideration addressed to the other's dignity' (Ricoeur, 496). At times, of course, it is that, but it needn't be and in its fundamental structure the address to the other may have little to do with the other's dignity and more to do with the offending other's hold on memory.

[15] P Bourdieu, *The Logic of Practice,* trans. Richard Nice, Stanford UP, Stanford, 1990, 127.

[16] This is not to say that one couldn't intentionally use imputation as a way of servicing reactive moral sentiments. One could spit out forgiveness as an insult. But the attraction of unilateral forgiveness in a good moral sense is that the symbolic violence is done against one's will, as it were. It is retracted even as it is enacted. And the intent in forgiveness is structurally an element of the retraction. The imputation is simply a necessary prelude to the retraction of guilt. But it functions to redistribute offense nonetheless.

[17] This assertion holds whether the forgiveness is public in the full ritual sense or whether it is interpersonal involving a theatrical space of two.

[18] I might connect this to what Emmanuel Levinas has called an 'after-verdict' in relation to justice, which Levinas associates with possibilities of mercy, but forgiveness, as I am construing it, operates outside justice and mercy and by a different logic, E Levinas, Entre-*Nous: Thinking-of-the-Other*, trans. Michael B. Smith and Barbara Harshav, Columbia, UP, New York, 1998, 230-231. Levinas recognizes that justice always involves some form of relation to a totality, some resistance to unilateral force: 'The I's relation to the totality, then, is essentially, economic' (Levinas, *Entre-Nous,* 27). Forgiveness, I would argue, doesn't work in quite this way.

[19] Ricoeur argues that the 'oneness' of self is at stake in the problem of memory (Ricoeur, 494-495).

Bibliography

Bourdieu, P., *The Logic of Practice.* Trans. Richard Nice, Stanford UP, Stanford, 1990.

Derrida, J., *On Cosmopolitanism and Forgiveness.* Trans. Mark Dooley and Michael Hughes. Routledge, New York, 2001.

Digeser, P. D., *Political Forgiveness.* Cornell UP, Ithaca, 2001.

Govier, T., *Forgiveness and Revenge.* Routledge, New York, 2002.

Griswold, C., *Forgiveness: A Philosophical Investigation.* Cambridge, New York, 2007.

Levinas, E., *Entre-Nous: Thinking-of-the-Other.* Trans. Michael B. Smith and Barbara Harshav. Columbia, UP, New York, 1998.

Murphy, J., 'Forgiveness, Self-Respect and the Value of Resentment'. *Handbook of Forgiveness*. Ed. Everett L. Worthington, Jr., Routledge, New York, 2005, 33-41.

Rice, A., and Kristeva J., *Forgiveness: an Interview*. PMLA 117.2, March 2002, 278-285.

Ricoeur, P., *Memory, History, Forgetting*. Trans. Kathleen Blamey and David Pellauer. Chicago UP, Chicago, 2004.

Solomon, R., *A Passion for Justice: Emotions and the Origins of the Social Contract*. Addison-Wesley, Reading, 1990.

Steve Larocco teaches literary theory and seventeenth-century poetry at Southern Connecticut State University in the US. He has published work on Shakespeare, John Donne and Greek tragedy. He is currently writing an interdisciplinary book on the ethical impulse.

Undoing What Has Been Done:
Arendt and Levinas on Forgiveness

Christopher R. Allers

Abstract
If it is true that to forgive a person *qua* offender involves forgiving the person's deed *qua* offence, what does it mean to forgive an offence? Focusing the argument around Hannah Arendt and Emmanuel Levinas, this paper will argue that forgiveness involves undoing or reversing a misdeed by reversing time and acting upon the past misdeed, cleansing and repeating it in the past, and making it *as if* it did not happen. Such an act of forgiveness, thus, releases the offender from the offensive past by giving the offender a new past, a new beginning, and the possibility of beginning anew. We will begin by focusing on Arendt's understanding of forgiveness in *The Human Condition*. One of the characteristics of action, according to Arendt, is that it is irreversible and cannot be undone. However, forgiveness, for her, performs the miraculous task of reversing an action that has consequences that one never anticipated. Forgiveness, then, is the undoing of what has been done for the sake of who did it. While Arendt later stopped talking about forgiveness as undoing what was done, we should not be too quick to jettison such an understanding of forgiveness and, instead, should hold to it, but take it in another direction. A direction in which we can take it is the one proposed by Levinas, who, in *Totality and Infinity*, discusses forgiveness in a way similar to Arendt's understanding in *The Human Condition*. Levinas, however, is more explicit about what such an undoing would entail; namely, forgiveness is a reversing of time that makes it *as if* the deed had not been done, *as if* the doer had not done the deed. In forgiveness, the forgiver acts upon the past and gives the offender a new, forgiven past that releases the offender from the past offence and allows for new beginnings. The deed has been done; yet, by forgiving, the past is cleansed and the future is opened for the offender to begin again *as if* the deed was never done.

Key Words: Forgiveness, action, Hannah Arendt, Emmanuel Levinas.

*****

'*... no one deliberates about the past, but about what is future and capable of being otherwise, while what is past is not capable of not having taken place; hence Agathon was right in saying: For this alone is lacking even to God, To make undone things that have once been done.*'
- Aristotle[1]

'What's done cannot be undone.'
- Lady Macbeth[2]

*'By the grace of forgiveness, the thing that had been done has not been
done.'*
- Vladimir Jankélévitch[3]

1.   'Love the sinner and hate the sin.'

We have all heard some version of this old Christian platitude,
which is actually a paraphrase of St. Augustine.[4] Perhaps one prefers this
slogan translated into a less religiously-charged vocabulary – 'love the person
and hate the offence,' 'love the doer and not the deed.' We often see such a
platitude sneaking in the back door of discussions about forgiveness: 'forgive
the sinner, not the sin,' 'forgive the offender, not the offence,' 'forgive the
doer, not the deed.' Whichever translation you prefer, such a catch-phrase
serve to get across the notion that we forgive the person and not the terrible
deed that they did. However, this trite and worn cliché, in my opinion, has
overstayed its welcome. It may have done some work in reminding us that we
should not condone sin, but whoever said that forgiving is synonymous with
condoning? Well, *Merriam-Webster Dictionary*, for one, and the *Oxford
English Dictionary*, for another. *Merriam-Webster* would have one believe
that to 'condone' is 'to overlook or forgive,' especially 'by treating (an
offence) as harmless or trivial.' The *Oxford English Dictionary*, likewise,
defines 'condone' as to 'accept or forgive (an offence or wrongdoing).'
While it may not be my place to haggle over definitions with *Merriam-
Webster* or the great *Oxford English Dictionary*, the Dictionary of
Dictionaries, I would like to step out of my place and say that to 'forgive'
does not mean the same thing as to 'condone,' particularly because
forgiveness is not an overlooking and does not treat anything as harmless or
trivial. Rather, a forgiveness worthy of the name is concerned with looking-
at (not overlooking) the most harmful and the most serious offences and
treating them as such. If they are overlooked, then offences are not forgiven,
but simply ignored or disregarded. If they are treated as harmless and trivial,
then offences are not forgiven; rather, we are wilfully deluding ourselves.
Forgiveness is not concerned with intentional ignorance or deliberate self-
delusion. Neither is forgiveness concerned with condoning in the sense of
tacitly approving (or accepting without disapproving); to forgive an offence
is not to tacitly approve it. Rather, you forgive an offence precisely because
you disapprove it, precisely because it is wrong, or else forgiveness would
not even be brought up. If you approved it, it would not need forgiveness.[5]

Forgiveness, rather, is a release, particularly releasing the doer from the deed. Forgiveness, then, is concerned with the doer, the offender, the sinner. This is understood in the Christian slogan – 'forgive the sinner' – therefore, in this paper, I am not going to argue that forgiveness is concerned with the sinner, the offender, the doer. We already know that. It is one of the presuppositions from which this paper springs and I am not going to focus on it. Yet, can a sinner be forgiven without in some way forgiving the sin? Can a doer be released from the deed, the misdeed, without in some way altering (in the act of forgiving, not prior to it) the past misdeed in order to release the doer? I would say no, and this is another presupposition of this paper – to forgive the doer is at the same time to forgive a misdeed. I do not think I will get away as easily with this presupposition, however, so I will briefly explicate why I think this is the case.

While one is not simply the sum of one's actions – that is, one is not exhausted by one's various inscriptions in the world, as Paul Ricoeur would say[6] – action, according to Arendt, does reveal and make manifest 'who somebody is.'[7] In light of this 'revelatory character' of action[8] – that is, since any particular act reveals 'who' the agent is – the agent is indissolubly bound to and, in an important sense, 'one' with the act. If it were the case, as Arendt argues, that deeds reveal 'who' a person is, then to forgive a person without forgiving the person's deed would be to forgive that person only up to a point. It would be to forgive the part of the offender who either has not offended in the past or will not offend in the future, but it is not to forgive the 'who' revealed in this deed, the offender *qua* offender, the part of the offender that has been offending and thus needs forgiveness. Forgiveness, rather, focuses on the 'who' revealed in this deed, on the instant of offending when the offender is, in an important sense, 'one' with the offence – so indissolubly bound to the offence that to forgive the offender also means to forgive the offence. As Vladimir Jankélévitch writes:

> Forgiveness aims at the thing that the wicked person did, an act that the evil person committed, a wrong that the evil person bears, or a misdeed for which the evil person made himself responsible. Forgiveness does not only forgive the being, it forgives the doing, or rather the having-done. It forgives the ravages of this being; it forgives the being for these ravages.[9]

With these two presuppositions in hand – that forgiveness is concerned with 1) forgiving the offender and that 2) to forgive the offender *qua* offender includes forgiving the offence – the purpose of this paper is to explore what it means to forgive an offence, sin, or misdeed. However, such an exploration, hopefully, will not amount to aimlessly wandering through the wilderness. I will chart out an itinerary that, while involving a few stops, leads toward a destination. The destination, and this is the thesis of this paper, is that forgiveness is undoing or reversing a misdeed by reversing time and acting upon the misdeed, cleansing and repeating it in the past, and making it *as if* it did not happen. Such an act of forgiveness, thus, releases the offender from the offensive past by giving the offender a new past, a new beginning, and the possibility of beginning anew. Arriving at such a destination will be a difficult journey; so let me lay out the itinerary. We will begin by focusing on Hannah Arendt's understanding of forgiveness as she expresses it in *The Human Condition*. Arendt sets the stage by discussing forgiveness as the reversing of the irreversible, the undoing of what has been done. One of the characteristics of action, according to Arendt, is that it is irreversible and cannot be undone. Forgiveness, as she understands it, however, performs the miraculous and impossible task of reversing an action that has consequences that we never anticipated. Forgiveness, then, is the undoing of what has been done for the sake of who did it. Here we see that, for Arendt, to forgive a doer is indissolubly tied to forgiving a deed and that forgiving a deed allows for the forgiven person to begin anew. However, Arendt claims that forgiveness is not concerned with misdeeds, offences, or sins, but with actions that 'get away from us,' from whose consequences we need to be released. While Arendt focuses forgiveness on reversing deeds whose consequences are harmful, I would like to focus forgiveness on harmful deeds themselves, on *mis*deeds, offences, or sins. Furthermore, Arendt is not quite clear as to what undoing a deed would look like, and she later stopped talking about forgiveness as undoing what was done or reversing the irreversible. I am not ready to jettison such an understanding of forgiveness, however, and would like to hold to it, but take it in another direction.

The direction in which I would like to take it is the one proposed by Emmanuel Levinas who, near the end of *Totality and Infinity* (in a section entitled 'The Infinity of Time'), discusses forgiveness (*pardon*) in a way similar to Arendt's understanding of forgiveness in *The Human Condition*.[10] Levinas has a more expanded notion of forgiveness, however, one that concerns the undoing or reversing of misdeeds. Furthermore, he is more explicit about what such an undoing or reversing would entail; namely, forgiveness is a reversing of time that makes it *as if* the deed had not been done, *as if* the doer had not done the deed. In forgiveness, the forgiver acts upon the past by repeating and cleansing it, and, therefore, the forgiver gives the offender a new past, a forgiven past, which releases the offender from the offensive past and allows for recommencement or new beginnings.[11] From here it will be a short walk to our destination. Both Arendt and Levinas discuss forgiveness in relation to new beginnings, rebirth, and recommencement, so keep your eyes peeled for this landmark along the way.

To begin, we will turn to Arendt's understanding of forgiveness as undoing what was done or reversing the irreversible.

2.   Arendt on Forgiveness: Reversing Actions and Releasing Agents

In *The Human Condition*, Hannah Arendt makes a distinction between labour, work, and action – the 'three fundamental human activities' which make up the *vita activa*.[12] Such activities are 'fundamental' because 'each corresponds to one of the basic conditions under which life on earth has been given to man' – labour corresponds to the biological process of life itself, work corresponds to the unnaturalness of human existence and the worldliness of the human artifice, and action corresponds to the human condition of plurality, to 'the fact that men, not Man, live on the earth and inhabit the world.'[13]

Action involves the possibility of new beginnings.[14] For Arendt, a person's capacity for action means that the 'unexpected can be expected,' the 'infinitely improbable' – or, better, the impossible – is possible, and such expectation of the unexpectable, such possibility of the impossible, is possible (as impossible) because each person is, by virtue of being born, unique, 'so that with each birth something uniquely new comes into the world.'[15] Action as beginning 'corresponds to the fact of birth' as the 'actualisation of the human condition of natality.'[16] Natality, for Arendt, in contrast to Heidegger's 'being-toward-death' and his preoccupation with mortality, is concerned with the new beginnings inherent in birth (*natalis*) and the concomitant capacity for beginning something new which each and every one of us has by virtue of being born.[17] That is, natality is concerned with both the possibility of newness inherent in birth itself and also the 'second birth' in which we 'respond to the beginning which came into the world when we were born' by inserting ourselves through word and deed into the human world and 'beginning something new on our own initiative.'[18] Action as a 'new beginning' then is a 'miracle,' for Arendt, in that any new beginning 'always happens against the overwhelming odds of statistical laws and their probability.'[19] Every act, every new beginning, 'breaks into the world as an infinite improbability' – that is, every new beginning is an impossibility that breaks in to (and breaks up) our horizon of possibility.[20] To quote Arendt at length:

> The miracle that saves the world, the realm of human affairs, from its normal, 'natural' ruin is ultimately the fact of natality, in which the faculty of action is ontologically rooted. It is, in other words, the birth of new men and the new beginning, the action they are capable of by virtue of being born. Only the full experience of this capacity can bestow upon human affairs faith and hope, those two

essential characteristics of human existence…It is this faith
in and hope for the world that found perhaps its most
glorious and most succinct expression in the few words
with which the Gospels announced their 'glad tidings'; 'A
child has been born unto us.'[21]

Natality, the capacity to begin ever anew, inherent in each individual by
virtue of being born, is our faith and hope that we are not condemned to some
fatalistic eternal recurrence of the same that what has happened did not have
to happen and does not have to happen again. Thanks to natality, we can
expect the unexpectable occurrence of the miraculous.

Action, for Arendt, is free; a freedom to do something that has not
been done before. As Arendt writes in her essay entitled 'What is Freedom?,'
action, 'to be free, must be free from motive on one side, from its intended
goal as a specific result on the other.'[22] This is not to say that when we act we
do so without motive or intended goals. Certainly, when we act we have
motives and goals and they are 'important factors in every act.'[23] However,
they are only 'determining factors,' that is, they give direction to our actions,
but 'action is free to the extent that it is able to transcend them.'[24] Such free
action is characterized by boundlessness, unpredictability, and irreversibility
– three (potentially hazardous) characteristics of action.

First, action is boundless. When we act, we do so into an already
existing web of human relationships, the 'medium where every reaction
becomes a chain reaction and where every process is the cause of new
processes.'[25] Action establishes relationships, opens limitations, and cuts
across all boundaries. Laws are meant to protect against the boundlessness of
action. While they may provide some protection, however, laws are never
reliable safeguards against such boundlessness.

Second, action is unpredictable. Laws, which may provide
protection against the boundlessness of action, are ultimately helpless against
the unpredictability of action. Action is unpredictable because of the 'basic
unreliability of men who never can guarantee today who they will be
tomorrow' and because it is impossible to foretell 'the consequences of an act
within a community of equals where everybody has the same capacity to
act.'[26] The only possible safeguard against the unpredictability of action, for
Arendt, is the making and keeping of promises. Promises create 'islands of
security' in the unpredictable 'ocean of uncertainty' that is the future.[27]
Promises are the uniquely human way of ordering the future, making it
predictable and reliable to the extent that this is humanly possible.[28]

Third, action is irreversible. Once one acts, the action cannot be
taken back and actions have consequences. It is irreversible in that the actor
is 'unable to undo what one has done though one did not, and could not, have
known what he was doing.'[29] The making and keeping of promises are not

absolute safeguards against the unpredictability of action and, therefore, we need some way in which to reverse the irreversible action. This is where Arendt brings in the faculty of forgiveness as the 'possible redemption from the predicament of irreversibility.'[30]

Forgiveness, for Arendt, is itself an action – a miraculous new beginning – creating a new situation. Forgiveness – as opposed to vengeance or revenge, which are predictable reactions with no power to unbind – 'can never be predicted; it is the only reaction that acts in an unexpected way and thus retains, though being a reaction, something of the original character of action.'[31] Furthermore, forgiveness is the 'only reaction that does not merely re-act but acts anew and unexpectedly, unconditioned by the act which provoked it and therefore freeing from its consequences both the one who forgives and the one who is forgiven.'[32] Forgiveness is an action that redeems the irreversibility of action in that 'forgiving attempts the seemingly impossible, to undo what has been done, and that it succeeds in making a new beginning where beginnings seemed to have become no longer possible.'[33] Forgiveness, by attempting the impossible task of reversing the irreversible or undoing what has been done, is a new beginning where beginnings appear to be impossible. However, I would like to add that although Arendt understands the possibility for new beginnings as a capacity of every human by virtue of being born, forgiveness as a new beginning also gives a new beginning to the one who is forgiven and this is precisely where a new beginning seems the most impossible. We will return to this later in our discussion of Levinas.

Forgiveness is, then, the undoing or reversing of '*what* was done' – the act – 'for the sake of *who* did it.'[34] Without being 'released from the consequences of what we have done' – that is, without being forgiven – 'our capacity to act would, as it were, be confined to one single deed from which we could never recover; we would remain the victims of its consequences forever, not unlike the sorcerer's apprentice who lacked the magic formula to break the spell.'[35] Forgiveness, for Arendt, is the mutual release of both the one who forgives and the one who is forgiven from the consequences of boundless, unpredictable, and irreversible action in order for it to be possible for life to go on, since, without forgiveness, we would be forever bound to the consequences of our original action and would lack the courage to ever act again.

There are two characteristics of forgiveness, as Arendt understands it in *The Human Condition*. On the one hand, Arendt understands forgiveness as a release, an unbinding of an agent from the consequences of an action.[36] On the other hand, Arendt holds that forgiveness is the undoing of what has been done for the sake of the one who did it.[37] These two characteristics are combined in *The Human Condition*, thus forging an understanding of forgiveness that focuses on forgiving the act in order to release the agent from its consequences, undoing what was done for the sake of the doer. Such an understanding of forgiveness attempts the impossible and miraculous task of reversing the irreversible in order to release the agent from the consequences of an action.

In her work on forgiveness after *The Human Condition*, however, Arendt goes on to separate these two characteristics, no longer speaking of forgiveness as undoing while still maintaining the understanding of forgiveness as release. After reading *The Human Condition*, W.H. Auden, in a letter to Arendt, questioned her claim that we forgive what was done. 'I was wrong,' Arendt concedes, 'when I said we forgive what was done for the sake of who did it.... I can forgive somebody without forgiving anything.'[38] Therefore, as she writes in her essay 'Some Questions on Moral Philosophy,' Arendt came to understand that 'it is the person and not the crime that is forgiven.'[39] Here we see that Arendt no longer understands forgiveness to be directed at the act in order to release the agent from the consequences of an action; rather, forgiveness is focused solely on the person. Therefore, forgiveness, for Arendt, is no longer concerned with undoing what was done; rather, it is concerned with releasing the agent from the act. Elizabeth Young-Bruehl writes that forgiveness as '*releasing* is much better for [Arendt's] purposes than *undoing* or *reversing* for it carries no implication that the deed is forgotten or dissolved in some way, while releasing implies being unbound from the past in order to go on: it is a letting go.'[40]

But is Arendt too quick in jettisoning her understanding of forgiveness as reversing the irreversible, as undoing what has been done? Does forgiveness as undoing necessarily imply that the 'deed is forgotten or dissolved in some way,' as Young-Bruehl says? Can you 'forgive somebody without forgiving anything,' as Arendt says? Can an agent be released from her act without in some way forgiving the act? Can one simply forgive an agent and not forgive the act? I think that she has jettisoned this understanding of forgiveness too quickly; the unbinding of the agent from the past deed is not possible without, in some way, undoing (altering, transforming) the past deed.

We will turn to Levinas shortly, but before we do, I would like to point to perhaps the main problem I have with Arendt's notion of forgiveness as undoing and releasing. Forgiveness, for Arendt, is concerned with undoing what was done in order to release the person from the *consequences* of action and not from the action itself because action, in the very specific, phenomenological way in which Arendt describes it, is an 'end in itself'[41] and is therefore 'good' in and of itself and does not need to be forgiven.[42] However, actions, as boundless and unpredictable, can become 'trespasses' (*harmartanein*).[43] 'Trespassing,' according to Arendt,

is an everyday occurrence which is in the very nature of
action's constant establishment of new relationships within
a web of relations, and it needs forgiving, dismissing, in
order to make it possible for life to go on by constantly
releasing men from what they have done unknowingly.
Only through this constant mutual release from what they
do can men remain free agents.[44]

Since action is unpredictable, when we act 'we know not what we do' and
every day we 'miss the mark.' Forgiveness, then, is not concerned with those
unpunishable and unforgivable 'offences' (*skandala*).[45] Forgiveness and
punishment are alternatives, for Arendt, in that they both 'attempt to put an
end to something that without interference could go on endlessly.'[46] A deed
that turns out to be unpunishable, according to Arendt, is also unforgivable,
and *vice versa*. Such a deed is an *offence* which 'since Kant, we call 'radical
evil'.'[47] Therefore, on the one hand, radically evil offences, for Arendt, are
outside of the realm of forgiveness and punishment.[48] In the destructive case
of 'radical evil,' Arendt repeats with Jesus: 'It were better for him that a
millstone were hanged about his neck, and he cast into the sea.'[49] On the
other hand, 'crime and willed evil' are outside the realm of forgiveness as
well.[50] Crime or willed evil are, according to Arendt's reading of Jesus, dealt
with at the Last Judgment which 'is not characterized by forgiveness but by
just retribution.'[51] In a word, forgiveness, for Arendt, is not concerned with
evil.[52]

Why can't evil deeds be forgiven? Arendt seems to underestimate
her own notion of natality (is not natality the capacity for new beginnings
where new beginnings no longer seem possible?) and makes forgiveness a
rather trivial matter that is too predictable, expected, and calculated (three
things she said forgiveness is not).[53] What is more unpredictable, unexpected,
and uncalculated than forgiving something that appears to be unforgivable?
Is there not always the possibility, by virtue of being born, for an agent to
begin anew, no matter how evil their actions may be, even after a so-called
'unforgivable' act? It may be better if they were never born, but why not
afford them the possibility of being reborn? Why not forgive?[54] While Arendt
focuses forgiveness on undoing what was done in order to release a person
from the *consequences* of an unpredictable and boundless action, I would like
to follow Levinas, to whom we now turn, and focus it on undoing what was
done in order to release a person from the action itself, from the deed *qua*
misdeed, from the offence and not simply from the consequences of an action
that has 'missed the mark.' Forgiveness, as I understand it, involves the
undoing of an offence, the reversing of a misdeed in order to release the agent
from the misdeed, from the offence as well as its consequences.[55]

3.   Levinas on Forgiveness: Reversing Time and Giving Time

In her discussion of forgiveness as reversing or undoing, Arendt is not clear about what such a reversal of the irreversible entails. What does it mean to 'undo' what has been done? Does she take such an undoing in a metaphysical sense in which the forgiver takes the place of Peter Damian's omnipotent God and, reaching back in time, 'physically' or 'literally' makes something that was done in the past not to have been done at all?[56] However Arendt would answer this question (and I doubt she would take undoing in such a metaphysical sense), I hold that forgiveness as undoing or reversing is not concerned with 'literally' or 'physically' changing the past in such a metaphysical sense, seeing as undoing the past deed in such a way would not only annul the past but would also annul the forgiveness, inasmuch as there would be nothing to forgive, the offender would become innocent having never offended to begin with.   Forgiveness does not make the offender innocent; it makes the offender forgiven. It requires that the past offence be left standing, or else there would be nothing to forgive, even as it requires that it somehow be undone or reversed. Therefore, rather than understanding the undoing or reversing in such a metaphysical sense, I will read this undoing or reversing in a 'purely ethico-phenomenological sense.'[57] In such a reading, I will turn to Levinas who has a more expanded notion of forgiveness, one that concerns the undoing or reversing of misdeeds, and, furthermore, he is more explicit about what such an undoing or reversing would entail; namely, forgiveness is a reversing of time that makes it *as if* the event never happened, *as if* the deed had not been done, *as if* the doer had not done the deed.

For Levinas, one can 'give the past a new meaning,' 'repair the past' by re-narrating it, putting it in a new perspective, thus freeing and opening up the future.[58]   This is not, however, the work of forgiveness, but the hermeneutical work of memory, the 'salutary character of succession,' in which the past is re-presented and repaired within limits, but time keeps marching on.[59] In the work of memory, the re-presenting of the past, the present is 'laden with all the past' and 'pregnant with the whole future' to the point of becoming bloated like the Fat Man who expanded himself and ate three hundred oxen and drank three hundred barrels of wine.[60] By re-presenting and remembering – which is what Arendt means by *teshuvah* or repentance[61] – one can retell one's past, find new meanings for one's past, and repair one's past, but only so much.[62] As Robert Gibbs stresses, 'it is *forgiveness* that changes the past, *not* repentance' or memory.[63] In and of itself without recourse to others, memory has its limits; it can only do so much, 'its age limits its powers,' as Levinas would say.[64] Without recourse to others – that is, without being forgiven – the past can be repaired, retold, and redescribed, but not to the point of changing it.

In contrast to the limited power of re-presenting the past, Levinas discusses what he calls 'the discontinuous time of fecundity' which 'makes possible an absolute youth and recommencement.'[65] This discontinuous time, beyond mere re-presentation, is the time of forgiveness in which forgiveness bequeaths a radical new beginning without which 'the I would remain a subject in which every adventure would revert into the adventure of a fate' and thus no adventure at all.[66] By discontinuous time, Levinas has in mind the parent/child relationship (or father/son relationship to use his nomenclature), in which the parent has new chances in the life of the child; the child represents a new beginning for the parent. 'My child is a stranger,' Levinas writes, invoking Isaiah 49, 'but a stranger who is not only mine, for he *is* me. He is me a stranger to myself.'[67] It seems that Levinas is not discussing the parent/child relationship in a strictly intergenerational, procreational, or biological sense here, and I would say that this discontinuity of time can be *re*generational, pertaining to the possibility of rebirth within the lifetime of a single person.[68] In a word, forgiveness is not only concerned with your flesh and blood child, but with your rebirth. When someone forgives an offender, the offender is given a new birth in the eyes of the forgiver. Forgiveness, then, is 'the very work of time'[69] since, as Levinas writes in *Time and the Other*, 'time is essentially a new birth.'[70]

Forgiveness, for Levinas, is paradoxical in the sense that it is retroactive, it changes and acts upon the past, as the very work of time it opens up the past itself. From the view of 'common time,' in which the present acts for the future but not the past (because the past is past and what's done is done), forgiveness 'represents an inversion of the natural order of things' in that it is a 'retroaction,' a reversing of time.[71] In remembering, we only bring the past forward, re-present the past, but do not go back to the past and change it. For Levinas, forgiveness 'refers to the instant elapsed' in that 'it permits the subject who has committed himself in a past instant to be *as though* that instant had not passed on, to be *as though* he had not committed himself.'[72] In forgiveness, what was done in the past is 'undone' not in some metaphysical sense in which one 'physically' or 'literally' changes the past, making it to be that what was done was never done, but, for Levinas, is only 'undone' in a 'purely ethico-phenomenological sense.'[73] Here the past is not manipulated, distorted, annulled, or abandoned and blotted out by forgetting. Forgetting, for Levinas, 'does not concern the reality of the event forgotten' and it 'nullifies the relations with the past.'[74] Rather, forgiveness, which is more active than forgetting, 'acts upon the past, somehow repeats the event, purifying it.'[75] The past is not re-presented in the present through memory, or nullified through forgetting, but repeated in the past. Furthermore, the past event is repeated, but repeated differently, *as if* it has not passed, *as if* it never happened, *as if* the doer had not 'committed' herself in action. Forgiveness is a 'rigorously *ethical* event' in which the other reverses time and repeats the past *as if* it had not happened and *as if* the agent had not committed herself, therefore, altering 'the *meaning* of the past, the *event* of the past, while preserving the past offence.'[76] *Historically*, the deed was done, but *ethically*, it is *as if* it had not been done.[77]

Such repetition purifies or cleanses the past event – the past is washed clean, not washed away – and 'conserves the past pardoned in the purified present.'[78] Forgiveness cleanses the past event and repairs it, according to Caputo, 'by repeating the past *as forgiven*.'[79] As Gibbs writes:

> Forgiveness achieves a freedom in relation to the past, by *repeating it* and *cleansing it*. To forgive is not merely to remember, not merely to give a new meaning to an old event, but is to change the past event, to conserve the change *[the forgiven past]* in the present. The repetition appears as repetition, as a doubled past, both the sinful one and the cleansed one.[80]

So while the event *did* happen (of course it did happen, for if it did not happen there would be nothing to forgive), it is repeated *as if* it did not happen. Such repetition purifies or cleanses the past event – the past is washed clean, not washed away – and 'conserves the past pardoned in the purified present.'[81] Forgiveness cleanses the past event and repairs it 'by repeating the past *as forgiven*.'[82] So while the event *did* happen, it is repeated in the past *as if* it did not happen and its reality is transformed in the present. By being forgiven, as Jeffrey Dudiak writes:

> It is not that my past is eliminated... but time will be relived, over and again, providing the possibility of a break with the past that is not heavy with this past, of a recommencement in time, liberated, time and again, with each passing generation, from fate.[83]

In forgiveness, I am given a new beginning, I become a child. Both pasts – the sinful one in which the event did happen and the cleansed or purified one in which it is *as if* the event did not happen – are conserved in the present. Therefore, forgiveness does not reinstate innocence, because the past did happen, yet, forgiveness acts upon the past making it *as if* it did not happen.[84]

Levinas then goes on to discuss forgiveness as constituting time itself. Departing from the tradition of phenomenology, time, for Levinas, is not the achievement of my consciousness, it is not of my doing, the future is not a 'future-present', a set of 'indistinguishable possibles which flow toward my present and which I would grasp.'[85] Rather, time comes from across an 'absolute interval,'[86] from the other as *tout autre*, who, according to Caputo, 'represents the absolutely unforeseeable future.'[87]   Caputo continues: 'The gift of forgiveness from the other belongs to the way the other, in forgiving me, gives me time.'[88] In forgiveness, this gift of time from the other is a gift of a new past, a cleansed sinful past, a forgiven past. I am released from my sinful past and given a new past, a forgiven past. In giving me my past, the other 'connects' the present to the past, 'unknots' me from my sinful past and 'reknots' me to my forgiven past (to use Gibb's translation).[89]   According to Caputo, '[b] y releasing me from my past, the other gives me a new past and hence a new future.'[90] Forgiveness, for Levinas, is the giving of time, the giving of a new birth.

4.   Conclusions and Beginnings
To conclude, we should focus on this mention of 'new birth' which reveals the most striking similarity between Levinas and Arendt. As Richard Kearney writes, 'Levinas (like Arendt)… promotes the idea of beginning-again-through-the-birth-of-another. Ethics as natality rather than mortality.'[91] For Arendt, natality is the capacity to begin anew that humans have by virtue of being born. For Levinas, we see the new birth or 'recommencement' coming from the other. The other gives me a new past, which releases me from my 'sinful' past, and, therefore, gives the possibility of a new future, a 'new chance for desiring and being good.'[92] By forgiving, the other gives me a new beginning.   I see these two understandings of new birth as complementary. The other gives me time, gives me a new past, and gives me a new beginning. In the eyes of the forgiving other, it is *as if* one did not do what one did, the forgiven person is released from what he or she did and therefore, is given a new beginning. Such a gift of a new beginning allows for the possibility of beginning anew – for the possibility of new beginnings in Arendt's sense – it allows for the possibility to 'capitalise' upon our capacity of natality (forgiveness *allows* for beginning anew, it is not given *on the condition that* you begin anew). Forgiveness gives a new beginning where one no longer seemed to be possible. Even when such a possibility to begin anew seems impossible, the other, by forgiving me, gives me a new past, gives me a new beginning in the sense of being reborn, thus, releasing this capacity from its bondage to the sinful past and making it possible to begin again. The Levinasian other gives a new beginning, a new birth by virtue of which natality, the Arendtian capacity for new beginnings – which each of us has by virtue of being born, and, I would add, by virtue of being *re*born, given a new beginning, a new birth in the Levinasian sense – is released from bondage in the act of forgiveness, of giving a new birth, of giving a new beginning from which we have the possibility of initiating new beginnings. In other words, in forgiving, which is a new beginning where new beginnings no longer seem possible, the other gives me a new beginning (in the Levinasian sense) that makes new beginnings (in the Arendtian sense)

possible. Forgiveness is that way in which humans give birth, continually, to the child of the future. Glad tidings, unto us a child is born.[93]

In calling Arendt beyond herself in a Levinasian direction, we can see that Arendt is on the right path when she discusses forgiveness as the reversing of the irreversible, or the undoing of what has been done for the sake of who did it. In order to forgive a person, the deed must be altered in some way; it must be undone or reversed making it *as if* it did not happen. Therefore, Arendt is correct to focus forgiveness, in part, on the deed itself and not simply the doer, and I think we should not be quick to jettison such an understanding of forgiveness. However, forgiveness, for Arendt, concerns undoing the deed in order to release the doer from the malevolent *consequences* of the action and not from the action itself. Forgiveness appears to be trivial, predictable, and calculable if it is relegated to only releasing agents from *consequences* of action and is not allowed to focus on misdeeds or offences themselves. At this point, we should follow Levinas and focus forgiveness on the deed *qua* misdeed, to release the doer not just from the consequences of a deed, but from a misdeed or offence itself (as well as its consequences). From here we can take Arendt's understanding of forgiveness as undoing or reversing, *mutatis mutandis*, in a Levinasian direction in order to explicate what such an undoing or reversing would entail. Forgiveness focuses on a past misdeed, reversing time in order to (retro)act upon the misdeed, repeating it and purifying it, undoing or reversing the misdeed, making it *as if* the misdeed had not been done, *as if* the agent had not committed the misdeed, thus, giving the agent a new, forgiven past. Forgiveness – as the undoing of what has been done – alters the nature of the past transgression, by repeating and purifying it, in order to loosen its hold on the perpetrator, giving a new beginning and making new beginnings possible where they no longer seemed to be possible. Thus, the perpetrator is released and reinterpreted in light of present and future possibilities as well as the forgiven past. The irreversible is reversed by reversing time, (retro) acting upon the action, repeating it *as if* it never happened, thus reversing or undoing the action and giving the agent a new past and the possibility of a new beginning. In such a way, to forgive the wrong-doer – to release the doer from the misdeed – one must forgive the wrong-done, the misdeed, while in no way condoning, overlooking, or approving the misdeed; rather, one must go back to the misdeed, repeat it and purify it, reverse it and undo it, make it *as if* it never happened, *as if* the doer did not do it. In forgiveness, what was done is undone, the irreversible is reversed.[94]

Notes

[1] Aristotle, *Nicomachean Ethics*, trans. D. Ross, Oxford University Press, Oxford, 1998, Book 6, Chapter 2, 139.

[2] Shakespeare, *Macbeth*, Act V, Scene 1. See Shakespeare, *The Complete Works of William Shakespeare*, Books, Inc., New York 1960, 1066.

[3] V Jankélévitch, *Forgiveness*, trans. A. Kelley, University of Chicago Press, Chicago and London, 2005, 164.

[4] In a letter to the nuns of Hippo (Letter 211, paragraph 11), Augustine writes: '*cum dilectione hominum et odio vitiorum.*' See St. Augustine, *Letters: 211-270*, ed. J. Rotelle, New City Press, New York, 2005, 25. Here it is translated: 'with love for the persons and hatred for their vices.'

[5] According to Charles Griswold:

> Broadly speaking, to condone is to collaborate in the lack of censure of an action, and perhaps to enable further wrong-doing by the offender. One may condone in the sense of accepting while not disapproving (by not holding the wrong-doing against its author), or in the sense of tolerating while disapproving (a sort of 'look the other way' or 'putting up with it' strategy). If forgiveness were condonation in either sense, it would certainly not be a virtue, and thus would no longer count as true forgiveness. The first amounts to complicity in or collusion with the wrong-doing, perhaps covered up by some form of rationalization. And of course, if its attempts exempts the wrong-doer from responsibility for the wrong action, it amounts to excuse. The second is compatible with continued resentment directed at the offender. But the aim of forgiveness is something quite different... (C. Griswold, *Forgiveness: A Philosophical Investigation*, Cambridge University Press, Cambridge 2007, 47).

Griswold is correct; forgiveness is not the same as condonation. He simply assumes, however, that 'true forgiveness' is a 'virtue.' Perhaps we should not be so quick to make such an assumption. Is not a forgiveness worthy of the name more about excess and superabundance than it is about moderation? Forgiveness may turn out to be nothing more than condonation, it's a risk. Perhaps a forgiveness worthy of the name does not put up absolute safeguards against condonation. Nevertheless, a discussion of virtue ethics and forgiveness is beyond the scope of this paper, so I am going to leave these claims unsubstantiated. I hope to return to them in some later work.

[6] P Ricoeur, *Memory, History, Forgetting*, translated by K. Blamey and D. Pellauer, The University of Chicago Press, Chicago and London, 2004, 490.

[7] H Arendt, *The Human Condition*, The University of Chicago Press, Chicago and London, 1958), 178. Hereafter *HC*. For Arendt's discussion of action as disclosing 'who' the actor is, see Arendt, *HC*, 175ff.

[8] Arendt, *HC*, 178.

[9] Jankélévitch, *Forgiveness*, 126.

[10] E Levinas, *Totality and Infinity: An Essay on Exteriority*, trans. A. Lingis, Duquesne University Press, Pittsburgh, PA, 1969.

[11] While Levinas focuses on the hope of *being forgiven* and has little to say about what it would mean *to forgive others*, I think that what he says can apply to both forgiving and being forgiven, to both times when I forgive and when I am forgiven. Levinas does focus on what it means to forgive in E. Levinas, 'Toward the Other', in *Nine Talmudic Readings*, trans. A. Aronowicz, Indiana University Press, Bloomington and Indianapolis, 1990), 12-29. However, his treatment of forgiveness in this work is too much of an economic exchange. Forgiveness is given on the condition of prior repentance. Conditional forgiveness, forgiveness given in an economy of exchange on the condition of repentance (*teshuvah*), is not true forgiveness. Although I will not be arguing this in this paper, forgiveness is unconditional, given when the offender is still sinning and with little or no intention to stop. However, I will not be dealing with this work in this paper; rather, as I said above, I will be applying Levinas' understanding of forgiveness as discussed in *Totality and Infinity* to both forgiving and being forgiven.

[12] Arendt, *HC*, 7.

[13] Arendt, *HC*, 7.

[14] This beginning is only one part of action (*archein*). There is also another side to action, namely acting in concert to see the action through (*prattein*). 'Here it seems as though each action were divided into two parts, the beginning made by a single person and the achievement in which many join by 'bearing' and 'finishing' the enterprise, by seeing it through.' (Arendt, *HC*, 189). (This has been, from the beginning of political philosophy, divided between two different stations in society; the ruler (*archein*) and the ruled (*prattein*). However, Arendt sees this as an attempt to control the unpredictability and irreversibility of action.)

[15] Arendt, *HC*, 178. In such contexts, Arendt often quotes a phrase from Augustine: *Initium ergo ut esset, creatus est homo, ante quem nullus fuit* (which Arendt translates as 'that there be a beginning, man was created before whom there was nobody' (Arendt, *HC*, 177.)). This quote is from Augustine, *De civitate Dei*, Book XII, Chapter 21. (Arendt mistakenly references this quote as coming from *De civitate Dei*, Book XII, Chapter 20.). Henry Bettenson translates this passage as: '[a]nd so to provide that beginning, a man was created, before whom no man ever existed.' Augustine,

The City of God, trans. H. Bettenson, Penguin Books, London 1984, 502. For some excellent work on the inaccuracy of Arendt's citation of the original Latin and the different ways she translates this phrase throughout her work, see D. Billings, 'Natality and Advent: Hannah Arendt and Jürgen Moltmann on Hope and Politics', *The Future of Hope: Christian Tradition amid Modernity and Postmodernity*, ed. M. Volf and W. Katerberg, Eerdmans, Grand Rapids, MI, 2004, 132-133, n.19.

[16] Arendt, *HC*, 178.

[17] Arendt, *HC*, 9. See also *HC*, 246 where Arendt implicitly distances herself from Heidegger when she writes that 'men, though they must die, are not born in order to die but in order to begin.' This is similar to Bruce Springsteen's 'Mary Queen of Arkansas' where he sings 'I was not born to live to die.' Bruce Springsteen, *Greetings from Asbury Park, N.J.*, Sony, 1973.

[18] Arendt, *HC*, 176-177.

[19] Arendt, *HC*, 178.

[20] H Arendt, 'What is Freedom?', *Between Past and Future*, Penguin, New York, 1968, 167.

[21] Arendt, *HC*, 247.

[22] Arendt, 'What is Freedom?', 151.

[23] Arendt, 'What is Freedom?', 151.

[24] Arendt, 'What is Freedom?', 151. See also H. Arendt 'Introduction into Politics', *The Promise of Politics*, ed. J. Kohn, Schocken Books, New York 2007, 194-195.

[25] Arendt, *HC*, 190.

[26] Arendt, *HC*, 244.

[27] Arendt, *HC*, 237.

[28] Although I will not attempt it in this paper, it would be interesting to discuss action in relation to Jacques Derrida's 'archi-promise.' For Derrida, language promises; namely, by speaking, I am promising to tell the truth, the whole truth, and nothing but the truth (but language is just a pointer and never delivers the 'thing itself'), even if you lie (and this is why a lie works, because by speaking you are promising to tell the truth). Perhaps we could say, in a similar way, that action promises; namely, by acting, I am promising (perhaps the universal, or justice, or whatever), a promise that I cannot fulfil (so we always need forgiveness). See J. Derrida, *Memoires: For Paul de Man*, trans. C. Lindsay, J. Culler, and E. Cadava, Columbia University Press, New York, 1986, 119 and H. Coward and T. Foshay, eds., *Derrida and Negative Theology*, SUNY Press, Albany, NY, 1992, 84-85.

[29] Arendt, *HC*, 237.

[30] Arendt, *HC*, 237. Here Arendt claims that forgiveness 'is one of the potentialities of action itself.' The consumptive cycle of labour is redeemed by work and the category of means and ends of work redeemed by action and speech. However, the redemption of the irreversibility and unpredictability of action 'does not arise out of another and possibly higher faculty' (as with labour and work); rather, the redemption is 'one of the potentialities of action itself' – namely, forgiveness and the making and keeping of promises. This is all questionable, however, in Arendt's own scheme. If forgiveness is 'one of the potentialities of action itself,' then forgiveness is not really unpredictable, unexpected, or miraculous. Amazing, perhaps, but not a miracle. Furthermore, in Arendt's scheme, forgiveness seems to be much closer to 'work' in that forgiveness in her scheme is not an 'end in itself' (like action), but seems to be just another means to an end. This all should be questioned more exhaustively; however, I only have time here to flag them on my way by.

[31] Arendt, *HC*, 241. Forgiveness, for Arendt, is the opposite of vengeance or revenge. Vengeance is a re-action against the original action. However, it does not put an end to the consequences of the action. Rather, 'everybody remains bound to the process, permitting the chain reaction contained in every action to take its unhindered course.' Vengeance is programmable, expected, predictable, and calculable; forgiveness is not. See Arendt, *HC*, 240-241.

[32] Arendt, *HC*, 241. Here we see that forgiveness, as a new action, frees both the forgiver and the forgiven from the consequences of the original action. This is another area of Arendt's discussion that should be questioned and, again, I am only pointing it out and moving on. Does forgiveness release both the forgiver and the forgiven? Should it? In this case, does forgiveness just become another self-interested project?

[33] H Arendt, 'The Tradition of Political Thought', *The Promise of Politics*, 58.

[34] Arendt, *HC*, 241.

[35] Arendt, *HC*, 237.

[36] See Arendt, *HC*, 237 and 240.

[37] See Arendt , *HC*, 237 and *HC*, 241.

[38] Arendt to Auden, 14 February 1960, Library of Congress. (Arendt's files do not contain the letter from Auden to which she was replying). See E Young-Breuhl, *For Love of the World*, Yale University Press, New Haven and London, 1982, 371.

[39] H Arendt, 'Some Questions on Moral Philosophy,' *Responsibility and Judgment*, ed. J Kohn, Schocken Books, New York, 2003, 95.

[40] E Young-Bruehl, *Why Arendt Matters*, Yale University Press, New Haven and London, 2006, 100.

[41] Arendt, *HC*, 206. Should Arendt also discuss forgiveness as an end in itself?

[42] While we cannot go into it in this paper, we should not forget what Arendt is doing in *The Human Condition*. She is not putting forward a political *theory* or a political *philosophy* to compete with other political theories or political philosophies. I would highly recommend (maybe with a few qualifications) Dana Villa's 'Arendt, Heidegger, and the Tradition', *Social Research*, Vol. 74, no. 4 Winter, 2007.

[43] Arendt, *HC*, 240 and n. 78.

[44] Arendt, *HC*, 240.

[45] See Arendt, HC, 240, n. 80 and Arendt, 'Some Questions on Moral Philosophy', 125.

[46] Arendt, *HC*, 241.

[47] Arendt, *HC*, 241.

[48] We have yet to take one of Arendt's footnotes seriously enough. In n.80 in Arendt, *HC*, 240, Arendt writes that offences are 'unforgivable, *at least on earth*' (my emphasis). This may bring to mind a Walter Benjamin quote that Arendt includes in her essay on Benjamin: certain thought things 'retain their meaning, possibly their best significance, if they are not *a priori* applied exclusively to man. For example, one could speak of an unforgettable life or moment even if all men had forgotten them. If the nature of such a life or moment required that it not be forgotten, that predicate would not contain a falsehood but merely a claim that it is not being fulfilled by men, and perhaps also a reference to a realm in which it *is* fulfilled: God's remembrance' (Arendt, 'Walter Benjamin, *Men in Dark Times*, Harvest Books, New York, 1970, 203. The quote can be found in W Benjamin 'The Task of the Translator', *Illuminations*, ed. H. Arendt, Schocken Books, New York, 1969, 70). This may serve to trouble Arendt's claim about forgiveness and human possibility. Perhaps forgiveness too retains its utmost significance if it is not *a priori* applied exclusively to humans. Unfortunately, such a discussion is beyond the scope of this paper.

[49] Arendt, *HC*, 241. Here, Arendt is quoting Luke 17:2.

[50] However, above we saw that Arendt writes that 'it is the person and not the *crime* that is forgiven' (Arendt, 'Some Questions on Moral Philosophy', 95. My emphasis.). It is interesting that she uses the word 'crime' here and not 'trespass.' Is this because she has broadened the boundaries of forgiveness to include the possibility of forgiving someone who has committed a crime?

[51] Arendt, *HC*, 240.

[52] See A Friedland's 'Evil and Forgiveness: Transitions', *Perspectives on Evil and Human Wickedness*, Vol. 1, No. 4, 2004, 24-47.

[53] Arendt, *HC*, 241.

[54] For a discussion of forgiveness as forgiving the unforgiveable, see K.E. Løgstrup's *The Ethical Demand*, trans. H. Fink and A. MacIntyre, University of Notre Dame Press, Notre Dame, 1997, particularly pages 209-213), J. Derrida's 'To Forgive: The Unforgiveable and the Imprescriptible', *Questioning God*, ed. J D Caputo, M Dooley, and M J Scanlon,: Indiana University Press, Bloomington and Indianapolis, 2001, 21-51), J Derrida's *On Cosmopolitanism and Forgiveness* (trans. by M Dooley and M Hughes, Routledge, London and New York, 2001, 27-60), and Jankélévitch, *Forgiveness*, 156-165.

[55] One could suggest that if an action is not simply a punctual moment in time, but something with consequences that extend into the future, that past actions have a history, a history of their consequences, then forgiveness can do transformative work on past actions by unpredictably changing their consequences.

[56] See P Damian's 'On Divine Omnipotence', in P Damian, *Letters*, vol. 4, trans. O J Blum, Catholic University of America Press, Washington D.C, 1998.

[57] J D Caputo, *The Weakness of God: A Theology of the Event*, Indiana University Press, Bloomington and Indianapolis, 2006, 229.

[58] Levinas, *Totality and Infinity*, 282.

[59] Levinas, *Totality and Infinity*, 282.

[60] Levinas, *Totality and Infinity*, 282. For the story of the Fat Man, see Brothers Grimm, 'The Six Servants', in *The Complete Fairy Tales of the Brothers Grimm*, trans. J Zipes, Bantam Books, New York, 2002, 437.

[61] See Arendt, 'Some Questions on Moral Philosophy', 111-112.

[62] Arendt, 'Some Questions on Moral Philosophy', 111. See also R. Gibbs, *Why Ethics? Signs of Responsibilities*, Princeton University Press, Princeton, NJ, 2000 349.

[63] Gibbs, *Why Ethics?*, 351. Capitalization in original.

[64] Levinas, *Totality and Infinity*, 282.

[65] Levinas, *Totality and Infinity*, 282.

[66] Levinas, *Totality and Infinity*, 282.

[67] Levinas, *Totality and Infinity*, 267. Levinas' emphasis.

[68] See Caputo, *The Weakness of God*, 229.

[69] Levinas, *Totality and Infinity*, 282.

[70] E Levinas, *Time and the Other*, trans. R.A. Cohen, Duquesne University Press, Pittsburgh, PA, 1987, 81.

[71] Levinas, *Totality and Infinity*, 283.

[72] Levinas, *Totality and Infinity*, 283.

[73] Caputo, *The Weakness of God*, 229.

[74] Levinas, *Totality and Infinity*, 283.

[75] Levinas, *Totality and Infinity*, 283.

[76] Caputo, *The Weakness of God*, 229-230.

[77] As Kierkegaard would say, alluding to Isaiah 38:17, in forgiving, the past misdeed is placed 'behind one's back' and when one 'turns to the one he forgives,' 'he cannot see what lies behind his back' even though he is still aware of it. (S Kierkegaard, *Works of Love*, trans. by H Hong and E Hong, Harper & Row Publishers, New York, 1962, 274-275). While the deed has still historically been done, when the forgiver faces the forgiven person the deed is not seen by the forgiver, but the forgiver still is not unaware of the deed. In this sense, the deed was done and the forgiver knows it was done, but when facing the person with the deed behind the forgiver's back, it is *as if* it was not done.

[78] Levinas, *Totality and Infinity*, 283.

[79] Caputo, *The Weakness of God*, 230.

[80] Gibbs, *Why Ethics?*, 351. Capitalisation in original.

[81] Levinas, *Totality and Infinity*, 283.

[82] Caputo, *The Weakness of God*, 230.

[83] J Dudiak, *The Intrigue of Ethics: A Reading of the Idea of Discourse in the Thought of Emmanuel Levinas*, Fordham University Press, New York, 2001, 276. Here, Dudiak makes reference to two passages in *Totality and Infinity*: 'Reality is what it is, but will be once again, another time freely resumed and pardoned' (Levinas, *Totality and Infinity*, 284) and 'The fact and the justification of time consist in the recommencement it makes possible in the resurrection, across fecundity, of all the compossibles sacrificed in the present' (Levinas, *Totality and Infinity*, 284).

[84] Levinas writes that '[t]he pardoned being is not the innocent being.' Levinas, *Totality and Infinity*, 283.

[85] Levinas, *Totality and Infinity*, 283.

[86] Levinas, *Totality and Infinity*, 283.

[87] Caputo, *The Weakness of God*, 231.

[88] Caputo, *The Weakness of God*, 231.

[89] Gibbs, *Why Ethics?*, 352.

[90] Caputo, *The Weakness of God*, 231.

[91] R Kearney, *The God Who May Be: A Hermeneutics of Religion*, Indiana University Press, Bloomington and Indianapolis, 2001, 68.

[92] A Peperzak, *To The Other: An Introduction to the Philosophy of Emmanuel Levinas*, Purdue University Press, West Lafayette, IN, 1993, 200.

[93] Luke 2:11

[94] I would like to thank Ronald A. Kuipers, Jeffrey Dudiak, and Shannon Hoff for their extensive and helpful comments on earlier drafts of this paper.

Bibliography

Arendt, H., *Between Past and Future*, Penguin Books, New York, 1968.

——, *The Human Condition*, The University of Chicago Press, Chicago and London, 1958.

——, *Men in Dark Times*, Harvest Books, New York, 1970.

——, *The Promise of Politics*, Ed. J. Kohn, Schocken Books, New York, 2007.

——, *Responsibility and Judgment,* Ed. J. Kohn, Schocken Books, New York, 2003.

Aristotle, *Nicomachean Ethics*, Trans. D. Ross, Oxford University Press, Oxford, 1998.

Augustine, *The City of God.* Trans. H. Bettenson, Penguin Books, London, 1984.

——, *Letters: 211-270*, Ed. J. Rotelle, New City Press, New York, 2005.

Benjamin, W., *Illuminations,* Ed. H. Arendt, Schocken Books, New York, 1969.

Billings, D., 'Natality and Advent: Hannah Arendt and Jürgen Moltmann on Hope and Politics'. *The Future of Hope: Christian Tradition amid Modernity and Postmodernity*, ed. M. Volf and W. Katerberg, Eerdmans, Grand Rapids, MI, 2004, 125-145.

Caputo, J. D. *The Weakness of God: A Theology of the Event*, Indiana University Press, Bloomington and Indianapolis, 2006.

Coward, H. and Foshay, T. (eds.), *Derrida and Negative Theology*, SUNY Press, Albany, NY, 1992.

Damian, P., *Letters*, Vol 4, Trans. O. J. Blum, Catholic University of America Press, Washington D.C., 1998.

Derrida, J., *Memoires: For Paul de Man*, Trans. C. Lindsay, J. Culler, and E. Cadava, Columbia University Press, New York, 1986.

——, *On Cosmopolitanism and Forgiveness*, Trans. Mark Dooley and Michael Hughes, Routledge, London and New York, 2001.

——, 'To Forgive: The Unforgiveable and the Imprescriptible' *Questioning God*, eds. J. D. Caputo, M. Dooley, and M. J. Scanlon, Indiana University Press, Bloomington and Indianapolis, 2001, 21-51.

Dudiak, J., *The Intrigue of Ethics: A Reading of the Idea of Discourse in the Thought of Emmanuel Levinas*, Fordham University Press, New York, 2001.

Friedland, A., 'Evil and Forgiveness: Transitions', *Perspectives on Evil and Human Wickedness*, Vol. 1, No. 4, 2004, 24-47.

Gibbs, R., *Why Ethics? Signs of Responsibilities*, Princeton University Press, Princeton, NJ, 2000.

Griswold, C., *Forgiveness: A Philosophical Investigation*, Cambridge University Press, Cambridge, 2007.

Jankélévitch, V., *Forgiveness*, Trans. by A. Kelley, University of Chicago Press, Chicago and London, 2005.

Kearney, R., *The God Who May Be: A Hermeneutics of Religion*, Indiana University Press, Bloomington and Indianapolis, 2001.

Kierkegaard, S., *Works of Love*, Trans. by H. Hong and E. Hong, Harper & Row Publishers, New York, 1962.

Levinas, E., *Nine Talmudic Readings*, Trans. A. Aronowicz, Indiana University Press, Bloomington and Indianapolis, 1990.

——, *Time and the Other*, Trans. R. A. Cohen. Duquesne University Press, Pittsburgh, Pennsylvania, 1987.

——, E.. *Totality and Infinity: An Essay on Exteriority*, Trans. Alphonso Lingis. Pittsburgh, PA: Duquesne University Press, 1969.

Løgstrup, K.E., *The Ethical Demand*, trans. Hans Fink and Alasdair MacIntyre, University of Notre Dame Press, Notre Dame, 1997.

Peperzak, A., *To The Other: An Introduction to the Philosophy of Emmanuel Levinas*, Purdue University Press, West Lafayette, IN, 1993.

Ricoeur, P., *Memory, History, Forgetting*, Trans. K. Blamey and D. Pellauer, The University of Chicago Press, Chicago and London, 2004.

Shakespeare, W. *The Complete Works of William Shakespeare*, Books, Inc., New York, 1960.

Villa, D. 'Arendt, Heidegger, and the Tradition', *Social Research*, Vol. 74, no. 4, Winter 2007, pp. 983-1002.

Young-Breuhl, E., *For Love of the World*, Yale University Press, New Haven and London, 1982.

——, *Why Arendt Matters*, Yale University Press, New Haven and London, 2006.

Zipes, J. (trans.), *The Complete Fairy Tales of the Brothers Grimm*, Bantam Books, New York, 2002.

Christopher R. Allers is an Adjunct Professor of Philosophy at Cornerstone University (Grand Rapids, MI) and a Sessional Instructor in Philosophy at the Institute for Christian Studies, Toronto (ICS) where he is also a doctoral student in the conjoint degree program between ICS and the Vrije Universiteit, Amsterdam. He is currently working on his dissertation on forgiveness which is tentatively titled *The Miracle of Forgiveness: Absurd Reflections on Ordinary Language and Common Pre-Understandings*.

Forgiving Grave Wrongs

Alisa L. Carse and Lynne Tirrell

Abstract

We introduce what we call the Emergent Model of forgiving, which is a *process-based relational* model conceptualising forgiving as moral and normative repair in the wake of grave wrongs. In cases of grave wrongs, which shatter the victim's life, the Classical Model of transactional forgiveness falls short of illuminating how genuine forgiveness can be achieved. In a climate of persistent threat and distrust, expressions of remorse, rituals and gestures of apology, and acts of reparation are unable to secure the moral confidence and trust required for moral repair, much less for forgiveness. Without the rudiments of a shared moral world – a world in which, at the very least, the survivor's violation can be collectively recognized as a violation, and her moral status and authority collectively acknowledged and respected – expressions of remorse, gestures and rituals of apology, or promises of compensation have no authority as meaningful communicative acts with reparative significance. Accordingly, we argue that repair in the wake of traumatic violence involves 'world-building,' which supports the ability of survivors to move from despair to hope, from radical and disabling distrust to trust and engagement, and thus from impotence to effective agency. Our Emergent Model treats forgiveness as a slowly developing outcome of a series of changes in a person's relationship to the trauma and its aftermath, in which moral agency is regained. We argue that forgiveness after grave wrongs and world-shattering harm, when it occurs, emerges from other phenomena, such as cohabitation within a community, gestures of reconciliation, working on shared projects, the developing of trust. On this view, forgiveness is an *emergent* phenomenon; it entails taking and exercising normative power – coming to claim one's own moral authority in relation to oneself, one's assailant, and one's community. The processes that ultimately constitute forgiving are part and parcel of normative repair more broadly construed.

Key Words: Apology, atrocity, forgiveness, genocide, moral repair, mutual recognition, reconciliation, resentment, respect, Rwanda, trauma, validation, voice, violence

*****

Sometimes, when I sit alone in a chair on my veranda, I imagine a possibility. If, on some distant day, a local man comes slowly up to me and says, 'Bonjour Francine.

Bonjour to your family. I have come to speak to you. So
here it is: 'I am the one who cut your mama and your little
sisters.' Or 'I am the one who tried to kill you in the swamp
and I want to ask your forgiveness.' Well, to that particular
person I could reply nothing good. A man, if he has had
one Primus beer too many and then beats his wife, he can
ask to be forgiven. But if he has worked at killing for a
whole month, even on Sundays, whatever can he hope for
pardon?

We must simply take up life again, since life has so
decided... Thornbushes must not invade the farms; teachers
must return to their school blackboards; doctors must care
for the sick in health clinics. There must be strong new
cattle, fabrics of all kinds, sacks of beans in the markets. In
that case, Hutus are necessary...We will begin to draw
water together, to exchange neighbourly words, to sell
grain to one another. In twenty years, fifty years, there will
perhaps be boys and girls who will learn about the genocide
in books. For us, however, it is impossible to forgive.
         --Francine Niyitegeka, Rwandan genocide survivor[1]

I see too many difficulties for us to exchange forgiveness
on the hills. Too many bad memories will grow again on
the fine words, like the bush in the middle of a plantation.
Someone who grants you forgiveness on a day of mercy,
who can't say he will take it back some other day in anger,
because of a drunken squabble? I can't imagine any
forgiveness capable of drying up all this spilled blood.
         --Pio Mitungirehe, Rwandan génocidaire[2]

1.   Introduction

Genuine forgiveness can be crucial to breaking cycles of violence
and destruction in ways that exceed fragile forms of stability grounded in
coercion, threat, or fear. Yet, in some cases, the risk of forgiving may be
greater than the risk of not doing so. In cases of grave moral wrongs,
forgiveness must be granted, if at all, only with utmost circumspection. In
this paper, we consider the nature and possibility of forgiveness in response
to grave moral wrongs, wrongs perpetrating what we call 'world-shattering'
harm. Our focus is on the Rwandan genocide. The demands of peaceful
cohabitation and national reunification pressure many Tutsi survivors, who
are a minority within a minority in Rwanda, to strive to forgive their former
neighbours who perpetrated slaughter, rape and wanton destruction against

them.[3] Memories of the atrocities make it difficult – and for many, impossible – to forgive, if by 'forgive' we mean, as Charles Griswold and others have held, 'to understand, to relinquish revenge and resentment, all the while holding the offender responsible.'[4] Many survivors seek personal freedom from the consuming hatred, resentment and fear that perpetuate their suffering and make the possibility of forgiveness remote at best. And some Rwandan survivors, like survivors of other genocides, claim to forgive their assailants. We want to try to understand how forgiveness might be possible and what it would entail for those who suffer world-shattering violation and loss.

To these ends, we explore a model of forgiveness we call the Emergent Model. This new account of forgiveness departs from the standard, Classical Model, according to which the victim extends forgiveness to the perpetrator as a result of a deliberate decision following a morally reparative transaction – a transaction aimed at securing forgiveness.[5] In the wake of world-shattering wrongs, we maintain that familiar forgiveness-seeking acts (e.g., gestures and rituals of apology, compensation, repentance) cannot have meaning as such unless a process of forgiveness is already firmly underway. Acts and gestures of these kinds can find no moral foothold – no shared and trustworthy moral order – in which to have reparative meaning and significance. They may carry familiar symbolism for survivors and perpetrators alike, but this alone is not sufficient for moral repair, for such symbolism is rooted in a world now lost to wanton destruction.[6] We believe that forgiveness is possible, even in the wake of grave world-shattering wrongs, but not without what we call shared 'world-building.' World-building, as we will explicate further, consists in cooperative work through which victims and perpetrators are joined in developing shared moral norms, embodied in emerging but stable social practices.

The Classical model successfully captures an important paradigm, suited to many cases of forgiveness in everyday life – cases concerning moral harms ranging from minor to serious. Griswold's account illustrates the Classical framework when he says:

> In the paradigmatic interpersonal scene that provides our touchstone, the offender has injured a specific individual; the offender asks the victim for forgiveness; which, if granted, is bestowed on the offender.[7]

On the Classical Model, moral injury is followed by a call ('please forgive me') and a response (positive or negative). Our concern with grave harms that shatter worlds raises the possibility of forgiveness emerging from a process not directed at forgiving in this way, in which the call and response are not central, not explicit, and if they occur, occur so late as to be largely symbolic. Griswold's account, like many Classical views, rightly emphasizes the importance of moral transformation in the offender, which brings about changes in the injured person's assessment of the offender. We agree that transformation of the offender is crucial to substantial forgiveness. In cases of grave wrongdoing, however, this model leaves the survivor too much at the mercy of the offender, taking forgiveness out of her hands while she awaits the call to forgive. We propose an alternative model, not as a substitute suited to all cases, but as one we believe helps make sense of forgiving grave, world shattering wrongs.

In cases of grave wrongs, forgiveness must emerge slowly, over time, and paradigmatically through endeavours bringing survivors and perpetrators into forms of cooperation – forms of cooperation that are not themselves directed to forgiveness. Through such cooperative endeavours, mutual recognition between survivor and perpetrator slowly evolves, beginning a process of moral transformation in which reparative acts can have meaning.[8] On the Emergent Model we propose here, forgiveness is, of necessity, a multifaceted, complex, and often jagged process, through which both trust and hope gain a foothold under conditions of perilous normative disorientation and moral insecurity, slowly contributing to conditions through which robust, and potentially enduring, forgiveness evolves.

2.   Sweeping Fear Away

On both the Classical and the Emergent models, paradigmatic cases of forgiveness bring the survivor a sense of freedom, escape from the haunting effects of the wrong committed against her. She experiences an abatement of animosity, fear or vengeance, and releases the wrongdoer from continued resentment. Édithe Uwanyiligira, a survivor of the Rwandan genocide of the Tutsi, says she chose to forgive in order to release herself from relation to the perpetrators:

> I know that all the Hutus who killed so calmly cannot be sincere when they beg pardon, even of the Lord. For them, the Tutsi will always be their enemy. But I myself am ready to forgive. It is not a denial of the harm they did, not a betrayal of the Tutsis, not an easy way out. It is so that I will not suffer my whole life long asking myself why they tried to cut me. I do not want to live in remorse and fear from being a Tutsi. If I do not forgive them, it is I alone who suffers and frets and cannot sleep. I yearn for peace in my body. I really must find tranquillity. I have to sweep fear away from me, even if I do not believe the soothing words of others.[9]

Expressing extraordinary resilience and resolve, Édithe seeks refuge from her suffering, freedom from the haunting effects of the violence committed against her and others. If successful, Édithe may find personal peace, inner tranquillity, even healing. Yet not every road to peace is a road to forgiveness.

The call and response framework does not fit in Édithe's case. Édithe does not seek apology, reparation, expressions of remorse, or pleas for pardon from her assailants, for she thinks these 'cannot be sincere.' Édithe is realistic in not trusting that those who committed grievous wrongs against her will respect her worth or face the wrongs they have committed. Remarkably, under the circumstances, Édithe maintains a clear sense of her own value and worth. She believes her peace, if it is found, will be found through disconnection from the perpetrator, abandoning all hope in the possibility of reconciliation and mutual understanding. It is true that the abatement of animosity, resentment, or vengeance, can bring psychic liberation. But on the view of forgiveness we articulate here, a unilateral shift of the kind Édithe undertakes is not in itself forgiveness. Forgiveness is not something the survivor can bestow, like grace, upon the perpetrator, nor does it consist in the achievement of inner freedom and peace, though it may bring both.

Forgiveness, when possible, both requires and itself helps to constitute a distinctive form of moral repair. Margaret Walker notes that victims of violent wrongs:

> need to know that others grasp the fact of the violation, its clear wrongfulness, the culpability of the perpetrator, and the reality of the harm and suffering caused them, in order to be validated. They need the affirmation of their entitlement to repair, and to be supported in seeking it or to have others seek it on their behalf.[10]

In order to *heal*, victims need to give voice to their experience of violation and loss and to know others in their community validate the wrongfulness of what they have endured. In order to *forgive*, victims need to be able to give voice to their experience and to receive understanding, validation and respect *from those who wronged them, those they would forgive.*

Crucially, on our view, *forgiveness entails the victim's taking and exercising normative power, thus establishing her moral status and authority in relation to her assailant and her community.* This reassertion of moral status cannot be a solely internal (or subjective) matter, as it is for Édithe. It must be inter-subjective, involving the acknowledgment and recognition by the offender of the survivor's moral status and, correlatively, of the nature and seriousness of the wrongs committed against her. If the offender does not acknowledge the survivor's moral status and authority, then what might at first seem to be forgiveness is better characterized as letting go or showing mercy, or perhaps even pardoning, excusing or condoning. Forgiving, unlike letting go, showing mercy, pardoning, and the like, is inherently relational.[11] This relationality is at the heart of the cruel challenge of forgiving grave harm. It asks that the survivor maintain a connection to the perpetrator, in seeking his moral understanding, recognition and respect.

On the Classical Model, a realignment of moral status and authority occurs through a transaction between victim and perpetrator: You wrong me; you later acknowledge your wrongdoing, express sincere remorse, and offer me an apology; I judge your apology to be genuine, demand (just) reparation, you meet my demands; I forgive you. In emphasizing a transactional dimension, the Classical Model rightly highlights the relationality of forgiveness; in emphasizing acts of apology, reparation, and the survivor's authority to grant or refuse forgiveness, it rightly highlights the survivor's moral status and authority. Both of these features – the relationality of forgiveness and the authoritative moral status of the forgiver – are key, we believe, to forgiveness properly understood.[12] But for forgiveness to be achievable through the Classical transaction, it must at the very least be possible for the perpetrator to *acknowledge* his or her act as wrong *in virtue of* his or her *recognition of the moral status and authority of the victim.*[13] Recognition of the moral status of the victim and acknowledgment of the wrong committed go hand-in-hand; both are essential to forgiveness. The Classical Model is thus viable only insofar as the survivor and the perpetrator engage *within a shared moral order,* one in which the moral status of the victim is securely established.[14] In the aftermath of world-shattering wrongs, no such order exists.

3.   World Shattering Wrongs

The Rwandan genocide, like all genocide, raises difficult questions about the nature of forgiveness. Although highly organized, the Rwandan genocide was intimate and personal. It was not action at a distance, but was enacted by Hutus, hunting, raping, beating, torturing and killing their Tutsi neighbours.[15] The devastation was swift and ferocious, leaving nearly a million dead, hundreds of thousands orphaned, and survivors who called themselves *bapfuye buhagazi* (the walking dead).[16]

When a world shatters, those whose world it was lose moral orientation. Language and action make little sense, reasons and motives become obscure, and norms that were formerly shared with others cease to have authority. The sense of safety and predictability is gone, so too is a framework of understanding in which the grievous moral damage endured might be voiced and validated.[17]

Four years after the genocide, Innocent Rwililiza, one of only twenty survivors of the six thousand who fled to the Kayumba Forest, said:

> A survivor cannot help always going back to the genocide.
> For someone who did not experience it, there is before,
> during, and after the genocide, and it's all life being lived
> in different ways. For us, there is before, during, and after,
> but they are three different lives, and they have broken
> apart forever.[18]

Innocent adds: 'The survivors tend not to believe that they are truly alive anymore – in other words, that they're still the same people they were before, and in a way, that's a little how they keep going.'[19] Like Innocent, survivors whose worlds are shattered often express a feeling of having 'outlived themselves,' of having occupied radically disconnected worlds, worlds impossible to reconcile and understand within one framework of meaning. This speaks to a sense of lost personal unity, of shattered identity. Claudine Kayitesi captures this sense of rupture when she says:

> Good fortune has offered me a second life, and I will not
> turn it away. But it will be a half-life, because of the
> complete break. . . . To be betrayed by your neighbours, by
> the authorities, by the Whites – that is a staggering blow. It
> can make one behave badly.... But to be betrayed by life...
> who can bear that? It's too much. You lose all sense of
> where the right direction lies. [20]

Claudine's claim to have been 'betrayed by life' reflects the scope of the devastation she and other survivors endure. The world in which they find themselves is one devoid of moral and social order. Violence and destruction have left no apparent bridge to the world that was lost; only chaos and debris remain.

When a world shatters, even the very meaning of words can change. Sylvie Umubyeyi, a survivor and now a paediatric social worker, says that 'the genocide has changed the meanings of certain words in the language of survivors, while other words have flatly lost their meaning, and anyone who listens must be very wary of these changes.'[21] Umubyeyi's observation is consonant with Simon Wiesenthal's remark, in *The Sunflower*, that in the concentration camps, the meanings of words became suspect, untrustworthy, because Nazis used them in connection to actions that were (at least initially) unforeseeable (and ultimately inconceivable in the terms of a familiar world, now lost). For example, 'registration,' which seems benign enough, often led to death: 'The oftener they registered us, the fewer we became.' In Rwanda, terms for agricultural activities became genocidal code – e.g., 'work' became 'killing,' 'clearing the tall trees' meant 'kill the Tutsi,' and so on. In both cases, the link between meaning and action is profoundly altered in a shift from the old world to the new. Wiesenthal captures the despair of lost meaning:

> It is impossible to believe anything in a world that has ceased to regard man as man, which repeatedly 'proves' that one is no longer a man. So one begins to doubt, one begins to cease to believe in a world order in which God has a definite place.[22]

Violence that shatters worlds destroys all regard for the sanctity of the victim's life, uses her body to demean and humiliate her, and targets and desecrates shared sources of meaning and value. In cases of moral atrocity (like genocidal murder, torture, and rape), the moral ground has given way to wanton destruction and degradation. There is no moral foothold for stable recognition of the victim's moral status. There is thus no shared normative framework in terms of which a perpetrator can understand, let alone sincerely acknowledge and repent, the wrongs he or she has committed. So too, the survivor's confidence in her own moral worth – her personhood – is often shaken, for she has lost both trust in the norms that define that personhood, and also her fluency in the language of those norms. Here, a process of forgiveness cannot be grounded in an existing moral order, nor is there a reservoir of trust on which to draw.

World-shattering wrongs thus resist forgiveness. In the Rwandan genocide, as in all genocide, the scale of the crimes committed was so overwhelming that forgiveness may seem offensive and appalling. Even talking about forgiveness in the face of atrocities is problematic. Claudia Card notes, "'resentful,' 'angry,' and even 'indignant' grossly under-describe characteristic moral responses to atrocities. We resent insults, cheating, and unfairness. But evils leave us speechless, appalled horrified, nauseated.'[23] Forgiveness, Card claims, cannot be the 'antidote to speechlessness, horror, nausea.'[24] Card anticipates our Emergent model in claiming that after atrocities, forgiveness should be granted, if at all, 'only slowly and with caution, depending on what the perpetrator does (by way of confession, apology, reparation, regeneration).'[25] Our view of forgiveness emphasizes the last of these, namely, *regeneration* – and, we would add, *generation* – of shared normative structures, a shared moral world, in which survivors and perpetrators can develop mutual moral recognition and understanding, thereby paving a way for the possibility of forgiveness.

4.   World-Building and Normative Repair

As we have emphasised, the challenge facing survivors of atrocity lies in finding a ground for moral repair in relationship with, rather than disconnection from, those who perpetrated heinous crimes against them.

Normative repair in the wake of traumatic violence involves what we call *'world-building,'* which is crucial to the ability of survivors to move from radical and disabling distrust to trust and engagement, from experiences of impotence to the possibility of effective agency, and thus from despair to hope.

Given scarce land and limited resources, survivors remaining in Rwanda have practical reasons to live and work together with perpetrators. As Francine Niyitegeka notes, survivors on all sides of the conflict must get back to the business of living.[26] Renewed relations among neighbours was necessary for restoring basic security, tending to needs for shelter, food and medical care, and rebuilding an economy. Yet the haunting ease with which neighbours had turned on neighbours with machetes – slaughtering, raping, and mutilating – made this prospect treacherous and unwise. It was imperative that a system ensuring basic security be established first. As necessary as such security would be, however, it could not come close to achieving moral repair, which requires developing a framework establishing mutual recognition of the moral crimes that had been perpetrated. As Walker writes:

> ...moral repair is served by authoritatively instating or reinstating moral terms and standards within communities where wrong may have caused fear, confusion, cynicism, or despair about the authority of those standards.... [M]oral repair is served by replenishing or creating trust among individuals in the recognition of shared moral standards and in their responsiveness to those standards and support of the practices that express and enforce them.[27]

Mere cohabitation with people who represent an enduring threat will not, of course, generate the conditions necessary for moral repair. If the perpetrator still, even quietly, accepts the genocidal project, or if lingering fears and doubts persist, survivors cannot begin to trust, much less to forgive. The question of persistent threat makes acts of apology, explanation, expressions of remorse, and other behaviours of the perpetrator suspect and potentially dangerous. The degree of damage done and the heinousness of the wrong committed make a difference to the very possibility of creating trust, and establishing mutual recognition and responsiveness to shared norms. Pio Mitungirehe, convicted génocidaire, voices the concerns of many when he says that he *'can't imagine any forgiveness capable of drying up all this spilled blood.'*

Worlds can be damaged to different degrees and in different ways. For a victim of a direct, individual crime, such as theft, rape, or kidnapping, in a non-conflict situation, it may be possible to return to a world shared with others – a world in which acts of theft, rape, or kidnapping are securely recognized as the violations they are.[28] Much may be lost and destroyed for the victims, but the world within which they have lived remains more or less intact. This is especially the case if the wrong committed against them is widely acknowledged as a wrong and their experience of the violation is validated and, ultimately, vindicated through protective and punitive efforts. This is not the case for the survivors of genocide whose world has shattered. In the before-during-after scenario described by genocide survivors, the world that has been so thoroughly shattered is lost; little remains to be rebuilt. Hope must lie in the possibility of creating a new world.

The new world under construction inevitably contains the debris of the past world, for there can be no historical or normative purity. The shattered fragments of the old world are painful reminders of loss, so survivors face the issue of how meaningfully to incorporate these shattered fragments without sinking under their weight. For those most alone, there is often little, if any, basis for trust in the power of shared norms of conduct and meaning that can validate and vindicate their experiences of grievous crime and loss. The sense of moral isolation and disorientation is profound. Those who flee may adopt a new world, slowly integrating into it, learning its norms, and gaining fluency. Those who remain must build a shared moral world together. Building a new world requires finding a 'we' – others with whom a collective sense of purpose and identity can emerge – one that fully incorporates a consciousness of the moral damage done.[29] This is especially difficult for survivors who must construct worlds with the very people who have committed atrocities against them.

In the case of world-shattering wrongs, the Classical model of transactional forgiveness falls short of illuminating how genuine forgiveness can be achieved. In a climate of persistent threat and distrust, expressions of remorse, rituals and gestures of apology, and acts of reparation are unable to secure the moral confidence and trust required for moral repair. Moreover, for such acts even to have meaning as forgiveness-seeking acts, more than a reasonable confidence in one's safety is required. The perpetrator's acknowledgment of wrongdoing and recognition of the survivor's moral status will need to be robustly secured and evidenced; it must be developed and integrated into shared moral understandings and expectations, through forms of positive, engaged cooperation that have gained stability. These achievements require survivor and perpetrator to move from mere cohabitation to interactive engagement, to interdependence and reasonable trust. In the absence of at least the rudiments of a shared moral world – a world in which, at the very least, the survivor's violation can be collectively recognized as a violation, and her moral status and authority collectively acknowledged and respected – expressions of remorse, gestures and rituals of apology, or promises of compensation have no authority as meaningful communicative acts with reparative significance.

5.   Emergent Forgiveness

On our model, forgiveness emerges, when it does, from the many phenomena involved in world-building, beginning with cohabitation within a community and small gestures of reconciliation, which slowly build trust. On this account, the perpetrator's acknowledgment of wrongdoing and recognition of the survivor's moral status develops over time through forms of positive, engaged cooperation. A culture of fragmented persons who live side by side with minimal and distrusting interactions will not create a normative moral order from which forgiveness can emerge.[30]

World building is not a solo activity; one always starts somewhere, with someone. In Rwanda, a major difference amongst survivors is between those who were radically alone as they fled to the marshes or the forests to hide and those who were hidden by someone, a caretaker offering a lifeline. Both were hunted, and lived with fear and despair. The hidden may often have had fears about their caretakers, because discovery would put the caretaker's own life at stake.[31] Nevertheless, those who had another person had a connection in the world, a person with whom their interests were intertwined, and this made a crucial difference to their post-traumatic resilience. Some who were left alone report that their psychological and emotional attachments were put on hold. Hope and trust were lost; confidence in the power of normative action was lost, even saying 'we' was lost.[32]

The ability to say 'we' is regained slowly. Forgiving grave wrongs is, as we have noted, of necessity a non-linear process that is dynamic, complex, and jagged. We see forgiveness emerging from world-building illustrated in a story we heard from a Rwandan priest we know:

> On a hill near Butare, a nun, Sister T, was working with Tutsi survivors, all women, bringing them together to do some weaving and sewing. At first no one spoke much, and some participated reluctantly. Slowly, without pressure, and by creating a safe haven, Sister T brought the survivors into a small daily community. Slowly isolation waned. Eventually, they began to open up to each other, talking first about mundane things and then about more serious matters. This process took some years, until the women began to think of themselves as a community.
>
> As the survivors worked together, wives of the génocidaires would walk by, one by one, carrying each

day's food to their imprisoned husbands. Every day, these
Hutu women would walk many miles to the prison and
back. Eventually, little by little, the Tutsi women developed
sympathy for their Hutu sisters, themselves imprisoned in
this routine of serving their husbands, over whose criminal
behaviour they lacked control. During the genocide, many
Hutu women enjoyed the benefits of their men's looting,
continued to feed the men, take care of their homes, and
failed to protect their Tutsi friends. Still, the Tutsi women
began to feel a connection to the Hutu women, for they too
had lost a great deal to the violence and destruction.
Eventually, they began to invite some of the Hutu women
to join their projects, and slowly, over time, the community
became integrated. Slowly, forgiveness emerged. There
was no single moment of decision to forgive, but there
were many small choices concerning inclusion and
exclusion, safety, what to share and what not to share, and
so on. These choices ultimately generated new relationships
that embodied forms of forgiveness.[33]

In the life of a genocide survivor, the move from isolation to limited
engagement to fuller engagement and trust is a significant journey of
increasing agency and self-articulation. The Tutsi women in Sister T's
collective first began in isolation, and very slowly began to interact. Their
interaction developed from sharing tools to working together in shared
enterprises. There was no clear moment when they moved from 'I' to 'We';
there was no definite moment when a collective moral identity was
established. Including the Hutu women was not an act of forgiveness, yet it
initiated a process of forgiving, a process in which suspicion and animosity
could abate and mutual understanding and acknowledgment could grow.

Imagine two (hypothetical) women from this collective, five years
after the genocide. Let Aimee be a Tutsi survivor and widow, and Berta be a
Hutu whose husband is in prison. After working together for several years,
Berta's question to Aimee is unlikely to be 'Will you please forgive me?' but
rather 'Have you forgiven me?' On the Emergent model, shared practical,
moral, and emotional pursuits change the urgency and timing of such a
question, submerging the importance of particular acts explicitly seeking or
bestowing forgiveness. In cases of world-shattering wrongs, apology and
reparation can be understood as such only once a process of world-building
has begun and key dimensions of forgiveness are already stabilized through
mutual recognition and respect. When Berta finally asks the forgiveness
question, she is not so much seeking a decision from Aimee, as seeking
mutual confirmation of the forgiveness already expressed in Aimee's actions.

When Aimee answers 'yes' to Berta, her affirmation is anchored in the world they are building together, one in which a shared moral understanding has gained a secure-enough foothold, despite appropriate and lingering fears.

It is important to emphasize that shared world-building is necessary but not sufficient for forgiveness. Not all community integration reveals emergent forgiveness; sometimes there is merely appeasement, acceptance, or letting go. To the question 'Have you forgiven me?' the answer might be either 'yes' or 'no'. The emergent view explains how 'yes' is possible, even in the absence of a concerted effort or explicit decision to achieve forgiveness, and outside a transactional model. Francine Niyitegeka's remarks, quoted at the outset of this article, about trimming thorn-bushes, teaching school, tending to the sick and selling beans in the market, mention actions that can all take place in the absence of forgiveness. Survivors and perpetrators can live and work side by side, establishing a basic normative order but without yet generating a shared moral identity, let alone a moral order in which persons are respected as such. A shared moral order in which the survivor's moral status is acknowledged and secure sets the stage for forgiving, but forgiving involves rebuilding trust and taking a new stance toward the grievous actions. The survivor's voice must be heard and validated. Francine's remarks suggest that if the genocide is to be taught in books, it must be recognized *as* genocide; it must be recognized as the moral horror that it is.

The reaction of the imprisoned Hutu husbands indicates some challenges of this emergent normative development. The men were at first angry, saying that the Tutsi could not be trusted and were trying to trick the Hutu women. Their wives went back to Sister T and said: 'The men need your help; they need to understand this process and the way things are now.' Facing their husbands' resistance, the Hutu women became more aware of the normative shifts they had experienced, and then sought ways to reinforce the changes for themselves, and ways to bring their husbands into the process. Sister T began to meet with the husbands in prison, but, until they were released, it was not possible for them to experience genuine connection to the emerging shared world of the women.

The Emergent Model holds that forgiveness can creep up on a person through a series of smaller practical and moral choices that do not aim at forgiving. This is a *transformative*, rather than cumulative, model; small choices, not themselves directed to forgiving, can lead to transformations in which the acknowledgement of wrongs and losses is integrated, gaining new and different meaning. Trust is rebuilt, slowly, as new norms and values are established in relationships and practices through which mutual respect and concern is realised.

We said earlier that one difference between the Classical model and the Emergent model concerns whether the survivor or victim undertakes

actions that are centrally aimed at forgiveness. Many normative phenomena
are emergent in the sense we wish to convey here. Consider a much easier
case, and a lighter example, to help to convey the structure of 'emergence': a
series of practical dietary choices can become *living as* a vegetarian, and then
suddenly one notices, saying 'ah, I see, I am a vegetarian.' In the 'ah-ha'
moment, one notices that one has been *being* a vegetarian for a long time and
undertakes a more explicit normative commitment under this more general
description. The standards governing one's choices, preferences, and
relationships have shifted, little by little. As a person lives as a vegetarian, the
burden of proof shifts as well, so that she comes to need a reason to eat meat
rather than needing a reason to avoid it. Moving away from prevailing dietary
norms of her culture, she embraces an alternative value system within which
she lives. She may, slowly, come to identify with other vegetarians, whose
vegetarian practices and commitments enrich and shore up her own.
Similarly, the survivors in Sister T's collective started a process, which
incrementally grew into commitments to fuller relationships than were
initially envisioned, so that slowly forgiveness emerged amongst them.[34]

On a similarly lighter note, the Emergent model looks to
developmental psychology for a metaphor for relations amongst those whose
worlds have shattered apart from each other and now take steps toward
reclaiming their own lives. Movement from solitude to parallel play to
interactive play is a developmental process that begins in childhood but that
we continue to traverse throughout our lives. Parallel play can ease us into
interactive play. Children are building worlds as they grow. There is the
world into which they are born and the norms they are striving to master, but
there is also the process of self-construction within that world, which
involves an interactive modification of that world. Shared worlds tend to be
constantly renegotiated, sometimes in small, imperceptible ways, sometimes
in explicit, even explosive ways.

The slow, painstaking process of rebuilding oneself and one's world
after grievous wrongs is in significant ways qualitatively different from the
healthy childhood process, to be sure. Yet it embodies a basic pattern of
human sociality and growth in the ongoing process of continually
renegotiated forms of interdependency that, with success, can yield
relationships marked by significant mutuality.

6.   Brave New Worlds
On the Emergent model, the practical and moral work of rebuilding
a world creates patterns of interaction that make forgiveness possible and
constitute its slow emergence, through small extensions of trust, and growing
mutual awareness and curiosity, understanding and respect. Significant
opportunities for change and growth must be possible – for the perpetrator,
the victim, and the circumstances in which they live. Both parties must be

brave. The perpetrator must face his own horrible actions, taking responsibility while moving forward into a more morally acceptable state. The survivor must be willing to seek moral recognition, understanding and respect from someone who committed grave crimes against her. Perhaps, with Aristotle, we must find the line between bravery and foolhardiness. Emergent forgiveness emphasizes the gradual growth of trust and hopefulness' while also recognizing the need for wariness. It is no accident that Sister T's collective began with women who, though in many cases complicit, were not the primary perpetrators of genocide. Facing the perpetrators was a later and risky stage in the process. This brave and painstaking work of building a shared world constitutes a process in which forgiveness can emerge.

The world-building dimension of forgiving in the wake of grave wrong tends to be obscured by thinking of forgiveness as a decision located discretely in space and time, changing the moral map. This is not, however, to deny that the elements of a complex and negotiated apology might contribute significantly to emergent forgiveness. In cases of world-shattering harm, it is not possible for forgiveness to be achieved directly through temporally discrete reparative acts and moral transactions, such as the call and response of 'Please forgive me' and the (seemingly) performative utterance 'you are forgiven.' Because such acts are largely symbolic, they can at most fortify a process of forgiveness already solidly underway. Emergent forgiveness is not realized through a direct decision to forgive, but through a complex set of actions and conditions, the completion of which may make the utterance of such a speech act anti-climactic, even if symbolically significant.

Of course speech and other actions intertwine in constructing new norms and practices; the strength and security of these new norms depend upon the degree to which speech and other actions mutually reinforce each other. Speaking and being heard are crucial aspects of personhood, and the validation that one receives when one's testimony is understood and appreciated reinforces the mutuality of the process of speaking-with, of living together, of sharing a world.

Fragile worlds are marked by dissonances amongst norms, speech acts, and actions of the body; such dissonances render the world unpredictable, unintelligible, and relationships untrustworthy. Generating reliable interpretive frameworks is crucial to building confidence, trust and hope. The survivor's moral status must be protected by a broader world, a world through which and in which shared moral stability is emerging. Until the survivor's moral risk is minimized by being collectively borne, forgiveness will not emerge. Walker writes:

> If no wrongs can be fully righted as no bell can be unrung,
> there is still plenty of room for reparative gestures that

work on the moral plane to relieve suffering, disillusionment, isolation, and despair. Too little is better than nothing, and small gestures can carry larger meanings or can be a starting point for a broader reconsideration of relationships between individuals and within societies.[35]

Rituals and gestures of apology and reparation – transactions between wrongdoers and those wronged – can stabilize and reinforce conditions in which forgiveness emerges. Nevertheless, their function in doing so depends on prior, ongoing, significant moral repair; their expressive success rides atop an already evolving moral world in which forgiving has taken root.

Although we have written as if emergent forgiveness asks each party to apprehend the reality of the other, we wish to emphasize that there is need for circumspection here. If forgiving requires mutual recognition, such that survivors and perpetrators alike come to see themselves through the eyes of the other, it is fraught with risk. Perpetrators have viewed their victims through eyes of hatred and contempt and may continue to do so. Adalbert Munzigura, a Rwandan génocidaire, offers a negative assessment of the prospect of mutual recognition, understanding, and empathy, between killers and survivors, saying:

> There are people in Kibungo who will be able to understand me, but only those who plied their machetes like me or more than me. The Tutsis, though – it's unthinkable for them to learn and understand. *You just can't ask them to see our actions as we did.* I believe their suffering will reject any kind of explanation. What we have done is unnatural to them. Perhaps patience and forgetting will win out; perhaps not.[36]

To be able to forgive, Adalbert suggests, the survivor would have to see the perpetrator's actions through the perpetrator's perspective. Adalbert believes this is likely to be impossible and, moreover, something we must not ask of a survivor. To be sure, such understanding risks further psychological damage and suffering for a survivor. Two questions loom here: How much does a survivor need to understand about the perpetrator in order to begin reasonably to trust, and, ultimately, to forgive? Just what will coming to sufficient understanding require of a survivor? These are questions for which there are no clear or simple answers.

Ideally, world-building allows the survivor and perpetrator slowly to develop empathy for each other. Empathy can promote mutual understanding and, when conditions are right, can serve the emergence of mutual recognition. Empathy can bring the personhood of the survivor into the heart of the perpetrator's understanding of her; this is stronger than mere acknowledgement and, if conveyed effectively, can strengthen the process of, and ground for, forgiveness. On the other side, the survivor who seeks to understand who the perpetrator is and how he could have done what he did will likely need to engage empathically with the perpetrator. Yet survivor empathy must be properly bounded, for there is great risk of moral compromise and of damaging identification with the perpetrator – absorption in, or internalisation of, a perpetrator's degrading view of his victims. [37]

In forgiving, the survivor has to, at the very least, see the perpetrator as a *person* rather than a *monster*, that is, as capable of sharing in a moral order, in spite of what he or she has done. The survivor must not be burdened with the task of the perpetrator's moral transformation, but without that moral transformation, a shared moral world will not develop

Asking for empathy on the part of a survivor – even properly bounded, morally healthy empathy – may be asking for too much. Perpetrators often resist acknowledging the harm they inflicted, the moral norms they violated, underestimating the full gravity of the wrongs they have committed. Shame and dissociation are obstacles to moral repair. Empathy poses moral risk if a failure of recognition persists on the part of the perpetrator. Forgiving is not always possible and not always desirable. Sometimes the practical, psychological, and moral perils for the survivor are too great, the obstacles impossible to overcome.

We have urged that in cases of grave moral wrongs, forms of emergent forgiveness make meaningful gestures and rituals of apology possible. Emergent forgiveness is also, in such cases, the most cautious, prudent, and ultimately stable form of forgiving. It is not a simple moral transaction or set of transactions aimed at achieving forgiveness, nor is it located in performative utterances that in and of themselves reconstitute moral relations. Emergent forgiveness is, rather, a slow constructive process of ongoing re-engagement in small ways, often in practical matters, that may add up to significant moral and normative re-construction. Practical realignment of relationships can open the door to moral growth that at an earlier stage may not be possible. Through world-building, survivors bravely shape a future in which they can be whole and healthy. When that world-building is done with the perpetrator, there is a chance for forgiveness. When it cannot safely be done with the perpetrator, there is no shared world for them. Archbishop Desmond Tutu says: '*Forgiveness is not some nebulous thing. It is practical politics. Without forgiveness, there is no future.*'[38] We hold that the practical politics of world-building constructs the future that sometimes brings about a safe and secure forgiveness.

Notes

[1] J Hatzfeld, *Life Laid Bare: The Survivors in Rwanda Speak*, translation: Linda Coverdale, Other Press, New York, NY, 2006, p.42.

[2] J Hatzfeld, *Machete Season: The Killers in Rwanda Speak*, translation: Linda Coverdale, Farrar, Straus and Giroux, New York, NY, 2005, pp. 206-7.

[3] Our focus on the Rwandan genocide is inspired by the work that one of us (LT) is doing with Rwandan refugees in Boston and her ongoing research motivated by a need to understand their situation and the very meaning of their survival.

[4] C Griswold, *Forgiveness: A Philosophical Exploration*, Cambridge University Press, Cambridge, 2007, p.47.

[5] We see this Classical model as the standard account now being developed by most contemporary philosophers addressing forgiveness, but it is developed very clearly in Griswold, who, like Walker, emphasizes that forgiveness is a process, but who also emphasizes the offender's request for forgiveness, and the victim's decision to forgive or not to forgive based on a judgment of a variety of criteria. Although forgiveness might often result from an explicit decision to forgive, even on the Classical model this can be implicit.

[6] The classical model would fit an explicit 'I forgive you,' as said in the Gacaca courts when a survivor meets the person who killed her entire family, but we know that often such statements are not freely made. The duress is significant. We know of no account of forgiveness that holds that a statement that one forgives, uttered under duress, or as a result of other forms of pressure or coercion, counts as forgiving.

[7] C Griswold, *Forgiveness: A Philosophical Exploration*, Cambridge University Press, Cambridge, 2007, p.47.

[8] For a distinction between 'reliance' (which is not normative) and 'trust' (which is normative, linking reliance to responsibility) see M.U. Walker, *Moral Repair: Reconstructing Moral Relations After Wrongdoing*, Cambridge University Press, Cambridge, 2006, pp. 79-85. On our view, reliance would develop into trust only if the parties are members of a shared moral world.

[9] J Hatzfeld, *Life Laid Bare*, translation: Linda Coverdale, Other Press, New York, NY, 2006, pp.173-4.

[10] M U Walker, *Moral Repair: Reconstructing Moral Relations After Wrongdoing*, Cambridge University Press, Cambridge, 2006, p. 19. See also Lazare, *On Apology*, Oxford: Oxford University Press, 2004.

[11] See, e.g., C Griswold, *Forgiveness: A Philosophical Exploration*. Cambridge University Press, Cambridge, 2007, pp.47-53, and 174.

[12] Margaret Walker's view of forgiveness is complex, and seems to straddle the Classical view and our Emergent Model, for she holds that forgiveness 'is a variable human process and a practice with culturally distinctive versions,' and yet she treats it as a decision. M.U. Walker, 2006. *Moral Repair: Reconstructing Moral Relations After Wrongdoing,* Cambridge University Press, Cambridge, p. 152. See 153 for her emphasis on decisions.

[13] L Tirrell, 'Apology, Promises, and the Politics of Reconciliation,' presented to *'Pathways to Reconciliation and Global Human Rights',* *Sarajevo 2005, sponsored by the United Nations Development Program in BiH, and The Globalism Institute of RMIT, AUS.*

[14] P Hieronymi, 'Articulating an Uncompromising Forgiveness,' *Philosophy and Phenomenological Research,* vol. 62, No. 3, May 2001, p.530. Also see C Griswold, *Forgiveness: A Philosophical Exploration.* Cambridge University Press, Cambridge, 2007, p.79.

[15] Darryl Li explains that in Rwanda, 'mass violence relied on social intimacy. Systematic identification and pursuit of Tutsi depended on the compilation of comprehensive lists at the local level; such surveillance, coupled with movement restrictions, made escape and anonymity extremely difficult. Moreover, the killing involved widespread denunciation and betrayal of friends, neighbours, and loved ones.' D. Li, 'Echoes of Violence: Considerations on Radio and genocide in Rwanda,' *Journal of Genocide Research*, vol. 6 (1), 2004, p.10.

[16] E Neuffer. *The Key to My Neighbor's House: Seeking Justice in Bosnia and Rwanda.* Picador, New York, NY, 2002, p.251.

[17] Walker eloquently articulates the important role in moral repair and survivor healing of giving voice to the moral damage done, and having one's experience of moral violation validated by others. (Margaret Walker, *Moral Repair: Reconstructing Moral Relations After Wrongdoing,* Cambridge University Press, Cambridge, 2006.) The importance of such articulation and validation is also explained in Maria Lugones and Elizabeth V. Spelman, 'Have We Got a Theory For You: Cultural Imperialism and the Demand for 'the Woman's Voice',' in *Women's Studies International Forum* vol. 6, no.6, 1983, pp. 573-581.

[18] J Hatzfeld, *Life Laid Bare,* translation: Linda Coverdale, Other Press, New York, NY, 2006, p.116.

[19] . Hatzfeld, *Life Laid Bare,* translation: Linda Coverdale, Other Press, New York, NY, 2006, p.117.

[20] J Hatzfeld, *The Antelope's Strategy: Living in Rwanda After the Genocide,* translation: Linda Coverdale, NY: Farrar, Strauss, and Giroux, 2009, p.7.

[21] J Hatzfeld, *Life Laid Bare,* translation: Linda Coverdale, Other Press, New York, NY, 2006, pp.217-218.

[22] S Wiesenthal, *The Sunflower: On the Possibilities and Limits of Forgiveness.* Schocken Books, New York, NY, 1998, p.9.

[23] C F Card, *The Atrocity Paradigm: A Theory of Evil.* Oxford University Press, Oxford, 2002, p.176.

[24] C F Card, *The Atrocity Paradigm: A Theory of Evil.* Oxford University Press, Oxford, 2002, p.176.

[25] C F Card, *The Atrocity Paradigm: A Theory of Evil.* Oxford University Press, Oxford, 2002, p.176.

[26] Even in more individualized atrocities, like sustained domestic assault, cohabitation may also be a social or economic reality.

[27] M U Walker, 2006. *Moral Repair: Reconstructing Moral Relations After Wrongdoing,* Cambridge University Press, Cambridge, p. 28.

[28] But see C Card, 'Rape Terrorism' in *The Unnatural Lottery: Character and Moral Luck,* Temple University Press, Philadelphia, PA, 1997, p. 97-117. Rape is complex, because the degree of world-shattering can be so variable.

[29] J Searle, *The Construction of Social Reality*, The Free Press, New York, NY, 1995.

[30] 'Normative repair' encompasses 'moral repair' but not vice-versa. Community norms include moral norms, but also include social and political norms that are not moral. Thus, on our view, moral repair can emerge from non-moral normative repair.

[31] See, for example, I. Ilibagiza, and S. Erwin. *Left to Tell: Discovering God Amidst the Rwandan Genocide*, Carlsbad, CA: Hay House, 2006, pp. 96-98, 134.

[32] John Searle develops a compelling account of collective consciousness in *The Construction of Social Reality*, NY: The Free Press, 1995.)

[33] We are grateful to Fr. Romain Rurangirwa for an account of these events. We take responsibility for the presentation here.

[34] This story is about world-building amongst women, who were neither the primary agents of the genocide nor bystanders. In general, the Hutu women stayed in their traditional roles, serving their men. Rwandan prisons contained approximately 3,000 women perpetrators, out of 100,000 prisoners overall. The Tutsi women, on the other hand, were among the primary targets; most were murdered, but among survivors over 80% suffered rape once or many times. So there is an asymmetry. Crucial to this story, however, is that the Tutsi women recognized shared oppression and reached out to the Hutu women across their differences, undertaking personal risk to express compassion. Also crucial is the absence of the men. As Nicole Itano reported in 2002: 'Hutu and Tutsi women in some areas have bonded together to shoulder the responsibility of caring for the thousands of genocide orphans, yet such cooperation has been made possible by the absence of the genocide's

worst perpetrators.' This was just before a massive release of prisoners, which would radically alter the sense of background safety. N. Itano, '3,000 Rwandan Women Await Trials for Genocide' Women's e-News, 12/20/02. http://www.womensenews.org/article.cfm?aid=1152
[35] M U Walker, 2006. *Moral Repair: Reconstructing Moral Relations After Wrongdoing*, Cambridge University Press, Cambridge, p. 37.
[36] J Hatzfeld, *Machete Season: The Killers in Rwanda Speak*, translation: Linda Coverdale, Farrar, Straus and Giroux, New York, NY, 2005, p. 194. Emphasis added.
[37] See A Carse 'The Moral Contours of Empathy,' *Ethical Theory and Moral Practice*, vol. 8, 2005, pp.169-195.
[38] Desmond Tutu, in S Wiesenthal, *The Sunflower: On the Possibilities and Limits of Forgiveness,* Schocken Books, New York, NY,1998, p. 268.

Bibliography

Austin, J.L., *How to Do Things with Words*. Harvard University Press, Cambridge, MA, 1975.

Brison, S., *Aftermath: Violence and the Remaking of a Self*. Princeton University Press, Princeton, NJ, 2001.

Calhoun, C., 'Changing One's Heart,' *Ethics*, Vol. 103, 1992, pp. 76-96.

Card, C.F., *The Atrocity Paradigm: A Theory of Evil*. Oxford University Press, Oxford and New York, NY, 2002.

———, 'Genocide and Social Death,' *Hypatia*, Vol. 18, 2003, pp. 63-79.

Carse, A., 'The Moral Contours of Empathy.' *Ethical Theory and Moral Practice*, vol. 8, 2005, pp. 169-195.

Govier, T., 'Forgiveness and the Unforgiveable,' *American Philosophical Quarterly,* Vol. 36, Jan 1999, pp. 59-75.

Griswold, C., *Forgiveness: A Philosophical Exploration*. Cambridge University Press, Cambridge, 2007.

Hatzfeld, J., *Life Laid Bare*. Translation: Linda Coverdale, Other Press, New York, NY, 2006.

Hatzfeld, J., *Machete Season: The Killers in Rwanda Speak.* Translation: Linda Coverdale, Farrar, Straus and Giroux, New York, NY, 2005.

Herman, J., *Trauma and Recovery.* Basic Books, New York, NY, 1997.

Hieronymi, P., 'Articulating an Uncompromising Forgiveness,' *Philosophy and Phenomenological Research,* vol. 62, May 2001, pp. 529-555.

Ilibagiza, I. with S Erwin. *Left to Tell: Discovering God Amidst the Rwandan Genocide.* Carlsbad, CA: Hay House, 2006.

Itano, N., '3,000 Rwandan Women Await Trials for Genocide' Women's e-News, 12/20/02. http://www.womensenews.org/article.cfm?aid=1152

Lazare, A., *On Apology.* Oxford University Press, Oxford and NY, NY, 2004.

Li, D., 'Echoes of Violence: Considerations on Radio and genocide in Rwanda,' *Journal of Genocide Research,* vol. 6 (1), 2004, pp.9-27.

Neuffer, E., *The Key to My Neighbor's House: Seeking Justice in Bosnia and Rwanda.* Picador, New York, NY, 2002.

Norlock, K., *Forgiveness from a Feminist Perspective.* Lexington Books, Rowman & Littlefield, Lanham MD, 2008.

Searle, J., *The Construction of Social Reality.* The Free Press, New York, NY, 1995.

Tirrell, L., 'Epistemic Aspects of Evil: The Three Monkeys meet *The Atrocity Paradigm,*' in *Evil, Political Violence, and Forgiveness: Essays in Honor of Claudia Card,* eds. A. Veltman and K. Norlock, Lexington Books Rowman & Littlefield, Lanham, MD, 2009, pp. 35-51.

——, 'Apology, Promises, and the Politics of Reconciliation,' presented to *'Pathways to Reconciliation and Global Human Rights', Sarajevo 2005, sponsored by the United Nations Development Program in BiH, and The Globalism Institute of RMIT, AUS.*

Tutu, D., *No Future Without Forgiveness.* Image, NY, NY, 2000.

Walker, M.U., *Moral Repair: Reconstructing Moral Relations After Wrongdoing.* Cambridge University Press, Cambridge, 2006.

———,'The Expressive Burden of Reparations: Putting Meaning into Money, Words, and Things' presented at Boston University Institute for Philosophy and religion, Conference on 'Reconciliation, Moral Obligation and Moral Reconstruction in the Wake of Conflict,' Friday, March 20, 2009.

Wiesenthal, S., Carga, H., Fetterman, B., *The Sunflower: On the Possibilities and Limits of Forgiveness.* Schocken Books, New York, NY, 1998.

Alisa L. Carse is Associate Professor of Philosophy at Georgetown University in Washington DC, where her research and teaching are centred in moral and political theory, moral psychology and gender studies. Her work on moral vulnerability, empathy, and trust explores the moral-psychological and existential repercussions of subordination for individual and group identity, effective moral agency and questions of social justice. She is currently working on moral implications of traumatic experience, and co-leading a project bringing neuroscientists and philosophers together exploring questions of self-governance and moral responsibility.

Lynne Tirrell is Associate Professor of Philosophy at the University of Massachusetts, Boston, where she works primarily in the philosophy of language, feminist theory, literary theory, and aesthetics. Working within inferential role semantics, she has written about metaphor, storytelling, pornography, silencing, hate speech and the functioning of derogatory terms, and issues surrounding authority and privilege. Most recently, she has been thinking about how public and official apologies work, and about the expressive dimensions of genocide.

PART II

The Right to Forgive

Moral Bystanders and the Virtue of Forgiveness

Linda Radzik

Abstract

According to standard philosophical analyses, only victims can forgive. There are good reasons to reject this view. After all, people who are neither direct nor indirect victims frequently feel moral anger over injustice and adjust their relationships with wrongdoers accordingly. Choices by third parties to forswear or overcome such moral anger and to normalize relations are subject to most of the same sorts of considerations as victims' choices to forgive. Furthermore, bystanders' reactions to wrongdoing often reflect either virtues or vices that are of a piece with what we normally describe as a forgiving or unforgiving disposition. In this paper, I reject the view that only victims can forgive by comparing the experience and regulation of moral anger by victims and bystanders. The virtues of victims and bystanders with regard to moral anger are so similar that there is no good reason to apply different labels. However, the recognition of forgiveness in bystanders offers us more than simple consistency. It also leads us to think about the role moral bystanders play in the maintenance of the moral community, as well as the ways in which this role can be abused or overstepped.

Key Words: Third party forgiveness, bystanders, moral community, virtue, indignation, anger, scandal, apology.

*****

1.   Indignant Bystanders

On a regular basis, the American media break out in a frenzy of moral indignation. The most famous case is surely the circus that surrounded the revelation of President Bill Clinton's affair with a White House intern, which lead to his impeachment hearing in 1999. More recently, the Governor of New York, Eliot Spitzer, was forced to resign when he was revealed to be a client of a high-price prostitution service. At that time, Martha Nussbaum wrote a newspaper editorial proclaiming her disgust with what she labelled 'a Puritanism and mean-spiritedness that are quintessentially American.'[1] Nussbaum's critique focuses on the public's tendency to become indignant over sex, specifically. However, I am more interested in these cases as examples of people feeling indignant over perceived wrongs to which they are mere bystanders.

Besides getting caught with one's pants down, the other way for a well-known figure to ignite a firestorm of moral outrage is to utter a racial epithet in public. In separate incidents in 2006-2007, actor Mel Gibson, comedian Michael Richards, radio talk show host Don Imus, and Senator George Allen were each caught using racist language against, variously, Jews, blacks, and Indians. Each case was followed by highly vocal and widely shared indignation. Repeated, carefully crafted public apologies by the transgressors followed. In the media and in living rooms across the country, the American public debated whether it should respond with forgiveness.

According to many theories of forgiveness, it makes no sense for members of the general public to discuss whether *they* should forgive Bill Clinton for cheating on his wife or Don Imus for using a racist insult against the players on the Rutgers University Women's Basketball team.[2] The victims of these wrongs have the standing to forgive. On some theories, loved ones of the victims (such as the Clintons' daughter or the players' parents) may have interests and identities so closely tied with the victims that they have the standing to forgive as well.[3] In some cases, a larger group of people might be considered secondary victims of the wrongful act (in the Imus case, perhaps black women generally were wronged by his words).[4] But victim status is what gives someone the standing to forgive. In the cases on which I am focusing, most of the commentators in the media were simply bystanders to the wrongs. According to leading theories, they and the general public they claim to represent cannot forgive.[5]

I would like to reject this view. I will argue instead that forgiveness is possible for third parties to moral wrongdoing and that, furthermore, a properly attuned disposition to forgive when one is a bystander to wrongdoing should be considered a moral virtue. I will suggest that, while there is often much to criticize in the outbursts of indignation that periodically occupy the American media's attention, these debates about forgiveness do not rest on a category mistake. In the latter part of this essay, I will sketch an account of third party forgiveness and highlight some of the distinctive issues this variant of forgiveness raises.

2.   Attitude-Based and Relational Accounts of Forgiveness

The most popular definitions of forgiveness these days present forgiveness as a relenting of the forgiver's negative attitudes towards the wrongdoer.[6] Although such attitude-based definitions of forgiveness frequently stipulate that only a victim's change in attitude toward a wrongdoer can count as forgiveness, I argue that the reactions of bystanders to moral wrongdoing can be so similar that there is no good reason to deny them the honorific label of forgiveness. Paul Hughes, for example, defines forgiveness as the overcoming or forswearing of moral anger toward a wrongdoer where one is motivated by morally relevant considerations.[7] Hughes argues against previous attempts to define forgiveness simply with respect to resentment (which is an emotion that is itself usually defined as something only a victim can feel) because he thinks that this too narrowly restricts the range of negative moral emotions that are negotiated in the aftermath of wrongdoing. Instead he identifies moral anger as the relevant emotion. However, Hughes then defines moral anger as anger over a wrong done to oneself.[8] This restriction seems to be not just arbitrary but also problematic.

Notice, we do not want to define forgiveness in relation to the modification of anger *simpliciter*. I might be angry because I lose a fair competition. The overcoming of such anger is not forgiveness. Only the overcoming of anger that reacts to a wrong deserves to be labelled 'forgiveness'. My anger is only moral anger when it is motivated not simply by the thought that 'it is me who hurts' but also by the recognition that 'no one should be hurt in this way.' If I am angered by wrongful harms only because they are *mine* and not also because they are *wrong*, then my emotion is not moral anger. It is an expression of mere self-love, not also moral judgment. The overcoming of that sort of anger does not deserve the label 'forgiveness'. On the other hand, when my anger is tied to the judgment that the harm was wrongful, then my anger is moral even if I was not the one harmed. To define moral anger as only the anger of a victim seems to misidentify what is moral about the anger.

Sometimes we feel a morally charged anger over wrongs done to people other than ourselves, even people with whom we have little or no personal connection. In the literature, this form of moral anger is usually labelled 'indignation'. P. F. Strawson identifies indignation as an analogue of resentment that 'rest[s] on, and reflect[s], exactly the same expectation or demand,' namely, 'the demand for the manifestation of a reasonable degree of goodwill or regard, on the part of others . . . towards all men.'[9] Many who were angered by Imus's characterization of the Rutgers basketball players were angered because it was a racist slur. The fact that they were not themselves on the team, or not themselves black, did not undermine their anger because the cause and justification of the anger was the wrong and not self-love.

Bystanders can feel moral anger. They can also overcome and forswear their anger in response to what seem to be morally relevant considerations. In the media coverage of the Imus scandal, a number of such considerations were offered as reasons for the modification of the public's indignation, such as Imus's repeated apologies, alternative interpretations of Imus's character and behaviour that did not excuse his comments but put them in a larger context, the claim that he had been punished enough, and hopes to encourage his moral improvement by a show of compassion toward him. The Rutgers players and coaches cited considerations such as these after a private meeting with Imus in which they offered him their own forgiveness. Why should we label their change in attitude toward Imus forgiveness but deny that label to the similarly motivated resolution of moral anger by members of the general public?

'Forgiveness' names not just a change in attitude but also a virtue. A forgiving person will feel a proportional degree of resentment when she is a victim of wrongdoing. Not to feel such moral anger would normally signify a failure of self-respect.[10] However, a victim who has a forgiving disposition will also be properly attuned to the moral considerations that, in most cases, call for the timely resolution of such resentment. Similarly, the virtuous person will be disposed to feel moral anger over the mistreatment of other people. Not to feel indignant, in certain circumstances, would fail to respect the victim. Yet the virtuous person will also recognize the moral considerations that support overcoming indignation. In both cases, the virtue lies between the vices of moral laxity or disrespect for human value, on one extreme, and self-righteousness or hard-heartedness, on the other.

The virtuous moderation of moral anger as displayed by victims and bystanders is so similar that there is no good reason to apply different labels. Indeed, it is hard for me to imagine that one could develop the virtue of forgiveness, which would be displayed when one has been victimized, if one did not also develop proper habits and dispositions when occupying the bystander position. We surely observe many more cases of wrongdoing as third parties than we experience personally as victims. Our notions of what sorts of wrongs are worth feeling angry about and what count as reasons for modifying anger are shaped by our experiences witnessing wrongs against others, sympathizing with the people directly involved, and regulating our own reactions to those wrongdoers.

The claim that bystanders cannot forgive is implausible if it is the claim that they cannot overcome or forswear their own moral anger toward a wrongdoer on the basis of moral considerations. Surely they can. Surely we have first person experience, as bystanders, of this sort of change. Once we recognize that bystanders do make decisions about what to do with their moral anger, it is easy to agree that these are decisions that can display either virtues or vices. Yet the view that only victims can forgive is so well entrenched that I suspect many theorists will take this argument to be a *reductio* of the theory of forgiveness from which it follows. If an attitude-based theory of forgiveness leads to the conclusion that mere bystanders forgive, then, they will say, that proves that forgiveness cannot simply be the overcoming or forswearing of moral anger. Forgiving must instead consist of a change that is not (merely) internal, but (also) external.

Some theorists prefer to define forgiveness as involving a change in relationships.[11] When one forgives, one stops relating to the wrongdoer as a wrongdoer. I would prefer to call this sort of process 'reconciliation' rather than 'forgiveness', but there is nothing to be gained in arguing over terminology. The normalization of relationships is certainly a morally significant reorientation deserving of philosophical attention. The point I would like to insist upon, however, is that a relational conception of forgiveness gives us no better reason to reject the possibility of third party forgiveness than an attitude-based conception does. In the aftermath of wrongdoing, victims are not the only ones who have to decide whether to normalize their relationships with the transgressor. At least some bystanders have to make such decisions as well. Imus's listeners had to decide whether to keep tuning in. His advertisers had to decide whether to continue sponsoring the program. Once again, it is hard to see why we should claim that there is a difference in kind between the choices victims face and the choices third parties face. Both seem to make decisions about forgiveness.

3.   The Right to Forgive

So far, I have argued that the leading conceptions of forgiveness are compatible with the possibility of third party forgiveness. In this section, I would like to consider a pair of objections that turn on the claim that only victims have a right to forgive. The first objection suggests that limiting such a right to victims protects wrongdoers from undue harm. The second objection limits the right to forgive by appealing to the interests of victims.

It is clear that both victims and bystanders may experience moral anger over a wrongful action. But while it is understandable and even good that ordinary members of the public were indignant over Mel Gibson's anti-Semitic tirade against the police officer who was arresting him for drunk driving, some commentators were disturbed by the public vilification of Gibson that followed, which included calls to other Hollywood figures to refuse to work with him in the future.[12] These actions were punitive and, one might charge, bystanders lack the proper standing to punish. Victims may act on their resentment. States may punish those wrongful acts that are also crimes. But, mere bystanders do not have a right to punish wrongdoing. Because they do not have a right to punish, one might argue, they do not have a right to forgive. Only the victim has a right to act on moral anger, so only he can choose to waive that right. Only the victim can forgive.

The question of whether social punishment for moral (as opposed to legal) wrongdoing is justifiable is an interesting and important one. Victims are usually allowed to express their resentment in ways that can be described as punitive in virtue of having a right to defend themselves against attack. There are surely limits on the means victims may take in defending themselves, which would include both considerations of proportionality and the reservation of some forms of power for the state alone, which we might justify in a Lockean fashion. Yet victims' legitimate means of self-defence certainly include things like verbal expressions of anger, denunciations, and demands for apologies and reparations. However, most conceptions of a right to self-defence, including Locke's, also permit third parties to defend the rights of people who are attacked.[13] Again, there will be limits on the means private individuals may take in defending others within a legitimate state, but the principle of defending the rights of others seems to justify an appropriately restrained expression of indignation. The principle seems to permit at least verbal expressions of anger, condemnations, and demands that the wrongdoer apologize to the victim and make proportional reparations to her. There is surely room for debate and further distinctions here, but for the moment it will suffice to point out that it is not obvious that bystanders lack any right to punish.

Furthermore, interesting though the question of social punishment is, it is not generally considered to be the same issue as forgiveness. When philosophers discuss the ethics of forgiveness the questions are how the victim should regard or relate to the wrongdoer, what her emotions and attitudes toward the wrongdoer should be, and whether she will restore voluntary relationships with the wrongdoer, *not* what the victim may or may not do to punish the wrongdoer. So, while issues of forgiveness and punishment are often quickly entwined, it is possible to separate them. Third parties might ask whether either justice or virtue require them to forswear their indignation and normalize relations with wrongdoers, even if they take no punitive actions.

For the sake of argument, let us deny the legitimacy of social punishment for moral wrongdoing. Let us stipulate that third parties who lack any special position of authority (such as being the parent of a young wrongdoer) are not justified in intentionally trying to make the wrongdoer suffer on the basis of and in proportion to the wrong, whether on retributive, deterrent, or moral education grounds. Even if we disallow third parties the right to punish, their indignation could still have a significant negative impact, one we might think ought to be tempered by forgiveness. Were a one-time Gibson fan to organize a boycott of his movies, it would be a case of social punishment. If a single fan is so angry he simply takes no more joy in seeing Gibson on the screen, his refusal to buy a ticket is not punitive. But if many fans feel the same way, and if film producers and financers know that they feel that way, the effect will be indistinguishable from punishment. The avoidance of voluntary business and personal relationships, subtle responses such as social withdrawal and emotional coldness by third parties, can harm a wrongdoer. Sometimes these responses are intended to be punitive, but sometimes they are just side effects of anger, disappointment, and mistrust. So even if we deny that third parties to moral wrongdoing have a right to punish, their decisions to forgive or withhold forgiveness are still meaningful and should concern anyone sympathetic to the interests of the wrongdoer.

A related concern about whether third parties have a right to forgive focuses not on the wrongdoer, but on the victim. A common worry among theorists of forgiveness is that, by recognizing the legitimacy of third party forgiveness, we will undermine or harm victims.[14] Any discussion of forgiveness must acknowledge that the victim of the wrongful act has a special kind of status. After all, the wrong is a wrong primarily because of what it does to its victim. It treats *her* as less than an end in herself. It violates *her* rights, insults *her* dignity and (often) causes the most harm to *her*. Given these special facts and given that the evaluation of reasons as sufficient to permit, justify, or compel forgiveness is one upon which reasonable people could disagree, it seems appropriate to recognize that the victim exercises a certain prerogative with regard to forgiveness.

Sometimes the claim that the victim has the prerogative to forgive is interpreted to mean simply that no one else can force or compel her to forgive.[15] This is a very weak prerogative, perhaps even a meaningless one. Insofar as forgiveness consists in a change in attitude, or insofar as the normalization of relationships includes some sort of internal change, no one could forgive for the victim. This isn't a prerogative; it is a psychological fact.

At other times, the victim's prerogative to forgive is characterized as a right to determine whether the wrongdoer *is forgiven* or *counts as forgiven*.[16] The idea seems to be akin to the religious equation of forgiveness with absolution. When a sin is absolved it is washed away once and for all. There is no such thing as a sin being absolved from one point of view but not another, absolved by God but not by the victim. It is either removed or it is not. If we were to conceive of forgiveness in this way, then there would be reasonable grounds for wanting victims rather than third parties to have the right to forgive. But the absolution model of forgiveness is not compatible with contemporary moral theories. Guilt is not something that can be washed away once and for all, so there are no grounds for worrying that third parties might erase the guilt without the victim having any say in the matter.

But the idea that a wrongdoer is to be marked or counted as forgiven can be given a social rather than a metaphysical interpretation. The right to forgive becomes the right to restore the wrongdoer's position as a member in good standing of the moral community. Perhaps when theorists assert that the victim has the prerogative to forgive, what they mean is that the victim's decision to renounce moral anger or normalize relations with the wrongdoer (or to refuse to do so) must be treated as authoritative for everyone else. According to this line of thought, the radio listeners' and advertisers' decisions to re-establish their usual dealings with Don Imus are properly guided by the basketball players' decisions about forgiveness. When bystanders respect a victim's prerogative, they treat her with the kind of dignity and respect for her moral agency that the wrongdoer had denied her. So in acknowledging the victim's prerogative to forgive, the bystanders help vindicate the victim and heal her wounds. On the other hand, when other parties offer forgiveness before the primary victim is ready to do so, they usurp her right to determine whether the wrongdoer will be released from the negative consequences of the moral transgression. Thereby, third parties appear to join the wrongdoer in suggesting that the victim is not a morally significant person.

However, while arguments for a victim's prerogative are usually taken as grounds for rejecting the category of third party forgiveness, there are a few ways of interpreting the prerogative that are actually compatible with third party forgiveness. On one version, let us call it the *permissive version*, no one else is allowed to forgive unless the primary victim forgives. If the primary victim forgives, then any secondary victims are free to make their choice. If secondary victims forgive, then bystanders make *their choice.*[17] The first decision permits but does not compel a decision to forgive from either secondary victims or bystanders. This may be the way the media saw the issue in the Imus case. The decision to forgive by the Rutgers Women's Basketball team was reported with interest but not taken to settle the issue of whether the public at large should forgive or whether Imus's show should remain on the air. If the permissive version is the correct understanding of the victim's prerogative, then granting the prerogative is consistent with the possibility that the reactions of bystanders could qualify as forgiveness (or refusals to forgive) as well.

A second reading of the prerogative, call it the *directive version*, grants the primary victim more influence by claiming that the primary victim's decision to forgive properly determines the reactions of any secondary victims and of bystanders.[18] When the primary victim forgives, then so must the others. When he declines to forgive, no one else may forgive either. This interpretation of the prerogative also allows that bystanders can forgive. However, my opponent may prefer this version since, here, the compassionate forswearing of moral anger is expressive of a virtue *of the victim*, not those who merely follow his lead. In response, I claim that even if we accept the directive version of the prerogative, there is still a virtue involved in allowing oneself to be guided by the victim into giving up indignation. In the media cases that have served my example here, victims' decisions to forgive are usually given very little weight. Indeed, most political wives who express forgiveness for the sexual misdeeds of their politician-husbands are received more frequently with pity or scorn than with deference. Assuming that their forgiveness is reasonable and sincere, and that they wield a directive prerogative to forgive, wouldn't the public that ignores or mocks their decisions to forgive be guilty of a vice? Wouldn't it be reasonable to describe that public as 'unforgiving'?

Of course, it is reasonable to wonder how autonomous a political wife's decision to declare forgiveness is, when she is under the hot lights of the media. This worry suggests that both versions of the victim's prerogative should include *ceteris paribus* clauses, which would in turn allow for even more situations where third parties must make independent decisions about whether to forgive. While the primary victim generally has the prerogative to forgive, it is possible for her to misuse that prerogative. She might offer forgiveness to the wrongdoer for the wrong reasons, perhaps reasons that end up condoning the wrong, or she might refuse forgiveness in a way that displays a vice such as hard-heartedness or a greedy desire for a disproportional reparation. Presumably such a misuse of her prerogative would leave bystanders free to make their own decisions about how they will view the wrongdoer.

Furthermore, in cases where the victim has died, is absent, or is simply uncommunicative about whether she forgives (and it would be too rude to ask her), bystanders are again left without authoritative guidance about what to do with their own indignation and so must make their own decisions. One might say that, in cases such as these, bystanders must retain their indignation. That claim is debatable. However, I will not pursue it because it does not deny that third party forgiveness is possible; it merely takes a particularly strong position on when it must be withheld. To sum up my argument in this section, the claim that the victim has a special prerogative, even a very strong prerogative, with respect to issues of forgiveness is compatible with recognizing the possibility that third parties can also do something that is reasonably labelled forgiving or refusing to forgive.

4.   In Defence of Public Indignation

A different sort of reason for denying the category of third party forgiveness is based on worries about the existence of bystanders' indignation rather than their resolution of it. Nussbaum's disgust with the American public in the case of Governor Spitzer seems to be based on the fact that the public was indignant over his sexual behaviour in the first place.[19] We could interpret this as the claim that people should not have felt indignant at all, or perhaps that they should not have allowed any personal feelings of indignation to influence their behaviour toward the Governor. I tend to think Nussbaum is right that we should keep our noses out of the consensual sexual affairs of public figures. A failure to respect privacy and reasonable differences of opinion about sexual ethics threatens more harm within the public sphere than the particular wrongs that are protested through our indignation. Our list of virtues should include the virtue of minding one's own business.

But, while this response may be appropriate to many cases of sexual transgression, we cannot claim that feeling or expressing indignation over wrongs done to other people is *never* appropriate. Nussbaum herself, after all, expresses indignation over what she takes to be an injustice committed against Governor Spitzer. Like Nussbaum, I wish Americans did not get so indignant over sex. But I am glad they get indignant over racism, I wish they were a bit more indignant over sexism, and I am horrified that they are not *much more* indignant over torture and the violation of *habeas corpus* rights.

Indignation is a means by which we show our solidarity with the victims of wrongdoing. It is a tool for constructing and communicating the norms that govern the moral community. Indeed, our indignation shows who we take to be included in the moral community. Senator George Allen knew that it would be intolerable to use a racist epithet against a black audience member from the podium of a campaign rally; but he repeatedly used a slur against S. R. Sidarth, a young man of Indian descent who was videotaping the event for a political opponent.[20] Allen seemed to assume that his audience would agree that Sidarth was an 'other' and so not within the scope of their moral concern. The public indignation that followed (and that ended Allen's bid for the presidency) showed him otherwise.

The observation that public indignation helps shape our moral communities reveals what bystanders have at stake in cases of public scandal. In this way, it may undermine my argument for third party forgiveness. Perhaps the general public are actually *indirect victims* of misdeeds such as Allen's. While Allen did not directly insult non-Indian members of the American public, perhaps he wronged them insofar as his actions threatened to make the society in which they lived a little bit worse – more divisive and more degraded. One might agree that members of the general public had the standing to forgive or refuse forgiveness, but only because they were not really bystanders; they were indirect victims.

However, I would like to resist blanket redefinitions of concerned bystanders as indirect victims. Indirect victims have claims of a stronger sort than anything I have attributed to bystanders, such as a claim to receive an apology or some form of reparations. Furthermore, even in cases where one counts an entire moral community as an indirect victim of the wrong, as one might in cases that involve racism by an unusually influential wrongdoer, the claim that we are indignant only in virtue of our own victimhood diminishes our moral capacities. Gibson insulted the police officer and our Jewish neighbours. Allen wronged Sidarth and the larger Indian-American community. Our anger over the mistreatment of particular victims reveals our caring about *them* –not just abstract norms, not just humanity as such, but particular human beings. Our ability to care about another person, even a stranger, for his own sake is one of our better features. When our indignation is primarily focused on the wrongful harming of someone else, we are properly considered third parties, not indirect victims.[21]

While indignation helps build and maintain moral communities, it can also be misguided and destructive. The American media sensations that have served as my examples in this discussion, perhaps especially those that revolve around sexual misconduct among consenting adults, frequently exemplify self-righteousness and *Schadenfreude* rather than genuine caring for one another's dignity and well-being. Furthermore, indignation, like resentment, is a moral emotion that, even when justified, can have a negative effect both on those against whom it is directed and on those who feel it. Just as one can be eaten up by resentment towards one's own abuser, one can be eaten up by indignation towards those who have harmed others. Those who closely followed the 2008 U.S. Presidential race may remember that some of candidate Hillary Clinton's supporters were so outraged at how she was treated by the media and the Democratic Party that they vowed to vote against their own political interests in protest. A handful of them were so angry as to express the thinly veiled (and morally depraved) hope that Barrack Obama would be assassinated before his nomination was finalized.[22] Such damaging forms of indignation are more likely when people closely identify with a victim, or when they see themselves as secondary victims of the wrongs. Many of the angriest Clinton supporters felt indirectly wronged. But even in cases where indignation is more clearly other-centred, it can be an obstacle to peace of mind and healthy relationships.

Since we cannot deny the legitimacy of third party moral anger as a category, we should recommend that this indignation and its expression in action be regulated by virtue. A virtuous bystander must strike the balance between moral laxity and vindictiveness, between compassion for the wrongdoer and solidarity with the victim, and between a concerned involvement with other people and respect for their privacy. I believe that this virtue deserves to be called forgiveness.

5.   Toward an Account of Third Party Forgiveness

When should bystanders forgive wrongdoers? When should they overcome or forswear their moral anger at a wrongdoer for offences committed against another person and when should they normalize relations? Surely, forgiveness is only a possibility when the moral anger is justified. This means that the offending act must violate a standard of morality that is at least reasonable.[23] Furthermore, the object of indignation must be reasonably believed to be responsible for the offending act in a way that is neither justified nor fully excused. I would also add that indignation is only justified when the wrong does not fall into the category of being none of the bystander's business.

It is difficult to define what counts as 'one's own business.' The question deserves a much better treatment than I am able to give it. But there are a few things that seem fairly clear. For example, many of the things that used to be placed in the 'none of my business' column were put there mistakenly. Whether the people next door beat their children is *not* none of my business, although respect for my neighbours' privacy means that I may not go snooping around in search of abuse without due cause. If I have credible evidence that children are being abused, then I cannot remain neutral (as people used to) simply on the grounds that they are not my children.

The moral injunction to mind my own business will generally apply to my efforts to uncover or know more about wrongdoing. It will also restrain the forms of response I may take to wrongdoing, such as punishing wrongdoers or informing others of the transgression. But in most cases, if I come across good evidence of something that is uncontroversially wrong, then any proportional feeling of indignation I feel will not be out of bounds.

There are surely exceptions here. Certain genuinely moral obligations can be bound up with particular communities or relationships in ways that would render an outsider's feelings of indignation unjustified. I can see that it would be morally wrong for the top striker on the Spanish national soccer team to stay up all night drinking before the championship match. His action would be seriously disloyal to his teammates and fans. But to feel anger at him myself, as a non-Spaniard and merely occasional soccer viewer, would be bizarre. It would be to claim a place in a community that I do not really have.[24] The overcoming of any such presumptuous indignation would not deserve the label 'forgiveness'. Some people feel that indignation over infidelity in other people's romantic or marital relationships falls into this category. Other people disagree, perhaps because they believe that sexual fidelity is something that should be socially encouraged or even subtly enforced by informal kinds of punishment. Whether a particular wrong is one's business or not can be a difficult call to make. The issue turns on questions about the role and scope of the moral community. More accurately, it turns on the fact that we belong to many overlapping moral communities – families, circles of friends, religious congregations, professions, nations, humanity as such – some of which legitimate our interests in intimate forms of wrongdoing and some of which do not. For the moment, I can merely note that so long as there are at least some cases where a bystander's indignation is justified, it is plausible to believe there are also cases where third party forgiveness is justified.

As with a victim's forgiveness, third party forgiveness may not condone the wrongful act. Giving up indignation because one decides that the victim deserved what she got or that the wrong is not worth caring about does not qualify as forgiveness. Third party forgiveness must be consistent with respect for the victim. It must also be consistent with respect for the wrongdoer. If one were to see the wrongdoer as less than a responsible moral agent (say, in virtue of being a child or being too contemptuous a creature to be held to moral expectations), then the forswearing of indignation would not count as forgiveness. So far, this parallels the standard account of a victim's forgiveness. In the third party case, we must add that the bystander may not relinquish indignation because of a lack of respect for himself either. If the bystander decides that he is not worthy to judge someone like the offender, we do not have a case of forgiveness.

This three-part requirement of respect follows from a general principle. In order to have a genuine case of forgiveness, moral anger must be given up (or relationships must be normalised) for a morally appropriate reason. Other acts that would not meet this principle include the bystander ceasing to resent because he has simply forgotten about the wrong or because his indignation is an obstacle to his working his way into a powerful wrongdoer's good graces.

Appropriate moral reasons for third party forgiveness would, I believe, include respect for the victim's special status in decisions about forgiveness. If the bystanders see that the victim has forgiven the wrongdoer for a morally permissible reason, then this provides them with a good (though not necessarily decisive) reason to forgive as well. Other good reasons bystanders may have for forgiving include those discussed in the literature on victims' forgiveness. Bystanders might be moved by a wrongdoer's repentance and attempts to make amends. They might come to see the wrongdoer's act in a broader context that does not excuse the wrongful action but helps them to separate the sin from the sinner. They might decide that the wrongdoer has already suffered enough. William Neblett's arguments against having an indignant character read like a standard defence of developing a forgiving character. In criticizing the tendency to hang on to indignation, Neblett argues that indignant people are more liable to aggressive behaviour, dishonest about their own moral flaws, and insufficiently compassionate towards wrongdoers.[25]

The overcoming of indignation is also likely to be controversial in just those cases where a victim's forgiveness is controversial. These include cases where moral anger is given up merely in order to achieve peace of mind or social harmony. Third party forgiveness will become entangled in further controversies as well, concerning its proper relationship to the victim's decision to forgive or to withhold forgiveness. The earlier discussion of the victim's prerogative points to some of the questions that will be at issue. There will also be special worries about how one might express third party forgiveness. Bystanders who utter the words 'I forgive you' are more likely to be greeted with hostility from a wrongdoer than gratitude. When bystanders declare their forgiveness, they bring the wrongdoer's attention to the fact that she has been under the shaming gaze of the moral community, and so third party forgiveness may well feel like a passive-aggressive punishment more than a gift of compassion.[26] If bystanders are to respect the privacy of wrongdoers, as well as victims, and to virtuously mind their own business, it might be appropriate for them to refrain from explicitly declaring the forgiveness they justifiably and virtuously feel.

6.   Conclusion

I have argued that the similarities in the moral anger experienced by bystanders to wrongdoing, as well as the choices they can make and the virtues and vices they can display, give us reason to stop defining 'forgiveness' in terms of victims' responses alone. I have tried to answer the most likely objections to extending the term to the case of bystanders, especially those that deny third parties the right to forgive. In closing, I would like to highlight some advantages to accepting the category of third party forgiveness.

First of all, allowing the possibility of third party forgiveness in our philosophical accounts of forgiveness simultaneously recognizes that bystanders make choices of moral significance and gives us many of the tools we need in order to determine what makes those decisions permissible or virtuous. Secondly, the category of third party forgiveness draws our attention to some additional moral problems of daily life that are genuinely vexing yet rarely theorized. What counts as a failure to mind one's own business? Is a tendency to mind one's own business a virtue? What are the limits of that virtue? Which bystanders have a right to express their indignation? Does the legitimacy of indignation justify social punishment for moral wrongdoing? If so, what forms of social punishment are permissible? There are few better rewards for altering our philosophical categories than the opportunity to do more, useful philosophy.[27]

Notes

[1] M Nussbaum, 'Trading on America's Puritanical Streak: Prostitution Laws Mean-spirited, Penalize Women,' *The Atlanta Journal-Constitution*, online edition, March 14, 2008, viewed April 2, 2009, <http://www.ajc.com/search/content/opinion/2008/03/13/spitzered_0314.html>.

[2] Imus referred to the team members, most of whom were black, as 'nappy-headed hos' - an insult that is both racist and sexist. The racism, rather than the sexism, was the focal point of most of the critics. Imus's popular radio show was cancelled as a result of public criticism and withdrawals by advertisers. It returned to the air within the year.

[3] See for example, Joram Haber, *Forgiveness: A Philosophical Study*, Rowman & Littlefield Publishers, Savage, Maryland, 1991, p. 49.

[4] See, for example, Trudy Govier and Wilhelm Verwoerd, 'Forgiveness: The Victim's Prerogative', *South African Journal of Philosophy*, vol. 21, 2002, pp. 97-111.

[5] It is much easier to cite those theorists who allow for third party forgiveness than those who deny it. The following writers offer brief but positive discussions of third party forgiveness: Christopher Bennett, 'Personal and

Redemptive Forgiveness', *European Journal of Philosophy,* vol. 11, 2003, pp. 127-144, at p.143; Claudia Card, *The Atrocity Paradigm: A Theory of Evil,* Oxford University Press, New York, 2002, p. 186; and Charles Griswold, *Forgiveness: A Philosophical Exploration,* Cambridge University Press, New York, 2007, pp. 117-119. Since first presenting a version of this paper at the second *Forgiveness: Probing the Boundaries* conference in March 2009, I have found three new, more fully developed defences of the category of third party forgiveness. They are: Alice MacLachlan, 'Forgiveness and Moral Solidarity', in *Forgiveness: Probing the Boundaries,* David White and Stephen Schulman (eds.), Inter-Disciplinary Press, Oxford, forthcoming; Glen Pettigrove, 'The Standing to Forgive', *Monist,* forthcoming; and Kathryn Norlock, *Forgiveness from a Feminist Perspective,* Lexington Books, Lanham, Maryland, 2009, pp. 115-135.

[6] Attitude-based theories include: Jeffrie Murphy's contributions to Jeffrie G. Murphy and Jean Hampton, *Forgiveness and Mercy,* Cambridge University Press, New York, 1988; Norvin Richards, 'Forgiveness', *Ethics,* vol. 99, 1988, pp. 77-97; Cheshire Calhoun, 'Changing One's Heart', *Ethics,* vol. 103, 1992, pp. 76–96; and Margaret R. Holmgren, 'Forgiveness and the Intrinsic Value of Persons', *American Philosophical Quarterly,* vol. 30, 1993, pp. 341–52.

[7] P M Hughes, 'What is Involved in Forgiving?' *Philosophia,* vol. 27, 1997, pp. 33-49.

[8] See Hughes, 'What is Involved in Forgiving?' p. 33 and especially n. 3 on pp. 46-47.

[9] P F Strawson, 'Freedom and Resentment', *Proceedings of the British Academy,* vol. 48, 1962, p. 200.

[10] Murphy and Hampton, *Forgiveness and Mercy.*

[11] Relational accounts of forgiveness are offered by Joanna North, 'Wrongdoing and Forgiveness', *Philosophy,* vol. 62, 1987, pp. 499-508; and Kim Atkins, 'Friendship, Trust and Forgiveness', *Philosophia,* vol. 29, 2002, pp. 111-132.

[12] The scandal reached such a level of intensity because Gibson had already faced charges of anti-Semitism in response to his film *The Passion of the Christ* (2004) and his failure to distance himself from his father's denial of the Holocaust. The apologies issued after his arrest addressed only that event and not the larger controversy. Many links to news items about the controversy are collected on the webpage, 'Mel Gibson DUI Incident,' *Wikipedia,* viewed October 20, 2009 <http://en.wikipedia.org/wiki/ Mel_Gibson_DUI_incident>.

[13] J Locke, *The Second Treatise on Civil Government,* Prometheus Books, Buffalo, New York, 1986.

[14] Govier and Verwoerd, 'Forgiveness: The Victim's Prerogative', 101; and Piers Benn, 'Forgiveness and Loyalty', *Philosophy*, vol. 71, 1996, pp. 369-383, at p. 380.

[15] Govier and Verwoerd, 'Forgiveness: The Victim's Prerogative', 101.

[16] Josek, Simon Wiesenthal's friend and fellow concentration camp inmate, powerfully suggests this view in Wiesenthal's memoir of his struggle over a dying SS man's request for forgiveness. Simon Wiesenthal, *The Sunflower: On the Possibilities and Limits of Forgiveness*, rev. and exp. ed. Harry James Cargas and Bonny V. Fetterman (eds). Schocken Books, New York, 1998, pp. 65-67.

[17] Of course, all of this would be complicated by the fact that there are often many primary and secondary victims, who will not necessarily agree on the question of forgiveness.

[18] There could also be hybrid versions of the victim's prerogative, according to which victims could have the right to direct some parties but only permit others.

[19] Actually, the cause of the indignation in Spitzer's case was far from clear and surely differed among observers. Nussbaum saw the anger as focused on Spitzer's participation in prostitution. Others concentrated on his marital infidelity. For many observers, however, the cause for anger was Spitzer's violation of laws he was elected to enforce or his hypocrisy in committing the very same crime that he energetically and indignantly prosecuted when he was the Attorney General of New York.

[20] 'Allen Quip Provokes Outrage, Apology', *The Washington Post*, online edition, August 15, 2006, viewed April 2, 2009, <http://www.washingtonpost.com/wp-dyn/content/article/2006/08/14/AR2006081400589.html>.

[21] Insisting that only victims can forgive would also rule out the popular notion of self-forgiveness. One might try to make room for self-forgiveness by counting the agent as an indirect victim of all of his own wrongful actions. This is not so much incorrect as it is beside the point. The moral anger a person directs at himself (guilt) has as its proper focus his mistreatment of his victim and not only his indirect mistreatment of himself.

[22] M Dowd, 'It's Over, Lady!' *The New York Times*, online edition, June 29, 2008, viewed October 20, 2009, <http://www.nytimes.com/2008/06/29/opinion/29dowd.html>.

[23] This condition allows us to resist the label 'forgiveness' for the forswearing of anger by someone who is operating with a faulty view of morality, such as a chauvinist who believes that men ought to be treated as superior sorts of beings but who habitually forswears his anger over perceived slights.

[24] Pettigrove argues that a bystander is only a potential forgiver if she shares 'a social context' with the victim and/or wrongdoer 'in which her purported forgiveness (or its absence) would matter' (Pettigrove, 'The Standing to Forgive').

[25] W Neblett, 'Indignation: A Case Study in the Role of Feelings in Morals', *Metaphilosophy,* vol. 10, 1979, pp. 139-152, at pp. 149-151. Neblett defines indignation as a larger category that includes both resentment and its third party analogue.

[26] Of course, a victim's forgiveness might be received in the same way.

[27] For their input and encouragement, thanks are due to Christopher Allers, Colleen Murphy, Glen Pettigrove, Robert R. Shandley, Marieke Smit, and David White.

Bibliography

Atkins, K., 'Friendship, Trust and Forgiveness'. *Philosophia,* vol. 29, 2002, pp. 111-132.

Benn, P., 'Forgiveness and Loyalty'. *Philosophy*, vol. 71, 1996, pp. 369-383.

Bennett, C., 'Personal and Redemptive Forgiveness'. *European Journal of Philosophy,* vol. 11, 2003, pp. 127-144.

Calhoun, C., 'Changing One's Heart'. *Ethics*, vol. 103, 1992, pp. 76–96.

Card, C., *The Atrocity Paradigm: A Theory of Evil.* Oxford University Press, New York, 2002.

Dowd, M., 'It's Over, Lady!' *The New York Times*, online edition, June 29, 2008, viewed October 20, 2009, <http://www.nytimes.com/2008/06/29/opinion/29dowd.html>.

Govier, T., and Verwoerd, W., 'Forgiveness: The Victim's Prerogative'. *South African Journal of Philosophy*, vol. 21, 2002, pp. 97-111.

Griswold, C., *Forgiveness: A Philosophical Exploration.* Cambridge University Press, New York, 2007.

Haber, J., *Forgiveness: A Philosophical Study.* Rowman & Littlefield Publishers, Savage, Maryland, 1991.

Holmgren, M. R., 'Forgiveness and the Intrinsic Value of Persons'. *American Philosophical Quarterly,* vol. 30, 1993, pp. 341–52.

Hughes, P. M., 'What is Involved in Forgiving?' *Philosophia,* vol. 27, 1997, pp. 33-49.

Locke, J., *The Second Treatise on Civil Government.* Prometheus Books, Buffalo, New York, 1986.

MacLachlan, A., 'Forgiveness and Moral Solidarity', in *Forgiveness: Probing the Boundaries.* David White and Stephen Schulman (eds.), Inter-Disciplinary Press, Oxford, forthcoming

Murphy, J. G., and Hampton, J., *Forgiveness and Mercy.* Cambridge University Press, New York, 1988.

Neblett, W., 'Indignation: A Case Study in the Role of Feelings in Morals'. *Metaphilosophy,* vol. 10, 1979, pp. 139-152.

Norlock, K., *Forgiveness from a Feminist Perspective.* Lexington Books, Lanham, Maryland, 2009.

North, J., 'Wrongdoing and Forgiveness'. *Philosophy,* vol. 62, 1987, pp. 499-508.

Nussbaum, M., 'Trading on America's Puritanical Streak: Prostitution Laws Mean-spirited, Penalize Women'. *The Atlanta Journal-Constitution,* online edition, March 14, 2008, viewed October 20, 2009, <http://www.ajc.com/search/content/opinion/2008/03/13/spitzered_0314.html>.

Pettigrove, G., 'The Standing to Forgive'. *Monist,* forthcoming 2009.

Richards, N., 'Forgiveness'. *Ethics,* vol. 99, 1988, pp. 77-97.

Strawson, P. F., 'Freedom and Resentment'. *Proceedings of the British Academy,* vol. 48, 1962, pp. 187-211.

Wiesenthal, S., *The Sunflower: On the Possibilities and Limits of Forgiveness.* rev. and exp. ed. Harry James Cargas and Bonny V. Fetterman (eds). Schocken Books, New York, 1998.

Linda Radzik is Associate Professor of Philosophy at Texas A&M University. She is the author of *Making Amends: Atonement in Morality, Law and Politics*, Oxford University Press, New York, 2009.

If God Cannot Forgive, What Becomes of Harmony?
The Strength of a Victim's Moral Prerogative Not to Forgive

Regan Lance Reitsma

Abstract
Would a divine being, a greatest conceivable being, have the moral authority to forgive all wrongs? Ivan, a character in Dostoevsky's *Brothers Karamazov*, argues that God cannot forgive wrongs to which He is a third party and so He cannot insure, as He promises, that He will bring about a 'new heaven and a new earth' in which all people are reconciled with each other. In this argument, Ivan appears to take the stance that a human victim is the only person who has the moral prerogative to decide whether or not to forgive his victimiser.

Key Words: Third party forgiveness, God, victims, moral prerogatives, liberty rights, the possibility of heaven.

*****

1.   Ivan's Twofold Challenge

Does God have the moral authority to forgive all wrongs? Ivan, a character in Dostoevsky's *Brothers Karamazov*,[1] insinuates - through a poignant story of the torture and murder of an eight year old boy - that there are wrongs that the Christian God doesn't have 'the right' to forgive, namely, (grievous) wrongs perpetuated by one human being against another. The malicious General, who tortures the young boy to death, Ivan might admit, has sinned against God: he has intentionally harmed someone God loves. But God isn't the general's only victim; the general has done the boy a direct (and very serious) wrong. To this act, God is a 'third party'; He is neither killed nor killer. (Pointedly, it is the boy, not God, who is mauled by dogs and robbed of a valuable future.) In Ivan's view, a third party to a wrong doesn't have the standing to forgive it, and so God doesn't have the standing – 'the right' – to forgive the boy's torture and murder.

Ivan means for this conclusion to lead to another. If God cannot properly forgive a human victimizer for what he has done to his human victim, how can God promise, as Christianity teaches, an 'eternal harmony'? The coming kingdom of God, 'the new heaven and the new earth,' proclaimed by the Christian scriptures is to be a community tightly stitched together (Revelation 21). In this kingdom, not only is God reconciled with each human citizen, but each human citizen is reconciled with every other: victim and victimizer will 'embrace'; 'the wolf will dwell with the lamb' (Isaiah 11). Ivan might admit that it is up to God to choose whether to repair

His broken relationships with sinners who have wronged Him, but he would insist that God doesn't have the proper standing to 'wash away' the wrongs we do to each other.[2] It is the boy's prerogative, and only the boy's, to decide whether to embrace the General. It would seem, then, that God cannot insure that all broken relationships are repaired. Any forgiveness God extends to the General would be, at best, 'secondary and incomplete.'[3] If so, Ivan asks, 'what becomes of harmony?'

Ivan's argument commits him to at least two important claims: first, that a victim has a type of freedom – a moral prerogative – to choose whether or not to forgive her victimizer and, second, that this moral prerogative is sufficiently robust to seriously threaten God's ability – despite His omniscience, omnipotence, and (one would think) wondrous ingenuity – to fulfil His heavenly promises. Ivan intimates that, to keep His promise, God would need to violate our moral prerogatives, something a morally perfect being presumably wouldn't do.

I agree with Ivan's first claim. In the very least, morality *often* requires a third party to give a victim significant 'space' to make a decision whether or not to forgive. Accordingly, there are cases in which a third party who attempts to influence a victim to forgive is guilty of being unduly intrusive. The difficult questions concern how robust the victim's moral prerogative is – what, exactly, does the prerogative forbid a third party from doing? – and whether God would be able to find a way to keep His eschatological promises without doing these morally forbidden things. These turn out to be far more complex and far more difficult questions than a casual observer might initially suppose.

Talk of heaven often, and often quickly, becomes silly. (Example: 'Eternity being interminably long, when the blessed become bored, will God inject new desires into them every so often so that they remain interested in their lives?') If you find yourself averse to reading on, afraid that my discussion will become ridiculous, let me mention two things. First, there will be, here, no reflection whatsoever about how big anyone's damn heavenly mansion will be. I intend to talk about things less silly than that. Second, theological discussions often prove to be very fruitful contexts for exploring everyday moral concepts and moral precepts. Ivan's objection, it turns out, will force us to examine very closely both what moral prerogatives are and how to determine whether, when someone says 'It's my prerogative to . . . ,' she is correct.

2.   The Story

Ivan means to challenge the belief, common among Christians, that God has the moral authority to offer forgiveness for all wrongs.[4] This challenge arises in the midst of another. Ivan tells the story of the eight year old boy, first and foremost, to argue against both God's moral perfection and

His sovereignty, His fitness to be King. The boy lived, along with his mother and two thousand other serfs, on the retired General's estate. While playing, the boy accidentally hurt the paw of the General's favourite hound, one of hundreds he owns. When the General discovered what had happened, he threw the boy into a cold, stinking dog kennel for the night. The next morning, the General summoned all of his servants, including the boy's mother, to a field where the boy had been brought. The General ordered the boy stripped naked, sent him running, and sicked his pack of hunting dogs on him. As the boy's mother watches, the boy is torn to pieces by the dogs.

Ivan finds it 'incomprehensible' that God did not intervene to prevent the boy's 'immeasurable' suffering. Being omniscient, God knew, the moment the General formed his malicious intention, what the General would do. Being omnipotent, God had the power, by a thousand upon a thousand means, to stop the General. And yet God did not stop him.[5] Presumably, being compassionate, God would not have wanted the boy to suffer so; being just, He would have recognized that the child didn't deserve to die. And yet God – our 'Father in Heaven' – stood by. Ivan demands to know why.

Ivan isn't the only person who demands to know why. The question why God doesn't intervene to prevent serious human suffering is older than him. The Hebrew prophet Habakkuk, seeing the tears of the oppressed, called out to God angrily, indignantly, 'I say 'Violence!' You do nothing' (Habakkuk 1). Some Christians don't seem to take Habakkuk as a model; they aren't quick to hold God to account. They seem content – too content, perhaps – to live without (more than an inkling of) an answer to the problem of evil. But out of solidarity with victims, Ivan insists he must have an answer, and an answer that makes sense to his 'Euclidean mind.' Ivan won't accept, for instance, an appeal to the doctrine of original sin, at least not if this doctrine means to say, in violation of the simple and obvious moral precept that scape-goating is unfair, that the boy deserves to suffer for the sins of his father, or his father's father. This is a doctrine, Ivan says, 'of the other world,' and he won't accept it. In other words, Ivan believes that the proper justification for God's inaction, if there is one, must cohere with our most obvious and most obviously humane moral ideals.

All this said, Ivan strikes a tone as wistful as it is indignant. He tells his devout brother, Alyosha that he does not want to 'rebel' against God. But he simply cannot agree to be a citizen in a kingdom whose almighty King doesn't prevent the serious suffering of innocent children.

Ivan's argument is subtly crafted, and he isn't theologically tone deaf. Vividly, with striking brevity, Ivan staves off a variety of rebuttals a believer such as Alyosha might think to give. For example, Ivan doesn't deny that God will attempt to make amends for His inaction; he imagines God taking the boy into His wondrous kingdom. But, Ivan protests, to give a child a wondrous good, even an eternity of happiness, does not atone for abandoning him to an episode of grievous suffering, however brief:

> I renounce the higher harmony altogether. It's not worth the tears of that one tortured child who beat itself on the breast with its little fist and prayed in its stinking outhouse, with its unexpiated tears to 'dear, kind God'! It's not worth it because those tears are unatoned for. They must be atoned for, or there can be no harmony. But how? How are you going to atone for them? Is it possible?

Also, Ivan supposes that God will punish the General. But retribution will not make up for what happened to the boy: 'What do I care for a hell for oppressors? What good can hell do, since those children have already been tortured? And what becomes of harmony, if there is hell?'

Notice, Ivan construes God as morally serious. As he imagines Him, God weighs moral considerations, and always and only does what He concludes is best. God's inaction, then, reflects his all-things-considered moral judgment: God thinks that He has adequate reasons not to save the boy. But this is precisely what Ivan objects to: a morally perfect being – even more, a loving father – would never judge anything more important than saving his own, innocent child from torture and death. God – perhaps exceedingly wonderful in manifold ways – suffers from defects of love, compassion, and justice; defects serious enough, Ivan thinks, to call into question His fitness to be King.

Notably, Ivan admits that the Christian vision of God's coming kingdom is morally inspiring. The reconciliation of broken relationships, the restoration of trust; how stirring to the morally sensitive soul. Ivan even suspects that, were he to see Jesus returning upon the clouds, he would fall to his knees, overwhelmed, and praise God. And so Ivan hastens to 'return his ticket' at once, to register his disapproval and to reject God's offer of kingdom citizenship before, beset by morally uplifting feelings, he forgets the 'unexpiated tears' of the eight year old boy.

It is at this point that Ivan insinuates that – for two reasons – God cannot properly forgive the General for what he has done to the young boy. First, Ivan believes that the General's crime is unforgivable, on the grounds that absolutely nothing could atone for the child's 'immeasurable' suffering. Second, Ivan appeals to the principle that a third party doesn't have the proper standing to forgive. No one, not even the boy's mother, has the moral prerogative to forgive the General:

> I don't want the mother to embrace the oppressor who threw her son to the dogs. She dare not forgive him! Let her

> forgive him for herself, for the immeasurable suffering of
> her mother's heart. But the sufferings of her tortured child
> she has no right to forgive.

The mother has the moral prerogative, Ivan begrudgingly admits, to choose to forgive the General for the tortuous grief the General has caused her own mothering heart. Ivan clearly thinks that forgiving the General for her own grief would be deeply misguided: a loving mother wouldn't attempt to forgive, and wouldn't be able, psychologically, to bring herself to forgive. But opting to forgive is, at least, up to her. However morally objectionable, the mother would be fully within her rights to make this choice.

Ivan insists, though, that the mother cannot forgive the General *for what he has done to her son*. Whether the General is forgiven for that act is not up to her. Ivan extends the argument: 'Is there in the whole world a being who would have the right to forgive and who could forgive?' If no one has this right, then God doesn't, either.[6]

3.   Ivan's First Argument: Forgiveness and Reparation

Let's take a moment to consider Ivan's first argument. If there are any unforgivable sins, the torture of innocent children is an especially strong candidate to be among them. But are there any?

Let's be clear about what is really at issue in Ivan's first argument. No doubt, in some particular cases there are strong moral reasons not to forgive – out of self-respect,[7] or out of solidarity with the perpetrator's other victims, or because it is clear that the perpetrator's request for forgiveness is insincere. But these 'reasons not to forgive' are not the salient issue in Ivan's first argument. Here Ivan is claiming – if we take his terse remarks at face value – that any (serious) wrong that cannot be atoned for, *ipso facto*, ought not to be forgiven. From this claim, it follows that an 'unsatisfiable' or 'irreparable' wrong can never be forgiven, *even if* there is no other moral reason not to, and – it would seem – *even if* there are other strong moral reasons to forgive it. Should we accept this thesis?

I don't think so. Ivan's view rejects a part of the Christian understanding of forgiveness that is especially compelling. If it is true – as it very much seems to be – that there are wrongs for which (complete) satisfaction is impossible, this strikes me as a reason to advocate a (forward-focused) conception of forgiveness that aims primarily at reconciliation and the creation of a shared future instead of a (backward-focused) conception that requires (complete) reparation for wrongs.[8] In some instances the act of forgiveness exemplifies a type of grace, a willingness to set aside the demand that moral debts be (entirely) paid up. And I think that this type of forgiveness can be justifiable: there are moral ends that are more valuable than securing reparation.[9] Ivan's moral principle 'no forgiving what cannot be atoned for' would make us, in the relevant cases, 'prisoners of the past.' According to this principle, even if each of the relevant parties wants to be free of the past, and even if each would be better off being free of it, they could not rightly practice forgiveness. What a baleful love of justice this principle represents.[10]

There is a second objection to Ivan's view that irreparable wrongs cannot properly be forgiven. Though the idea is far-fetched, let's assume that the General has become authentically and deeply repentant. Does Ivan mean to say that the boy himself, the General's primary victim, would be wrong to forgive the repentant General? Ivan seems to be committed to saying so. He intimates that a grievous wrong should not be forgiven if it is impossible for the victimizer to make proper satisfaction. Since no act can undo the historical fact that the boy spent a night in the stinking kennel and a morning being torn apart by dogs, and since the boy's suffering is 'immeasurable,'[11] the General – unable to change the past, and having only finite resources for compensation – has no way to make adequate amends and so, by Ivan's reasoning, can't be forgiven. This would be a strange view for Ivan, of all people, to take. After all, he is arguing for a victim's moral prerogative to choose whether or not to forgive. Why would Ivan, who is stressing the victim's moral freedom, tie the victim's hands in this way?

Whatever you happen to think of Ivan's first argument, let's move on to his second chain of reasoning, which is the argument I intend to focus on. What should we think of Ivan's belief that third party forgiveness is impermissible and so God cannot promise an eternal harmony?

4.   Divine Forgiveness and Human Moral Prerogatives

Ivan's second argument is a version of the argument that God's forgiveness would violate important considerations of justice: in this case, God's third party forgiveness would violate, Ivan thinks, the victim's moral prerogative.

To make this argument clear, we should begin by making an important distinction. There are – for lack of a better phrase – two 'broad methods' by which a third party might conceivably violate a victim's moral prerogative. First, he might do this by being unduly intrusive, say, by putting excessive pressure on the victim when she is in the midst of deciding whether to forgive. Second, he might violate a victim's prerogative without 'interfering' in any way with the victim's process of decision-making, say, by ignoring her decision after it has been made, or by failing to even consider whether she has chosen to forgive. The reason it is important to distinguish between these two broad methods is that the moral case against excessive influence is different than the moral case against ignoring the victim.

Let's begin with the moral objections to ignoring the victim. Consider a case in which one of your moral prerogatives is ignored. Your doctor fails to respect your 'do not resuscitate' order. Your moral prerogative to decide what happens in and to your body entails that you ought to be granted the authority to determine which end-of-life medical procedures you will not receive. The doctor's behaviour raises important moral questions about her attitudes toward you. Why isn't she granting your decision the authority it deserves? Does she think she has more authority over the course and duration of your life than you do? But then she isn't taking you seriously as a person who has the ability, and the moral authority, to make decisions for yourself.

Likewise, if God were to behave as though your victimizer's wrong is 'washed away' when you have not forgiven it and his 'debt is paid' when you haven't accepted reparation or chosen mercy, this would suggest that He is failing to take you seriously. If you have a moral prerogative to choose whether to forgive, then you must be given the opportunity to make the decision, and your decision must be taken as authoritative. Presumably, if God were to ignore your decision, it wouldn't be because He is literally ignorant of it. Being omniscient, He knows what you've decided. And so, if God behaves as though all is well between you and your unforgiven victimizer, He is straightforwardly violating the dictates of justice. He isn't granting your decision (not to forgive) the authority it deserves.

Let's grant this argument, for the moment. And let's imagine that God simply won't wash away wrongs against you pre-emptively, and He won't fail to respect your decisions about forgiveness. Could God fulfil His eschatological promises even so?

You could easily imagine a Christian thinking that even if God assiduously respects the prerogatives of victims, He will find a way to persuade (many of) them to exercise their prerogatives to choose forgiveness. Someone taking up Ivan's argument might claim that this optimistic line of thinking raises the question whether an active, campaigning God would end up being guilty of intrusiveness instead. We do tend to think that, at least in a wide range of cases, a third party not only lacks the standing to determine whether a wrong is forgiven, but is under important moral restrictions in promoting forgiveness. Wouldn't these restrictions apply to God? Wouldn't it also be unduly intrusive for God, as a third party, to attempt to 'influence' victims to forgive?

Anne Minas thinks so. Let's take a look at her argument. Minas has us imagine that you hear of a case, in a faraway place, in which a husband cheats on his wife. If you don't know either the betrayer or the betrayed, would you think to campaign for the forgiveness of the husband? Presumably, you have far too much good sense: you recognize that it's not your 'place.' But if you did attempt – in a public way – to acquire forgiveness for the husband, Minas claims, you would be guilty of being intrusive and 'high-handed.' Minas regards this type of advocacy for forgiveness as 'intrusive' because you simply aren't an interested party to the dispute, and so you shouldn't act as though the couple's relationship is your business. Minas regards it as 'high-handed,' presumably, because you aren't, we might say, a properly appointed member of the 'morality brigade.' It's not your proper role, your appointed task, in society to ensure that everyone chooses to behave, in each instance, in the morally most laudable way. Even if forgiving would be a praiseworthy thing for the wife to do, it's not your place to put significant psychological pressure on her to forgive – say, by furrowing your brow at her and saying, 'Why won't you forgive? A good person would.' Minas seems to liken God's promotion of forgiveness to your intrusive, high-handed, and altogether inappropriate attempt to acquire forgiveness for the husband.

This (version of the) argument is glib, and Glen Pettigrove has a good response to it.[12] He remarks that people often take comfort in the idea that God has forgiven their wrongs, and even when the primary victim has not forgiven them. This comfort might seem, at a glance, morally misguided. Say that the cheating husband, John, comes to think that God has forgiven his betrayal, though he recognizes that his wife, Sally, has not. As John is taking comfort in God's forgiveness, we might wonder 'what about Sally?' Isn't John ignoring her, his primary victim? Pettigrove diffuses this worry by arguing that God can be seen as a secondary victim, and so He has some standing to forgive the husband. He is not being unduly intrusive, for He is not a 'mere' third party.[13]

First, Pettigrove implicitly makes an important distinction that Minas fails to consider. In the case of the cheating husband, you have no relationship whatsoever with either the betrayed wife or the betraying husband. And so, you certainly have no standing whatsoever to attempt to acquire forgiveness for John. You are a third party – neither betrayed nor betrayer. But, more pertinently, you are not a secondary victim. If you are a decent person, capable of imaginative identification with other human beings, you might suffer the minor, internal wince that accompanies hearing of a serious wrong to any other human being. But this does not make you, in any important sense, an interested party or a real victim. As I will discuss later, there are serious limitations on how involved any mere third party should be in attempts to influence victims to forgive.

God, however, if He loves each person, will be – not merely a third party, but also – a secondary victim whenever His children are harmed.[14] Moreover, if God has a prior relationship to John, John's betrayal can count not only as a betrayal of his wife, but as 'letting God down' or as a violation of, say, his covenant with God. This does not mean that God's act of forgiveness repairs the relationship between John and Sally. Pettigrove's account reveals, and only attempts to reveal, that God is not being unduly intrusive when He forgives John. (For all Pettigrove says, God's forgiveness of John is 'secondary and incomplete.')

Pettigrove's general argument is supported by a corresponding insight about friendship. Your close friends have more latitude (than strangers) to exert influence upon you, in manifold ways: to tease you, to ask you whether you really want to be seen in public with those pants on, to press you not to let your anger boil over, to encourage you not to give up on a long-desired goal. One reason, though certainly not the only reason, to have close personal friends is to have people around who know you well enough to be able, as it were, to 'keep you in line.' Accordingly, a good friend might well do no wrong when he challenges your reluctance to forgive. His remarks do not so clearly count as intrusive and high-handed. He has more latitude; there are fewer moral barriers between you and him. Correspondingly, there are serious restrictions upon the behaviour of strangers and mere acquaintances. They can certainly silently hope that you forgive, and maybe even express pleasure if you do, but they have very little right to exert pressure on you.

If this strikes you as correct, it seems to follow that that the level and types of 'influence' that it is morally permissible for a third party to exert depends, at least in part, on the level and type of relationship the third party has with the victim. If there is no relationship, the right to influence is, in the very least, highly restricted. But if you have a close relationship with the victim, your 'right' to influence the victim's decision is less restricted. This will turn out to be an important point to keep in mind. It seems to suggest that God's own right to influence victims will vary according to His relationship with them.

Pettigrove points out another reason why John might take comfort in God's forgiveness. God's act of forgiveness bodes well for him. God is, by hypothesis, an impeccable judge of the reasons for and against forgiving. If He forgives John, this is presumably because He sees that the grounds for forgiving John are sufficiently strong. John might take comfort, then, that Sally will eventually come to see these reasons, too.

Pettigrove's remarks address Minas' version of the 'don't be intrusive' argument satisfactorily. But Ivan's version of the argument doesn't imply, uncharitably, that God has no personal connection to human victims, or to human victimizers. On the contrary, Ivan could admit that God does. Ivan suggests, instead, that the central problem arises not merely because God is a third party, but because Christianity proclaims a future harmony that God can't bring about, at least not without violating important moral prerogatives. Ivan points out that God has magnificently grand intentions. He promises to stitch people together into a tight-knit community. (Whatever else you might say of the Christian God, He isn't aiming low.) But it isn't His prerogative to reconcile, among other people, John and Sally. If it is Sally's moral prerogative to choose whether to forgive John for what he has done to her, then only Sally is able to determine whether the relationship between her and John is repaired, and so whether they have a future. This reconciliation is ultimately in her hands, not God's. This is what prompts Ivan to say, if God is not the agent who determines whether human victims and their human victimizers reconcile, 'what becomes of harmony?'

5.   Taking Stock
Ivan's challenge, his second argument, doesn't constitute a disproof of the prediction 'God will bring about a new heaven and a new earth'. Even if there are (significant) moral restrictions upon third party influence, and even if God obeys these restrictions assiduously, it does not follow, as a matter of logic, that God will fail to fulfil His promises. But Ivan's challenge does create a puzzle for thoughtful Christians. Several responses to the puzzle seem simply to raise additional problems and hard questions. Consider the following terse exchanges.

If God respects the moral prerogative of victims not to forgive, will His kingdom be very tightly stitched together but considerably smaller than He Himself hopes? Not only does 'smaller but purer' sound chilling, couldn't the biblical passages that declare 'to the world' the 'good news' of Jesus' second coming be charged with false advertising? If few people will actually benefit from this event, why regard it as good news 'for the world'?

Will God respect the moral prerogatives of victims, forgive a vast number of people – though only for their sins against Him – and subsequently permit His kingdom to be splintered when some of its citizens are unwilling or unable to forgive each other? But then isn't all the talk of 'harmony' and 'wolf dwelling with lamb' misleading? If old wounds persist unhealed in God's kingdom, in what sense is this kingdom truly a harmony?

Will God make it a prerequisite of citizenship in His kingdom that citizens forgive all of their (repentant) victimizers? But then isn't God, in His advocacy for forgiveness, not only being intrusive and high-handed, but 'heavy-handed,' too? Even good people might find it difficult, for moral or psychological reasons, to forgive the perpetrators of the most serious wrongs against them. And so, isn't requiring forgiveness too much to ask?

Notice: Ivan's challenge is driven, in part, by the loftiness of the Christian vision. God aims for the reconciliation of God and humanity and a community with a valuable shared future. No doubt, in our everyday lives, the act of forgiveness sometimes aims for less lofty goals. Say Tina discovers that a fellow office worker has spread false rumours about her, and she comes to resent the perpetrator. She resolves not to speak with him anymore. After a time, Tina might decide to give up her negative feelings and her resolution. Though she has no desire to create a close, personal relationship with her co-worker, she is willing to talk business with him, when it is necessary for the business's success. It seems natural to call Tina's act an act of forgiveness even though it does not aim at a 'tightly-stitched, shared future.' This, however, does not seem to be the type of forgiveness envisioned by the metaphor of God's kingdom. This kingdom is an image of a community in which people do not merely lack resentment. They 'embrace.' They sit, trustingly, with previous victimizers.

The question, then, is whether God can bring about this level of harmony while adequately respecting the moral prerogatives of human victims. Ivan has serious doubts.

6.   The Complicity Argument

To be fair, I should mention the possibility that Ivan is making a third argument against God's moral authority to practice and to promote forgiveness.[15] According to this third argument, it's not merely that God's authority to forgive is called into question because He is, with respect to acts such as the General's, a third party. The central problem is that God is complicit in the boy's suffering. Because God could have prevented this suffering, He thereby has 'forfeited' any right to influence the boy's decision whether to forgive the general.

To speak in favour of this argument, there are cases in which it would be morally unseemly for a close friend – yes, even a close friend – to encourage forgiveness. George is close friends with both Jack and Gabriella, who are married to each other. George is at a raucous party with Jack, who has had far too much to drink and is flirting with another woman. George watches as Jack and this woman head off to a bedroom. He knows Jack will deeply regret this liaison, but a lack of personal courage (as George himself would admit) keeps him from stopping Jack. (The salient point: George did not perpetrate the wrong, but he is implicated in it.) Later, Gabriella finds out about the affair, and about George's complicity. Feeling (twice) betrayed and (twice) deeply wounded, she confronts George: 'you didn't stop him?' It would be very troubling to find George, moments later, pressing Gabriella to forgive Jack: 'This relationship needs to be mended, and you hold the key. Forgive Jack.' The problem is not merely that George is (selfishly) pressing this claim upon Gabriella too soon, long before she's ready, when the wounds are yet raw. Gabriella would seem to be justified in thinking that there is a special reason that George, whatever his present motives, cannot put any pressure on her to forgive: 'If you were so concerned about this relationship being strong, why did you stand by and let Jack rip it apart?' Whatever moral latitude George once enjoyed, he has it no longer.

To generalize, someone who is implicated in a wrong cannot properly exert psychological pressure on the victim to forgive that wrong. Whatever (meagre) 'right' a mere third party might have to encourage forgiveness, and whatever (greater) 'right' a close friend has, this type of 'right' is forfeited by the person who is implicated in the victim's mistreatment. In Ivan's view, this principle of forfeiture applies to God. God's failure to prevent the boy's suffering calls into question His fitness to be king, and it entails that He is no longer morally permitted to press the boy to forgive the General.

I think this is a very serious argument. Clearly it borrows much of its force from the force of the problem of evil. To attempt to respond to it would require that I discuss whether God has sufficient justifications for not preventing the boy's suffering. Not only would I be hard-pressed to get God off the hook (in a few pages, no less), attempting to do so would take me far afield from some of my central concerns: for instance, a discussion of the 'shape' of the victim's general moral prerogative not to forgive. And so I don't intend to address this 'complicity' argument. That said, I will incorporate one of its insights into my own general view.

7.   Responses to Ivan's Second Argument

Let's return to Ivan's second argument, the challenge at the heart of this discussion, and sketch several responses.

Perhaps the strongest Christian response to Ivan's challenge appeals to a mystery, something a 'Euclidean mind' would be unwilling or hard-pressed to grasp. But I'll limit my discussion to 'Euclidean' responses.[16] This isn't because I am unwilling to consider the possibility of a mystery, but because I would prefer to press everyday moral thinking as far as it will go before I entertain more inscrutable ideas. In that spirit, let's move forward.[17]

One response is to argue – contrary to Ivan's main premise – that third party forgiveness is, at least in some instances, morally acceptable. I think it is. If a thoughtful son believes, on good evidence, that his dead mother would likely have forgiven her business partner for a financial indiscretion, he might 'forgive' the offending party on her behalf. This 'forgiveness by proxy' strikes me as a legitimate practice. (The son isn't, for instance, ignoring his mother's decisions; he's making an honest attempt at deciphering what she would have decided and respecting this 'counterfactual' decision.)

The weakness in this response is that the cases in which third party forgiveness seems most acceptable do not seem to help against Ivan's challenge. Even if you agree with my judgment about the case of the son's 'forgiveness by proxy,' it doesn't help Christianity. If we are assuming, for the sake of argument, that human beings will have a conscious existence after biological death, there is no need for a proxy to settle the question whether to forgive the General on behalf of his victim; the boy will be able to choose, in the fullness of time, whether to reconcile with the General. Even if the boy's mother could justifiably forgive the General by proxy, this decision, at best, would only be able to serve a communal purpose in the 'here and now,' and not in the 'there and later.'

A second response is that Ivan's argument is grounded in a mistaken conception of God's kingdom. The (morally uplifting) metaphors commonly used to describe this kingdom suggest that its citizens have deep, personal connections with each other. But perhaps Kant's picture of the Kingdom of Ends is closer to the truth about what God's kingdom would and should be like. In the Kingdom of Ends, each citizen properly respects the humanity of every other, and, presumably, any citizen who owes another a debt – financial or moral – would make a serious attempt to seek forgiveness and make amends. But this doesn't imply that each pair of citizens in the Kingdom of Ends has a close, personal relationship and, in any important sense, a 'shared future.' To make the Kingdom of Ends a living reality, perhaps a victim will only need to come to trust his victimizer sufficiently to co-exist in the community and to set aside any demand for (further) reparation. A community, even a wondrous community, can persist without strongly affectionate ties between each of its members. If so, then the aim of forgiveness, even in God's kingdom, will not invariably be the 'lofty' goal of a 'shared future.' Secondary forms of forgiveness, which aim at less lofty goals, might be sufficient in some cases.

This response, though it raises pertinent questions about what an ideal human community would be like, does not resolve the case of the eight year old boy. The question remains 'What if the General repents, but the boy will not forgive?' Could God properly require that the boy forgive, whether in the lofty or less lofty sense? It would be 'more' to ask the boy to have a close, personal relationship with the General, but it would already be 'a lot' to ask him to be willing to co-exist with the perpetrator of his torture and death. In brief, to defend this response, we would still need to think about how much freedom to choose whether to forgive a victim really has.[18]

A third response disputes the eschatological implications Ivan draws. It does not follow from the claim that God lacks the moral prerogative to forgive, or even to compel forgiveness, that people will not choose to. If God were to respect the moral prerogative of victims to decide whether to forgive (very serious) wrongs against them, this would make it logically possible, of course, that His kingdom would not come to be – just in case none of us decided to forgive. But everyday experience tells us that forgiveness is often practiced within the human community, and so God might have very good grounds to be optimistic that an eternal harmony, with a significant population, will come about. (More proactively: if people are more likely to forgive under certain conditions, God could try to create those very conditions to maximize the rate of forgiving.)

Not to mention, (if we set aside the complicity argument – yes, a 'big if') would God violate the moral prerogative of victims were He merely to encourage them, with all the (morally legitimate) persuasive skill He is able to muster, to forgive? Your doctor, after all, does not violate your moral prerogatives when she gives you professional advice about the best course of action. And even if God is not morally permitted to compel people to forgive their victimizers, this doesn't constrain Him from attempting to inspire them – by being very forgiving Himself (Matthew 18) – to choose a radically forgiving spirit. Can you plausibly accuse people who set a good moral example of exerting, thereby, 'undue pressure' on bystanders?

This third response has a significant virtue. It construes God as leaving some of the 'kingdom-making' acts of forgiveness to people, and so construes human beings, attractively, as co-creators of God's kingdom. There will be Christians who are already inclined to think that God, by choice, has given up some of His control and some of the 'space' of His sovereignty by creating creatures to which He has given the freedom to make personal choices. At the same time, this response is somewhat conciliatory. It grants a significant measure of Ivan's argument. It places the hope of an eternal harmony into a constrained (though freakishly capable) God's hands.

A fourth response is less conciliatory, but more controversial. What if God were to actively pursue an eternal harmony by making forgiveness, or even a forgiving spirit, a requirement of admission into His peaceable kingdom? According to this proposal, to be a citizen in His kingdom, it is necessary to forgive all (serious) wrongs done to you, at least all wrongs done by repentant victimizers who are also members of His kingdom.[19] Kingdom membership truly has its costs: you must embrace, or at least work (in good faith) to embrace, any of your victimizers who are also members of God's kingdom.

This response would certainly provoke the objection that God would be 'respecting' the direct victim's moral prerogative in name only. To say 'It is your choice whether to forgive,' but 'threaten' ostracism, some might say, doesn't properly respect the victim's prerogative. But there are ways for a thoughtful Christian to respond to this objection. In particular, it's not clear that God's demand would constitute an implicit 'threat.' First, the claim 'you will not make it into my kingdom' will seem to be a threat, of course, if it is taken to imply that a failure to be in God's kingdom is, *de facto*, a ticket into a grievously painful hell. It will seem to be less of a threat, if it is not. (I'm going to leave the question of universal salvation to the side.) Second, presumably the demand to forgive, or to have a forgiving spirit, would not be the only moral demand God would make upon citizens of His kingdom. There would be expectations on citizens to love neighbour, to do justice, and to walk humbly with God, as well. Presumably, a peaceable kingdom of the type God wants to create could not exist and persist if its citizens are not, among other things, deeply committed to the moral practices that stitch a society together. The argument could be made that a deeply forgiving spirit is also a necessary condition for the creation and sustenance of an ideal community, an eternal harmony.

A pattern has emerged. The second, third, and fourth responses call for us to consider the victim's prerogative (not) to forgive more carefully. How robust is this prerogative? What types of behaviour does it protect the victim from? Is the prerogative a prerogative against every third party, or only against any 'mere' third party, and not against close friends? Are there ways to encourage a victim to forgive that are likely to be effective but not inappropriately intrusive? In summary, what, exactly, is the 'shape' and 'strength' of the victim's prerogative?

8.   What is a Moral Prerogative?

Ivan's remarks advert to 'rights talk.' The mother has no 'right' to forgive the General, Ivan says, for what he has done to her son, and neither, he thinks, does any third party. I have interpreted Ivan as gesturing at the concept of a victim's 'moral prerogative' (not) to forgive. What, generally speaking, are moral prerogatives? What morally valuable thing(s) do they protect? Are prerogatives untrumpable? Or can (some) prerogatives be outweighed by other moral considerations? If we could answer these questions, perhaps we would be in a better position to analyse the 'shape' and 'strength' of the particular moral prerogative Ivan posits.

I don't happen to know of any general analysis of the concept of a moral prerogative. In my view, a moral prerogative is a type of moral right, a species of 'moral liberty right,' which attempts to protect a person's dignity by limiting the ways others can 'interfere' with her decision-making.

To make my case, let me begin by speaking generally of moral rights. A moral right is defined in terms of the moral obligations it entails. Any moral right, by its very nature, creates a moral obligation, not to violate it. If we are to understand moral rights properly, it is crucial to recognize two things. The first is that *your* moral rights do not tell you what morality requires *you* to do. Instead, *your* moral rights place moral obligations *on others*. For example, your right to free speech places moral obligations on other citizens, and your government, not to suppress your speech. It would be morally wrong, a violation of your moral right, for someone to gag you so that you cannot campaign, publicly, for a political cause you care about. The second crucial point is that you might have a moral right to do something morally wrong. This might initially sound paradoxical. But it's not. The purpose of your moral rights is to protect you, not to indicate how you ought to behave. Consider a few cases. Even if the political cause you want to campaign for is morally objectionable, it would be wrong, even so, for others to gag you. Also, if you were to have a moral right to gamble, this would mean that it is wrong for other people to stop you from gambling. For instance, it would be morally wrong for an anti-gambling group, however well-meaning, to blockade the casino, preventing you from getting in. Your moral right protects you from their interference. And this is true even if your going to the casino is an imprudent or even an immoral use of your money. If you have promised your spouse that you will not use your daughter's college education fund on slots, it would be morally wrong for you to head to the casino with that money. Your behaviour both risks little Sarah's future education and constitutes a broken promise. All this said, it isn't the anti-gambling group's place, however well-meaning they are, to prevent you from gambling. Your moral rights protect you from this type of (paternalistic and moralistic) interference.

These two 'crucial points' fit with the claims Ivan makes about the moral prerogative (not) to forgive. Ivan clearly thinks that this 'right' places obligations on other people. The boy's prerogative places restrictions upon his mother: according to Ivan, she cannot properly forgive the general on her son's behalf; and on God: He cannot act as though all is well in heaven and earth when the boy hasn't opted to forgive. Also, Ivan clearly thinks that the question 'what do I have a moral right to do?' is distinct from the question 'what would it be morally right for me to do?' Recall, Ivan thinks that, even though a good mother *wouldn't* choose to, the boy's mother has the 'right' to forgive the general for the suffering he has caused her. In other words, Ivan admits that the mother has the 'right' to forgive the general, though (he judges) it would be the wrong thing for her to do. The decision is up to her, and he hopes that she makes a good one.

So far, I've identified a moral prerogative as a type of moral right. We can identify, more specifically, what type of moral right it is. It is standard to make a distinction between two types: claim (or positive) rights and liberty (or negative) rights. A claim right differs from a liberty right in terms of its 'shape.' A claim right is a right to be provided with some good or service. It operates, we might say, as an 'open hand'; if you have a claim right to a free public education, this would mean that when you show up at your local public school at the age of five and demand, in your squeaky voice, an education, the government is under a moral obligation to give it to you. A liberty right, on the other hand, is a right to freedom from interference. It operates as a 'shield of protection.' Take, for instance, the moral right to property. Your right to property entails that other people ought not steal from you, or to use your laptop or your television set without your consent. The basic idea here is that 'you get to decide' how these objects – your telephone and your television set – are used, and by whom.

A victim's moral prerogative to forgive should be regarded as a liberty right. It isn't a claim right. It's not that the victim should be given some good or service by someone. Instead, the victim's prerogative protects him from having his decisions disregarded – 'ignored,' as I put it earlier – and from being subjected to excessive pressure to forgive. This prerogative restricts, this is to say, interference. As I see it, a moral prerogative is a 'species' of liberty right. Some (though not all[20]) liberty rights protect your 'space to make decisions.' The phrase 'it's my prerogative to' connotes 'I should be given the freedom to' or 'you would do wrong to stop me from making my own decision about'. For instance, if someone who intends to fritter away his coins in a slot machine were to announce 'It's my prerogative to use my money as I see fit,' he is suggesting that 'interference' with his (admittedly poor) decision would be inappropriately intrusive. It's not your place to decide how he spends his money.

Now that we have an analysis of moral prerogatives, we can begin to ask questions about how much moral authority we should give to them. In my view, to speak very generally, moral rights ought to be taken very seriously. They protect something very important, human dignity. The doctor who ignores your 'do not resuscitate' order is not taking you seriously as a person. You ought to be treated with dignity, and so permitted to make important decisions about your life for yourself. That said, I regard even some of your most significant moral rights as 'trumpable.' For instance, your moral right to property places significant moral restrictions upon people with respect to your material possessions. In normal circumstances, it would be wrong for someone not only to steal from you, but to use your belongings without your consent. This is true even if their using your things would not harm you in any way. If someone were to wander into your house, without your consent, to watch your television, he does you wrong, even if his behaviour does no more harm to you than to increase your electrical bill by a few cents. Your moral right to property places serious restrictions on other people, including the government, from 'interfering with' your belongings.

But say a jogger comes across a serious car accident in front of your house when you aren't home. She doesn't carry a cell phone when she is out running. No one is around to help. After knocking on your door, she decides to enter your house – obviously, without your consent – to use your telephone to call for emergency help. I submit that she has done you no wrong. The health and life of the accident victims are more important, morally, than your right to choose who does (not) use your telephone. It is clear that if we are to take your moral rights seriously, we can't treat any and every garden-variety reason as sufficiently weighty to trump your moral rights. But there do seem to be cases in which moral rights are outweighed, by other moral rights or by other very weighty moral considerations. It seems to follow that if you want to understand a particular moral right, you need to think about how much it would take to trump it.

Clearly, moral rights are very complicated creatures. This must be at least part of the explanation why our public debates about rights claims often do not go well. When we want to determine whether a particular 'I have a moral right to...' claim is true, we need to ask several questions; namely: What moral obligations would this moral right create? Who would, and wouldn't, be under these moral obligations? And under what conditions, if any, would these moral obligations be outweighed? These are the questions we should ask about the right (not) to forgive.

9.   The 'Shape' and 'Strength' of the Prerogative (Not) to Forgive

Let's return to Ivan's second argument. Ivan thinks that it is the victim's moral prerogative to choose whether or not to forgive his victimizer and that God would likely have to violate this type of prerogative to fulfil His promises. Either He would have to ignore the authoritative decisions made by victims who choose not to forgive or He would have to put an inappropriate level of pressure on unforgiving victims, to get them to change their minds. Either behaviour could be construed as treating the victim with a lack of dignity; his decisions should be given the proper authority, and he should be given the 'space' to make them.

I agree with the claim that God would not ignore a victim's proper role in the process of forgiveness. Not only would God be averse to violating important considerations of justice, but if God really wants the victim and victimizer to be reconciled – if that is His main goal – it wouldn't make sense for God to ignore the victim. Without the victim's act of forgiveness, the relationship would not actually be repaired. Presumably, God then will be sensitive to the victim's essential role in the process of reconciliation.

Ivan's claim that God would need to put undue pressure on victims who are reluctant to forgive is, in the end, harder to assess. If God were to aim to change the minds of people reluctant to forgive, the obstacles do seem massive. For instance, if my analysis is correct, then the restrictions against a mere third party are significant. Since many people don't regard God as a close friend, these restrictions would seem to apply to God. Would God need to establish a proper relationship with such victims before he begins to advocate for forgiveness? Could He manage to?

At the same time, is there any argument that the victim's moral prerogative is so robust that it ties God's hands completely? I don't see what this argument would be. It is very important to make a distinction between coercive and non-coercive influence. Some types of influence are coercive and so dignity-violating: no doubt, a victim is protected, by morality, from threats and undue pressure. But some types of influence – setting a good example, for instance – cannot plausibly be construed as coercive. And very generally speaking, I personally would not want to construe the victim's moral prerogative as so robust that it makes it wrong, at a communal level, to engage in moral conversations about the merits of forgiveness. A community that does not have these conversations, it seems to me, simply fails to take people – and their capacity to think and to reflect – seriously by a different route. A culture that doesn't hold discussions about big ideas hardly treats its members in a dignifying way. In brief, God would have to work through, and only through, means of influence that are not coercive and dignity-violating.

(Coercion can be subtle, of course; but wouldn't God be able to make the relevant subtle distinctions?) This means, in the very least, that it is possible that God will be able to fulfil His promises.

In the end, there is something speculative both about Ivan's argument and about the tradition Ivan is criticizing. His argument, as I've construed it, is committed to making (pessimistic) predictions about what God will be able to accomplish through legitimate means. How will things come out? It seems hard, at some point, to know what more to say. Is God going to be able, even if He respects the prerogatives of victims, to stitch together a significant community of forgiving people? Can we say any more than (the somewhat cloying) 'Stay tuned'?

Before ending this discussion, it seems we should consider the following type of case, a case in which a victim resists forgiving his victimizer *even though* the weight of moral and prudential considerations call strongly for forgiveness. There are, no doubt, such cases. Say the relationship between two old and very close friends, Samson and Delilah, has been seriously breached, by Delilah. The wrong done by Delilah was serious, though not grievous. Samson is understandably deeply hurt, but the wrong is not so serious that it threatens, by itself, to render his life unhappy. Instead, what it threatens is his relationship with Delilah, which has been very important to him. Immediately after the wrong, it was poor good sense for Samson to wonder whether they would ever be able to stitch things back together. That said, as time has passed, Delilah has come to see her wrong in the fullness of its profound ugliness. Accordingly, she has become deeply remorseful. She has tasted bitter guilt, swallowed her pride, offered significant satisfaction, and requested forgiveness – patiently, several times. Delilah's wrong has also done collateral damage. Samson's and Delilah's close family and friends have been hurt by her behaviour, too. Not only has the sense of being wronged festered in Samson, his family and friends hate to see him suffering the way he is. And Delilah's family and friends also hate to see her so full of remorse and so clearly distraught, a suffering that forgiveness would begin to release her from. This means that each relevant party – the victim, the victimizer, and the secondary victims – would be personally benefited were Samson to choose to forgive. Samson has been given time to make his decision whether to forgive. But despite the time, despite Delilah's sincere remorse, despite his family's advice, despite how much the wound continues to fester in him, and despite how much it would benefit his friends and family, Samson is unwilling to forgive.

What to make of a case such as this? I want to suggest that this story gestures at two limitations on the victim's prerogative. Here is the first. If we imagine that Samson's family has given him the 'space' to make his decision, attempting to influence him not through coercive mechanisms but by appealing only to considerations he generally cares about – his own long-term welfare, say – there is no moral case against their behaviour. They aren't unduly intrusive strangers. They recognize that, without Samson's forgiveness, the relationship will not be reconciled. In other words, they aren't ignoring his decision; they have come, in time, to rue it. They wish he would choose to forgive. Samson's prerogative is real, and it has been respected. But his choice not to forgive is wrong; it is, in the very least, morally regrettable that he won't forgive. How, we might ask, should Samson's family and friends regard Delilah? In a case such as this, the victim's friends and family have to decide what to do if Samson continues to be unwilling to forgive. Though I think friends and family should, in some cases, be unwilling to forgive a perpetrator out of solidarity with their beloved, the beloved can't, it seems to me, 'hold them hostage.' Must Samson's family continue to treat Delilah as an offender simply because he is unwilling to forgive her? I don't think so. Of course, the relationship between the victim and his victimizer hasn't been reconciled. But the responsibility for this breach, at some point, begins to shift from Delilah to Samson, and this begins to free Samson's family to make their own peace with Delilah. The relevance of this to our eschatological discussion is that, if my reasoning here is correct, then a victim can't keep his properly remorseful victimizer out of God's kingdom. Whatever freedom his moral prerogative gives him, it doesn't properly give him the power to do that.

The second decision that Samson's family will have to make is how to think about Samson, given his decision not to forgive. If Samson has not forgiven, the old friendship remains broken, of course. It is true that the victim holds the key to reconciliation. But Samson's behaviour begins to call into question his own character. It seems to me that Samson can be expected by morality to do what is in the interest of the people he clearly loves and by prudence to do what really is in his own interest. His prerogative protects him from dignity-violating intrusiveness, but it doesn't protect him from the moral or the prudential judgment that he is choosing badly. He can be treated as morally and personally responsible for his reluctance. If I'm right about the nature of prerogatives, his prerogative doesn't protect him from this judgment.

10.   Last Things

The Christian tradition – in some strains – endorses some strikingly radical practices when it comes to forgiveness. Jesus' followers are to be willing to forgive not only 'once or twice,' or even 'seven times,' but 'seventy times seven times.' (And do you really expect that Jesus will let you hold a grudge the four hundred and ninety first time you've been wronged by the same individual?) A follower of Jesus is, the scriptures say, to forgive his enemy. And Jesus himself was willing to forgive those who crucified him, with the shockingly charitable 'for they know not what they've done.' This theology is not the voice of what we often call common sense. It is a call to a radically forgiving way of life.

And yet this risky and morally counterintuitive outlook does have its allure. It presents a God who is more forward-focused than backward-looking. He is fully righteous and just, but even more loving and merciful. Once you see how much God has forgiven you, how will gratitude not lead you – Jesus seems to insist – to go and do likewise? The tradition thinks it is speaking with God's own voice when it invites people to 'See, taste the fruits' of this forgiving Spirit. Even if moral prerogatives have a very important moral function, especially in a fractured society in which people cannot trust each other to obey important moral boundaries, does the existence of moral prerogatives really call into question the ideal at the heart of this Christian vision? I find it very hard not to admire a community in which people are stitched together by practices of forgiveness.

I'm not sure, but perhaps the New Testament's idea is that each person will be put, in the fullness of time, into something similar to Samson's situation. We've all been seriously wronged. But if your victimizer wants forgiveness, given that this forgiveness will make such a profound community possible – for you, for your victimizer, and for others – will you not forgive? Maybe God's promise is supposed to imply that He thinks that people, in these circumstances, will forgive. God is, Christians might suppose, an impeccable judge of the reasons to forgive. Maybe, they might argue, we'll come to see these reasons, too. And there certainly would be something baleful if a significant number of people were to exemplify Samson's persistent unwillingness to forgive the Delilahs among us.

Notes

[1] F Dostoevsky, *The Brother's Karamazov*, translated by Constance Garnett, MacMillan, 1912.

[2] A number of biblical passages, though they do not explicitly claim that God will engage in third party forgiveness, suggest that 'those who believe' will have their sins 'washed away' and will enter the kingdom of God (e.g. Acts 10). These passages simply don't make clear whether God's act of forgiveness merely 'washes away' sins against Him, or whether it also 'washes away' wrongs done to others, too.

[3] J Gingell, 'Forgiveness and Power'. *Analysis*, vol. 34, 1974, pp. 180-184.

[4] For the sake of clarity, I propose we call wrongs done to God 'sins', in which case Ivan's argument doesn't attempt to argue that there are *sins* that God can't forgive. Ivan's challenge is to the claim that God has the moral authority to forgive all *wrongs*. In his view, God can't forgive wrongs not done to Him.

[5] Notice that God would not have to violate the General's free will to prevent the boy's death; He could let the General form his malicious intention freely and sick the dogs, then prevent the consequences of this act. You do not, after all, violate the free will of an assassin by pushing your friend out of the way of his bullet. Preventing the consequences of a free decision is not the same thing as interfering with the process of making the decision.

[6] Is God a special case? If what Christians think of Him is true, God certainly isn't a garden variety agent. 'Perhaps, then, the restrictions that apply to a garden variety human agent,' someone might argue, 'do not apply to God.' I don't intend to pursue this line of thinking in this chapter.

[7] D Novitz, 'Forgiveness and Self-respect'. *Philosophy and Phenomenological Research*, vol. 58, no. 2, June 1998, pp. 299-315. Novitz's argument that a person who has adequate self-respect will not always be willing to forgive seems to directly challenge Jesus' advice to Peter in Matthew 18 to 'forgive seven times seventy times.' It's unclear, though, that Jesus is advancing a general moral principle that all of us should follow, or something more like a requirement that his disciples and followers, those people who believe that God has forgiven them for a multitude of sins, should be willing (out of gratitude, presumably) to forgive others time and time again. Also, see Matthew 14.

[8] It doesn't follow from what I have said that backward-looking considerations are irrelevant, merely that in some cases they are outweighed by forward-looking considerations.

[9] Journal article: A Minas, 'God and Forgiveness'. *Philosophical Quarterly*, vol. 25, 1975, pp. 138-150. Minas also argues that God, being morally perfect, can't forgive because, to do so, He'd have to ignore the call of justice. In her version of this argument, if someone has done a (serious) wrong, this calls for punishment. If God, instead of punishing the wrong doer, forgives him, then He has not balanced the scales of justice. This argument suffers from several objections. First, it conflates forgiveness and mercy. Second, Minas' argument fails to consider whether there are moral considerations that, in some cases, outweigh considerations of desert. Presumably, the primary point of forgiveness, in most cases, is reconciliation. When a child seriously betrays her father's long-standing trust, the father's act of forgiveness aims to repair their relationship so their shared future will have the same value as their shared past. One way to signal forgiveness is to show mercy. Even if the act of mercy violates a tenet of justice, I don't think the father would be wrong to show mercy. This is relevant to this essay because the Christian tradition attributes this type of moral calculation to God Himself: He is fully righteous but even more merciful; just, but even more

loving. Nothing Minas says indicates that this is a morally problematic calculation.

[10] It's an ever-present danger, of course, that we fail to take seriously how grievous a wrong was and how difficult it'd be for the victimizer to provide adequate reparation. But isn't it possible for a victim to be *both* adequately sensitive to these considerations *and* to choose reconciliation even so?

[11] There is sometimes something unseemly about quibbling over 'just how much' someone has really suffered. This type of parsing seems insensitive. Would it be unseemly and insensitive, then, to quibble over whether the boy's suffering is, strictly speaking, 'immeasurable'?

[12] G Pettigrove, 'The Dilemma of Divine Forgiveness'. *Religious Studies*, vol. 44, 2008, pp. 457-464.

[13] Not to mention, John's 'taking comfort' in God's forgiveness is entirely consistent with his continuing to earnestly and anxiously desire forgiveness directly from Sally. He needn't be ignoring her.

[14] Another argument for the claim that God, as a greatest conceivable being, does not have the capacity to forgive because the proper object of forgiveness is a harm suffered and God cannot suffer any harm. God, having no body, cannot suffer physical harm. And He cannot suffer emotional harm either: would a greatest conceivable being feel insulted, for instance, when betrayed? There are at least two problems with this argument. First, it makes the controversial assumption that being open to emotional harm is by its very nature a weakness. If God were prone to stewing over minor slights, He would, of course, lack a proper sense of His own dignity. But if a parent cares about her child, she thereby opens herself up to possible harms: if the child suffers, she will suffer with him. This harm is a reflection of her love, a part of the 'logic' of a loving relationship. But loving is not a personal shortcoming, and she wouldn't be a better person if she were unharmed by the suffering her children. Why not think the same things about God? Second, set aside the question whether a divine being can suffer emotional harm. Even if He cannot, it does not follow that He can never be sinned against. A person can be wronged without suffering physical or emotional harm. If someone lies to me, he has wronged me, even if I don't feel aggrieved, and even if his lie doesn't have any negative effects upon my life. Ivan's challenge, notice, does not turn on Minas' assumptions. He might admit that God is often wronged, or even that God suffers emotionally when His beloved children are seriously wronged. Ivan is committed only to the much weaker, and very plausible, assumption that God is not the only victim of human wrong doing.

[15] It is also possible that Ivan is directing his objections at a particular theological doctrine I haven't mentioned. There is some textual evidence that

he is objecting to the idea that all human suffering has a significant purpose or that the boy's suffering was somehow necessary for the eternal harmony to obtain. Such a doctrine, though, isn't my interest.

[16] Someone might argue that God has a special prerogative to forgive. Though a human third party does not have the right to forgive, a divine being has the moral authority to wash away a wrong even if the victim does not decide to forgive it. This would naturally provoke the question what grants God this special status. I don't intend to pursue any type of approach that is tantamount to saying 'God can do whatever He wants; He's God.' Neither, in my view, would the mere fact that God created us, or is omnipotent, grant God this special authority. The argument would need to appeal to arguments more 'Euclidean' than that.

[17] Also, the responses I will suggest in the main body of the text are responses to the worry that God will, in any attempt to create a new heaven and a new earth, violate moral prerogatives by the 'method' of intrusiveness. Though I think there are cases in which it is morally permissible for someone to 'ignore' a past wrong (see endnote #18), it seems as though Christians (if they want to successfully address Ivan's second argument) will largely have to argue for God's 'right' to promote a forgiving spirit.

[18] Another response might go like this. There are cases in which people are perfectly justified in acting as though wrongs have been forgiven even though the standard apparatus of a public apology, a public declaration of forgiveness, and a formal decision about reparation didn't occur. This idea seems to have been endorsed in a fictional story. In 'Babette's Feast,' Dinesen tells the fictional story of a small community of pious Lutherans who have grown weary of each other and bitter about their life together. Several of the members of this very small sect have very old, lingering grievances against each other. Despite their unwavering commitment to a simple life, free of all worldly luxury, they happen to come together – largely against their heart's desires – for an unexpectedly wondrous feast. In the midst of all of the good food and good wine, spirits warm, conversation livens, and long-absent laughter returns. These old friends, long aggrieved, begin to see their old gripes and grumbles as small and petty: 'you fool, you cheated me!,' one bellows as he laughs. The grievance is remembered, but no longer held against the perpetrator. In this context, the idea seems to be, there is no need to go through a public ritual in which victimizer formally apologizes and victim formally accepts; the wrongs are swept away in the warm tide of grace. This response does suggest that there would be no need, in an ideal community, for formal mechanisms to address all past wrongs. Sometimes wrongs are properly 'swept away' in a warm tide of grace. This response, though, is not clearly able to speak to grievous wrongs, whether by

a stranger or by a friend. Grievous wrongs do seem to require formal mechanisms.

[19] There is scriptural support for this view. When Peter asks Jesus how often he must forgive someone who persists in wronging him, Jesus tells Peter that he must forgive continuously, 'seven times seventy times' (Matthew 18). And Jesus gives an explanation: he points out how often God has forgiven Peter. The passage suggests that Jesus' followers are under an expectation to forgive. It is a requirement of gratitude.

[20] On the other hand, some liberty rights do not: the moral right to life, for instance. It entails that other people are under a moral obligation not to kill you (unjustly). This moral right protects your life itself, not (merely) a set of decisions about your life.

Bibliography

Dinesen, I., 'Babette's Feast'. *Anecdotes of Destiny and Ehrengard*. Vintage, 1993, pp. 19-60.

Dostoevsky, F., *The Brother's Karamazov*, translated by Constance Garnett, Farrar, Straus, and Giroux, New York, 1990.

Dworkin, R., *Taking Rights Seriously*, Cambridge, 1977.

Gingell, J., 'Forgiveness and Power'. *Analysis*, vol. 34, 1974, pp. 180-184.

Minas, A., 'God and Forgiveness'. *Philosophical Quarterly*, vol. 25, 1975, pp. 138-150.

Novitz, D., 'Forgiveness and Self-Respect'. *Philosophy and Phenomenological Research*, vol. 58, no. 2, June 1998, pp. 299-315.

Pettigrove, G., 'The Dilemma of Divine Forgiveness'. *Religious Studies*, vol. 44, 2008, pp. 457-464.

Regan Lance Reitsma is Assistant Professor of Philosophy and Director of the Center for Ethics and Public Life at King's College in Wilkes-Barre, Pennsylvania. His research interests are in ethics and rational decision-making.

PART III

Forgiveness and the Judeo-Christian Tradition

From the Religious to the Political Apology: How the Religious Prehistory of Apology Makes Sense of Collective Responsibility

Danielle Celermajer

Abstract

Political apologies, that is, apologies made by representative political leaders on behalf of the nation for grave wrongs of the past, became part of international landscape in the latter part of the twentieth century. For many members of the nations or communities on whose behalf such apologies were made, they represented a critically important dimension of 'dealing with the past' at the same time as constituting transformed political futures; but for apologies' critics, they violated key principles concerning moral individualism and the modernist liberal principles that only individuals can be agents and only individuals can be held responsible for wrongful acts. In seeking to find a way of making sense of the type of collective responsibility encoded in the political apology, this chapter interrogates collective forms of repentance in the sphere of religion, and specifically collective repentance in Judaism. Addressing the assumed sharp divide between the ways in which modern liberal communities deal with past wrongs and conceptualise responsibility and the modalities in which wrongs and responsibility are addressed in religious or even theo-political contexts, it argues that the dichotomies are overdrawn and thus obscure the continuities between religious and contemporary political practices of apology. Specifically, it suggests that the manner in which Judaism understands the relationship between collective and individual responsibility provides a template for rethinking that relationship in our own context. More specifically, it argues that in apologising, the collective is not assuming responsibility for the action, which rightly adheres to the individual, but is rather recognising its role in creating and sustaining the ethical context in which individuals make choices about how to act.

Key Words: Apology, collective responsibility, liberalism, penance, Judaism.

*****

1. Making Sense of Repentant Politics

Looking around the world, from the best-known case of South Africa, to the myriad lesser-known sites where communities in strife have been adopting and adapting practices of forgiveness and apology, one cannot but notice that 'the repentant mode' has made a bold entry onto the stage of contemporary politics. Indeed, collections and books such as this one, which both document and seek to make sense of this novel form of political action, now constitute a well-populated sub-genre that crosses disciplines and continents.[1] For the most part, when forgiveness and apology are taken up as methods for dealing with social and political violations in the past, they are classified as one of a number of strategies or institutions that come under the rubric of 'transitional justice', and thus understood as one of the means that political communities are trying out as they struggle to move beyond the entrenched conflicts and divisions that are the legacy of past violations.[2] This classification certainly makes sense, given that transitional processes have become one of the most important features of post-1989 geopolitics, with polities all over the world combining a range of strategies, including truth commissions, trials, compensation, reconciliation and public memory projects as well as apology and forgiveness to deal with their particular pasts. What this functional classification of apology and forgiveness leaves out, however, is a specific analysis of *these* modalities of dealing with the past, of what it is that apology and forgiveness *do* by way of 'dealing with the past'. In other words, observing that they are ways of dealing with the past says nothing of the way in which they do that work.

As evidenced in this volume, there are a number of disciplinary, methodological or epistemological approaches that one might take in interpreting political apology and forgiveness. For example, one might study particular examples and track what happens to people involved in them; one might conduct a philosophical analysis of the concepts; one might undertake comparative studies of different cases to detect commonalities and distinctions; or, one might speak with people who have forgiven, apologised, or refused to do so to discern their intentions, responses and phenomenological experience. In this chapter, I take a somewhat different route, focusing not solely on contemporary practices, but rather on what I suggest represents the intellectual or metaphoric predecessor of the political apology, the religious apology. That is, in seeking to better understand the contemporary phenomenon of representative collective apologies for past wrongs, this chapter will draw an interpretive line back to the practices and understandings of collective apology as it functioned in the sphere of religion, and draw on these to illuminate some of the questions that dog our understanding of the contemporary practice.

Religion is of course a vast and internally diverse field, and there no doubt exist practices that bear at least a family resemblance to contemporary modes of forgiveness and apology in a number of world religions.[3] In this brief analysis, I deal only on practices of apology in Judaism, focusing in particular on those forms of apology that, like the contemporary political apology, are concerned with collective wrongdoing and thereby take as their repenting subject not the individual wrongdoer, but the collective. The specific question that this chapter asks is then how practices and understandings of collective apologies in Judaism can help us to make sense of the collective responsibility that contemporary apologies seem to imply.

Such a move to what I call the religious underpinning of the political apology will strike many readers, particular students of politics, as not only odd, but as politically, ethically, and epistemologically problematic. After all, one of the primary features of contemporary liberal democratic polities is their secularity, or, more precisely, their adoption of secular processes and laws, carefully forged so as to ensure that they neither favour nor reflect the interests of any particular religious group, but stand equidistant from all religious imaginations and commitments. Moreover, beyond secularity's concern for equality of treatment, there is a whole raft of core differences between the principles underpinning modern liberal politics and those underpinning religious communities, all of which would suggest *prima facie* objections to looking to religious practices to explain secular political practices. Indeed, contemporary liberal politics sees itself as structurally opposed to the theo-political forms that it replaced in a number of critically important ways. In particular, whereas the laws and organising principles of religious communities are necessarily aligned with the thick moral tenets of the particular religion, liberal politics excludes thick or absolute moral commitments, entrenching only those rules necessary to stabilise and sustain its own political processes (constitutional principles, for example).[4] Similarly, whereas theo-politics places the source of political order, right and truth in some transcendent realm of revealed truths outside of the political community itself, in contemporary liberal politics, the political community must itself be the source of its own revisable norms and rules. Further, and particularly pertinent to the question this chapter asks, one of the major points on which modern liberal politics distinguishes itself from pre-modern theo-politics is that it prioritises individual identity, responsibility and freedom over collective identity and responsibility. In somewhat stark terms, we modern liberals see ourselves as having left behind the highly problematic ontologies of pre-modern theo-political forms, where individuals neither had the freedom to choose their own paths (including their conception of the good life), nor were they held responsible solely for what they chose along those paths.

These general distinctions between secular and religious or theo-political forms are particularly pertinent in considering the apology, given that when one apologises, one is presumably apologising in reference to a standard of what is right and wrong or good and bad, and if that standard is associated with a transcendent absolute, it will hardly be useful in dealing with conflicts that are often themselves the outcome of particularistic identities. Moreover, for moderns, insofar as apology implies responsibility for wrongdoing, we would require that only individuals can apologise and that collective apologies, particularly those with a theological scent, hark back to problematic conceptions of responsibility to which we no longer adhere. If then, repentant modes of action have been transmitted to and picked up by contemporary liberal democratic political communities from the sphere of religion, one must view this transmission with considerable concern, and assess whether the apology that has been transmitted carries with it elements of theological politics that are structurally problematic for liberal democratic political communities.

In this regard, I should make clear that I am not suggesting that the apology that has been picked up in contemporary politics has anything specifically Jewish (or even religious) about it. I am rather suggesting that the historical experience of collective apology in Judaism (and thereafter Christianity) provided a cultural template or a possibility that has been inscribed in our cultural and historical imaginations, and that this template, being thus available, has been taken up to meet contemporary concerns and social and political aspirations In this sense, my return to religious contexts is in the manner of Walter Benjamin's model of the collector, who picks up the fragments of the past that lie broken around his feet to make sense of the present.[5] Though connected with their past, in their present incarnation, these fragments of apology would no longer be thoroughly embedded in the meta-narratives of their original location. They have undergone a 'sea change,' to become something 'rich and strange.'[6]

What I will argue in this chapter is that a careful interpretive reading of both practices and commentaries on apology, as developed originally in Judaism, and then picked up in Christianity, provides a framework for making sense of contemporary political apologies. Moreover, it does so in a manner that not only avoids the concerns one might have about theo-political forms, but also elucidates the particular work that apologies do in contemporary politics. Perhaps even more importantly, because the apology in Judaism is primarily oriented around collective rather than individual wrongdoing, it provides a uniquely useful template for understanding contemporary apologies, whose collective quality has, in itself caused significant conceptual problems in an age committed to moral individualism. Before moving to an analysis of the understanding and practices of apology in Judaism, therefore, I begin by setting out the problem of collective responsibility in relation to collective apologies and exploring how contemporary political theory has tried to make sense of this problem.

2.   Political Apologies and the Collective Subject

Political apologies, the class of acts with which this chapter is concerned, are, significantly, apologies made by representative leaders on behalf of a group, most often a nation, that is thereby rhetorically located as being in some sense responsible for the wrongs in question.[7] It is precisely this collective quality that has given rise to one of the major criticisms that has been raised against contemporary political apologies; that is, that insofar as they attribute responsibility for past wrongs to an undifferentiated collective, they violate basic principles of moral individualism. This alleged violation is no small matter, given that one of the foundational ontological premises of modernity is that only individuals are capable of action, because only individuals have the agency that is the prerequisite of action and accountability. Correlatively, it is morally suspect to hold collectives such as nations, in whose name apologies are given, responsible for those wrongs.

This type of objection was well illustrated in the debate over whether the Prime Minister of Australia should apologise on behalf of the nation for the forced removal of Aboriginal and Torres Strait Islander children from their families. This debate followed the release, in 1997, of *Bringing them Home*, the report of the National Inquiry into the Forced Removal of Aboriginal and Torres Strait Islander Children from their Families, which had documented, in excruciating details, the systematic policy that had existed in Australia from 1910 to 1970, whereby Indigenous children were removed from their natural families and placed in institutions, foster or adoptive homes.[8] The report had, amongst its 57 recommendations, called on Australian governments and sub-state institutions that had been involved in removal, to apologise to Aboriginal and Torres Strait Islander people for the harms they had incurred.[9] Despite the widespread public support that the apology recommendations garnered, the then Prime Minister, John Howard, steadfastly refused to apologise for ten years until he lost office, catalysing an extraordinary political debate in Australia about responsibility, race and apology. Particularly relevant here is that one of the major justifications that he gave for his refusal was that, so he argued, an apology on behalf of Australians unfairly blamed individuals for wrongs that they had not committed. As he stated during one of the parliamentary debates over this issue, 'To say to them that they are personally responsible and that they should feel a sense of shame about those events is to visit upon them an unreasonable penalty and an injustice.'[10] What he was voicing, in every day terms, was what one might call the liberal objection to claims about collective responsibility, or collective identity: individuals alone and not collectives are capable of being moral agents, and as such, it is both a category mistake and a violation of the principle of moral individualism to blame collectives for wrongdoing.

What made matters still more difficult for those seeking to justify a collective apology, was that many of the wrongs that were the subject of the apology had been committed before many contemporary Australians had even been born. Similarly problematic was the fact that many Australian citizens had not been born in Australia at all, but had come as migrants or refugees, thus presenting a challenge for those seeking to explain how they could also legitimately be brought under the umbrella of collective responsibility. As the Prime Minister asserted, in a rare piece of solidarity with migrant Australians, 'you can't really apologize on behalf of people who moved here in the last ten or fifteen years and never knew anything about this.'[11] In both cases, what was being challenged was thus not only the notion that there could be a collective identity and associated collective responsibility, but the claim that this collective identity could cross time, encompassing members who had not even belonged to the community at a time when the wrongs were committed.

The Australian Prime Minister's objections in this regard were by no means idiosyncratic or uniquely linked to this particular wrongdoing and call for apology. On the contrary, they were highly representative of one of the principle tensions that wrack contemporary debates about how to deal with the past. Certainly, a number of the processes that have been adopted to deal with past wrongs, most prominently the new international and hybrid criminal trials, focus exclusively on individual responsibility, thus remaining true to our modernist commitments to individual responsibility. Others, however, including public memorials, societal reconciliation processes and representative apologies all attribute some type of responsibility to the collective in which the wrongdoing took place, or to the group to which the particular wrongdoers belonged. It may be a stretch to claim, as Howard did, that processes of collective repentance or reconciliation visit an unreasonable 'penalty' upon members of the group, but undoubtedly, these approaches to dealing with the past do implicate the collective in the narrative of wrongdoing and to the extent that this attribution comes into conflict with commitments to moral individualism, it requires a cogent justification.

In the Australian case, where the public was intensively engaged in debating the rights and wrongs of apology, there were a number of 'non-theoretical' attempts to finesse this problem of collective responsibility. The first was to try to attach responsibility entirely to institutions, most importantly the state that had passed the laws sanctioning removal, but also the Churches and other sub-state institutions such as the police that had been involved in removal. Thus, for example, when the Commonwealth objected to apology on the grounds that it misattributed blame and apportioned inter-generational responsibility, the Australian Human Rights and Equal Opportunity Commission responded by pointing out that the Commonwealth was well aware that 'the state' is an institution that transcends any particular government in power (located at a distinct time), and, as such, the contemporary state inherits the debts (as it does the surfeits) of its earlier incarnations.[12] By way of analogy, the Commission pointed to the arena of international law, where each government inherits the legal commitments, economic debts and so on of its predecessor governments.

This move both worked at a logical level, and conformed with the original recommendations, that had in fact called on apologies from precisely those institutions. The problem was that it failed to capture precisely that dimension of the apology that so powerfully touched the Australian population and what speaks to people all over the world who become involved in apology movements. That is, that political apology is not a purely institutional response. On the contrary, in contradistinction to the criminal legal responses to wrongdoing, which often alienate society and individuals, even the victims themselves, insofar as they come under the mediation of highly formal institutions, apologies seem to uniquely capture the sense that wrongdoing and suffering involve people and society itself. Tens of thousands of Australians had planted hands to make their apologies in the 'Sea of Hands' public performances, had signed Sorry Books and had joined sorry marches, and for them, the Prime Ministerial apology was also their apology.

A second move, attempting to retain this soft social referent, but to avoid the problems of collective attribution, was to redefine the apology as an act that did not imply responsibility at all, but rather expressed empathy with the victim, as in, 'We are sorry that (you are suffering)', in place of 'We are sorry for (what we did)'. What this strategy did was move the apologising Australian people out of the position of the one responsible for wrongdoing, to place them next to the victims, as if those apologising were no more than bystanders in a drama that touched them, much as one is touched when one witnesses any suffering. Ironically, it was Sir Ronald Wilson, one of the co-authors of *Bringing them Home*, who most famously suggested that apology was properly understood as an expression of sympathy, not responsibility.[13] The problem with this move was that it solved the problem of collective responsibility only by removing the question of responsibility altogether, thereby missing what was perhaps most poignant about the apology; that is, that it did implicate everyone in the violations that had occurred.

The third and most productive move was to alter the way in which the type of responsibility associated with apology was described, specifically by substituting the language of shame for the language of guilt. Underpinning this linguistic shift was an understanding that whereas guilt points a highly exacting finger of responsibility to the perpetrator, shame implies a more amorphous sense of association with the wrongdoing that was more compatible with the relationship that the collective had with the wrongs in question. As one writer put it:

> Guilt is not the same as shame and trying to get out of one
> doesn't let us out of the other. Guilt [...] operates in the
> realm of personal breach. Shame, on the other hand,

> operates in the realm of honour and dishonour [...] while
> guilt is often limiting in that it draws down into individual
> acts of wrongdoing, shame can in a sense be a spur back
> into our common humanity.[14]

The advantage of this move was that it retained the connection with the
people of Australia with the wrongs in question, but seemed to offer a way of
severing the link between them and the actual commission of the wrongful
acts that guilt normally implies. Accordingly, this move even appealed to
conservative intellectuals firmly committed to moral individualism. As
Robert Manne, a well-known conservative commentator put it:

> Because guilt for wrongs done is always a matter of
> individual responsibility, an idea of collective guilt
> genuinely makes no sense. An individual cannot be charged
> with the crimes of others, [...] however talk of sharing a
> legacy of shame is quite another thing.[15]

While it is difficult to assess how Australians actually made sense
of the collective apology, it is clear that one way or another, many of them
did so. One saw this perhaps most clearly in the massive public support that
the official apology, delivered by Howard's successor, Kevin Rudd,
received, when he delivered it at the opening of the first new parliament in
February 2008.[16] What one can say is that the linguistic turn to shame,
combined with the incessant and powerful narratives of the suffering of the
many Indigenous Australians effected by removal, combined with a growing
recognition of the previously unacknowledged bloody and cruel history of
colonisation were sufficient for people to understand that the wrongs of
removal went beyond the particular individuals who had put children in
trucks and driven them away, and beyond those who had physically and
sexually abused Indigenous children in institutions and foster homes.
Nevertheless, this assumed consensus was not accompanied by a clear
theoretical articulation that set out, analytically, how it was that a collective
could be responsible, but only individuals can act.

Turning from practice to theory, there has been little attempt to
specifically theorise the collective responsibility associated with apologies.[17]
Nevertheless, contemporary literature on responsibility can offer some
elucidation on collective responsibility. Beginning with Joel Feinberg's
groundbreaking essay on collective responsibility, a number of theorists have
recognized the inadequacy of the variations one might draw out of the idea of
the responsible individual and have sought to shift their perspective from a
formal analysis of the responsible institution to a more sociological analysis
of the cultural context in which wrongdoing occurs.[18] For Feinberg, what

was critical in justifying collective responsibility was a recognition that violations may in themselves be discrete, but they take place in a broader cultural context that in some way legitimises them, despite their formal classification as 'wrongs'. The classical case for Feinberg concerned the systematic and pervasive environment of racial discrimination in the United States, within which particular acts of violence were perpetrated against blacks, but his analysis clearly has broader reach.[19] This broader cultural context thus forms the effective link in the chain between the individual perpetrator and the broader collective, along which responsibility can also travel. Feinberg's approach provides the basic template for a family of theories that ground collective responsibility in discriminatory cultural contexts.

Larry May, for example uses the concept of 'dispositions' to justify collective attribution, because dispositions 'create a climate of attitudes in which harm is more likely to occur.'[20] Like Feinberg, May identifies the pertinent collective characteristic in this zone of *disposition*, as distinct from decision, action or even authorization. Building on this notion, David Miller supplements his more institutionally formal 'co-operative practice' model of collective responsibility with the 'like-minded group' model, noting that the latter can capture in its net all those who, even without *acting* or formally assenting, implicitly supported the manifest wrongful acts through their shared 'general attitude.'[21] This shift away from action or even authorization is what permits Miller to trace collective responsibility without having to meet the more onerous conditions required for institutional responsibility, such as fair decision making procedures. Iris Marion Young's term 'social connection' does similar work in casting the net of responsibility over a group of people standing in the background, or off to the side of the actual wrongdoing, but who share a social or cultural space that one senses is the ground for the actual wrongdoing.[22]

What these different theorists are all suggesting is then that to grasp the intuition that collectives can be responsible without also making the problematic claim that collectives can or did 'act', one has to hypostasise some type of shared disposition or attitude that is both common to all members of the collective and one of the necessary conditions for the wrongs to have taken place. Thus, even though members of the collective did not take part in committing the particular act, they did share in the environment that rendered that action not only possible, but even likely. In the Australian case, one can see how applicable this theoretical framework is. For white Australians may not have actually themselves removed Indigenous children from their families, but they have certainly been part of, or even constituted, a political culture pervaded by racism and the generalised denigration of Indigenous Australians. That removing children so brutally and systematically, in utter contempt of the rights of their families, was not only possible, but a relatively unnoticed part of Australian law and policy for sixty years of Australian political life, speaks volumes for how Indigenous Australians were held for non-Indigenous Australians.

This pervasive social and institutional culture of racism was perhaps most poignantly laid out in the massive five-volume report of the *Royal Commission into Aboriginal Deaths in Custody* (RCIADIC), released to Australians and the international community already in 1990. This report provided an extraordinarily comprehensive picture of the historical abuse of the rights of Aboriginal peoples and their contemporary disadvantage measured against every socio-economic indicator.[23] It covered not only the disadvantage suffered in the context of the administration of law, policing and the penitentiary system, but linked this problem with the systematic disadvantage of Aboriginal people, documenting their situation with respect to education, housing, health, employment and infrastructure. Most importantly for our purposes, the Royal Commission contextualised these specific disadvantages within the *political* history of colonization; the policies of integration and assimilation, the non-recognition of land rights, and civil and political inequality and exclusion. It framed them not as discrete acts of discrimination or inequality, but as part of a pattern of non-recognition that was a constitutional dimension of the post-colonial Australian state. Thus, by the time that *Bringing them Home* was released in 1997, the link between specific acts of violation and the failure on the part of Australia as a nation to recognise Indigenous Australians as co-equal citizens and subject of rights was well established.

Still, this conceptual framework for collective responsibility had not been systematically connected with the apology as such. Certainly, one could draw on this framework to mount a viable argument against those critics who demanded that any collective attribution committed a moral offence. What was left unexplained, however, was why *apology* in particular might be the mechanism through which this dimension of responsibility had come to be expressed, or how apology was uniquely suited to expressing it. For this explanation, I suggest that we need to turn to the history of collective apologies in the sphere of religious practice.

3.   Collective Apologies in the Sphere of Religion

At first glance, religion may seem an odd place to look for interpretive tropes for deciphering the political apology and not only because of the structural distinctions between political secularism and religion outlined earlier. The more specific problem with turning to religious apologies is that, whereas the apologies with which we are concerned are collective, religious apologies would seem to be essentially individual. After all, the dominant image of religious repentance in the Western imagination is that of the lone penitent in the darkened confessional, looking into his or her heart and seeking a very personal and private form of inner transformation. The archetypal religious apology would thus seem to be very far from the public collective form of apology that characterises the contemporary political apology.

If one looks beyond the screen memory of the individual apology, however, and digs a little deeper into the histories of religious practice, one finds that even within Christianity, this private confessional form was a relatively late entry onto the scene, with its image pasting over a far longer history of collective forms. In the first centuries after Christ, the church's penitential practices were highly public and involved the entire community. It was only as a result of the highly political processes of the Council of Trent (in the mid-sixteenth century) that the sole sanctioned rite of penance in the Catholic Church came to comprise an individual, private ritual, where the penitent exchanged words of contrition for forgiveness and absolution.[24] And indeed, since Vatican II called for the creation of new forms of repentance, two collective forms of penance have re-entered Church practice. Nevertheless, the Roman Catholic concept of repentance and the private individual form have been considered synonymous, and there has been little recognition of the fact that there had been, nor the possibility that there could be, other forms or conceptualisations.

In Judaism, by contrast, collective public repentance has been the principal form of penitential practice, stretching back to the earliest forms of ritual rites up into the present, and it is deeply embedded in Jewish theology. On *Yom Kippur*, for example, the entire Jewish community comes together and communally repents its wrongdoings of the previous year. Critically, in saying that it comes together to repent its wrongs, I do not mean that the people gather as a collection of individuals each apologizing for his or her own wrongs at the same time, but that they repent *qua* community, as the corporate body *Knesset Israel*.[25] In pre-rabbinic temple Judaism, the rituals of repentance entailed sacrifice and other purification rites involving the whole community, or the High Priest acting on behalf of the whole community, but with the destruction of the second temple is 75 CE, the sacrificial rites were replaced by verbal expressions of repentance in the liturgy, by other forms of *teshuvah* (the acts of repentance including compensation) and by acts of justice or charity (*tzedakah*). For our purposes the most relevant strand is the verbal expression of repentance in the form of penitential prayers, now performed in the synagogue.

This corporate expression of repentance is perhaps most apparent in the penitential prayers that dominate the *Yom Kippur* liturgy.[26] The various prayers are articulated in three basic ways: aloud by the rabbi on behalf of the community, privately and silently by each person and *aloud by all members of the congregation on behalf of all members of the congregation.* In the latter case, where each member of the congregation confesses a common list of sins individually, but in unison, the voice of the prayers is first person plural: 'we have sinned against you'. The experience is literally of a single sound as the voices of the pray-ers come together: each person singularly, but also as part of the common voice, speaks his or her responsibility and regret for every sin, whether or not he or she has individually committed it.

This is but one example of a rich history and indeed contemporary practice of collective and public repentance in Judaism and in various Christian churches, including, as noted above, in contemporary Roman Catholicism. What they represent is an unambiguous, long-standing recognition, in ritualised forms, of the responsibility that the entire community holds for all of the wrongs that take place within that community. In these forms of collective repentance, there is a clear recognition that there is a connection between the community *qua* community and the acts of wrongdoing that occur within its midst, irrespective the question of which individuals within the community actually committed the wrongful acts. The community both recognises its part on the aetiology of wrongdoing and picks up this responsibility in the form of apology. The first question for us must thus be how these two forms of responsibility, individual and collective, are reconciled in this context. The second question is: how does apology attend to the responsibility of the collective and how does it do its work of altering the collective in such a way that it will no longer sustain such wrongs?

Before answering these analytic questions, however, it will be important to return to the objections that turning to collective religious apologies may well be rising in the mind of the reader. That is, even if the existence of the collective religious apology would seem to offer an alternative to the private individual religious model seemed to offer, and thus rendering it more compatible with the contemporary form, it only raises other, more serious problems. The mere fact that Judaism (or Christianity) provides an essentially collective trope for interpreting contemporary collective apology does not mean that it is a suitable or morally desirable one for modern liberal political communities. In fact, as canvassed earlier, standard modernist understandings of religious collective practices maintain just the opposite. Modern political forms were established to counter the assorted vices of theocratic corporatist political forms. In place of their allegiance to a transcendent metaphysics, we limited ourselves to the mundane and human; instead of aligning ourselves with thick, heteronymous values (God's laws), we preferred 'thin' values established by autonomous citizens and always open to revision by a new crop of autonomous citizens; rather than external ritual we chose either authentic individual commitment or rational, 'disenchanted' institutions;[27] and perhaps most importantly, in place of crude collectivism and its failure to respect the unassailable principle of moral individualism, we opted for individual responsibility.

If this characterization of religion's collective apology is correct, then it hardly provides a useful interpretive frame for making sense of the collective apology and, more particularly, for how the collective apology inscribes collective responsibility in a manner compatible with modern commitments to moral individualism. If religion's collective apology is guilty of absolutism, heteronomy, empty externality and gross collectivism, then all of this disqualifies it from functioning as a legitimate mechanism in contemporary liberal politics.

Undoubtedly, an anachronistic reading of the collective rituals of religious repentance would see in them precisely the type of collectivist ontology and understanding of transpersonal responsibility in which moderns no longer believe and which we no longer tolerate – understanding as we do that individuals and not collectives are responsible for the wrongs they commit. A more careful reading of the tradition suggests, however, that the collective responsibility articulated here is not on the same register as the individual responsibility. If one reads the interpretive texts of the traditions, one sees how they manifest a conceptual scheme in which individual and collective responsibility do not operate in a zero sum game, but fold into each other to provide a richer picture of responsibility for systematic wrongdoing.

To enter into this alternative scheme of responsibility (and indeed ontology), one might begin by recognizing the critical link that Jewish thought and practice forges between individual sin, or wrongdoing, the foundational covenant, or founding principles of the community, and the role of the people in upholding the covenant. For Jews, every ethical precept and thus every individual choice about right and wrong is underpinned by a primary law or covenant, which was neither given to nor accepted by the individual, but was, at the point of origin and thereafter given to, *and accepted by*, Israel (the people not the state) as a collective. That is, although individuals may make choices about right and wrong, their moral orientation is always already given by the collective adherence to certain principles. One finds a range of teachings throughout Judaism about the collective nature of the law. The sages expressed this conception metaphorically, for example, when they taught that:

> It [the law] can be compared to people on a boat. One took out an awl and began boring a hole in the boat beneath his seat. The others said to him, 'What are you doing?' He replied, 'Is that any concern of yours? [I am not boring a hole beneath your seat] but only under mine'. They said: 'But you will sink the whole ship, and we will all drown'.[28]

The point here is not that there is no space for individual dissent or no possibility of evaluating particular laws, but that it is logically impossible to think of someone's obligations to Jewish laws entirely outside the corporate body. Because law logically requires plurality, no single abstract person could abide by the laws outside the fact of the body of Israel. The law *qua* law, as an authoritative organizing system, logically precedes specific laws or adherence to laws. And at this level the law, like the grammatical structure of a language, or the notion of property, only exists if it is held up at a number of locations. Absent general respect, the law cannot work as a meaningful and authoritative mechanism for regulating social relations, and so cannot work for any single individual. Without this structural starting point, only anarchy, not autonomy, is possible.[29]

When individuals fail to uphold the law, they are no doubt responsible for the contravention. Once one understands the corporatist nature of law, however, one must also recognise that this individual dimension of responsibility is only part of the story. Most especially when these contraventions are not mere aberrations but part of a systematic and recurring pattern of wrongdoing, one has to look beyond the individual to recognise that responsibility also falls on the community that has failed to provide a sufficiently compelling normative context. The individual is responsible for taking the wrongful action; there is no question here of a mega-agent. However, the normative judgment that allowed her to act in this way did not exist in a vacuum, but was embedded in a normative framework for which everyone was responsible. It may have been an individual man who committed acts of violence against a particular woman, or a particular white person who treated a black person with contempt, but each did so within a context where the value of women and blacks was systematically and collectively diminished. The individual acted, but the collective provided the context in which he or she acted, and it is at this level that the collective is also responsible.

Where individual actions are this located within a broader context of the framework of collectively embraced moral dispositions, the economy of the relationship between individual and collective responsibility changes significantly from one in which they stand in a zero sum game. That is, the assumed economy of that relationship is one where the individual *or* the collective is responsible for wrongdoing, and the amount of responsibility attributed to one is subtracted from the sum of the other's responsibility. Under this alternative schema, we recognise that individuals may be responsible for an action, but the community is responsible for the moral framework and parameters of meaning from which individuals draw both their identity and the dispositions to act. When the collective takes responsibility, it is for this contextual moral framework that it is taking responsibility and not the action itself.

This analysis then takes us to our second question which was how the apology represents an acknowledgement of the distinct dimension of responsibility that adheres to the collective, and how it might effect the work of altering the collective, in a way that we expect our institutions for 'dealing with the past' to do. That is, one would look to such institutions not only to recognise the wrong that has been done, but in some way to alter the responsible party so that it does not repeat the offence. How then would apology alter the collective?

To answer this question, one must stay very close to the nature of the responsibility that the collective holds. Recall, it is not responsible for the action, but for the normative framework in which actions occur and more specifically, for providing the context of meaning in which individuals evaluate what is right and wrong. If one returns to the collective prayers of *Yom Kippur*, these can now be re-interpreted as performative speech acts that acknowledge the failure of the community to uphold the specific norms with sufficient strength to prevent individual wrongdoing. Thus, the Old Testament theologian Von Rad argued that offences against the sacral order implicated all members of the community, not because of the deep ties of blood, but because the offence threatened the order itself and the set of relationships which organized the community and its social function.[30] Sin is not attached to a number of individuals by virtue of their proximity to the wrongful action, but rests at the level of organizing principles in which they, qua collective, are located; that is, in the covenant.

In this sense, the collective apology represents a return to the covenant, to the foundational constitution that the community forged, where it laid out rightful principles for action and for relations between people. In apologising, the community recognises that it has violated its original promise to treat all members equally or to respect the dignity of all human beings. It recognises that although it constituted itself as a community in which killing is not permissible, it has allowed killing to occur, that even though it constituted itself on the principle of equal respect, it has operated in a manner that some people are systematically disrespected. And further, in returning to those covenantal promises, in apologising, it makes them once again.

Of course, in some cases, the original covenantal or constitutional principles or promises may have themselves been the source of the problem. Thus for example, the community may have been formed on the basis of the exclusion of certain types of people (women, blacks, the disabled) from the circle of those accorded equality and respect. This was certainly the case in Australia, where the Australian state was formed on the basis of the systematic exclusion of Indigenous peoples and disrespect for their humanity. In this case, the apology marks not a simple return to those principles in their original form, but an universalisation of those principles, one demanded by those whose humanity they have denigrated. In the Australian case, for example, it marks recognition that the constitutional principles of equality and respect have systematically and structurally excluded indigenous people, and that a full realisation of those principles cannot tolerate such exclusion. When the collective apologises, it is thus 'recovenanting', reconstituting its foundational identity and orienting principles so that the normative context with which the individuals act more powerfully grounds their action in principles of equal respect and negatively sanctions the wrongs that were once implicitly permitted.

Interestingly, when the Swiss political philosopher Karl Jaspers sought to make sense of the questions of guilt and responsibility in the wake of the *Shoah*, he not only recognised the need to articulate a more variegated map of responsibility, but also that there was a form of collective responsibility of precisely this nature.[31] Jaspers was certainly alive to the dangers of collective attribution, the very category mistake that had allowed for the mass murder of Jews *qua* Jews. Nevertheless, he also recognised that those who had not themselves committed the wrongful acts were nevertheless responsible for 'moral failings,' the 'countless little acts of negligence, of convenient adaptation of cheap vindication, and the imperceptible promotion of wrong' which make evil possible and 'cause the conditions out of which both crime and political guilt arise.'[32] This dimension of guilt he called political guilt, and beyond that lay what he called metaphysical guilt, that guilt that all human beings bear by virtue of their co-humanity with those who commit grievous wrong. Indeed, when he speculated on how one might appropriately pick up on this dimension of responsibility (as one would, for example, meet individual criminal responsibility with punishment), he suggested 'penance and renewal.'[33] Though without making this explicit, what Jaspers was articulating was precisely this connection that had historically, in the realm of religion, been drawn between the contextual guilt of the collective and the work of penance.

Read this way, the collective, performative modes of religious repentance do not contravene the basic commitments to moral individualism that lie at the heart of secular liberalism, but rather enrich what has become an attenuated conception of the aetiology of wrongdoing. Such collective attributions certainly do not cancel out individual responsibility, nor do they implicate all members of the collective with the sharp finger of direct responsibility. What they do, however, is insist that we look beyond the decontextualised action and recognise that in the background was a systematic normative frame in which many people were implicated. This more complex ontological map is surely perspicacious in the context of the violations that become the subject of transitional and historical justice, violations that, in the main consist of systematic wrongdoing against degraded and marginalised groups of people.

Read back against this richer interpretive and practical history, one can thus begin to articulate an understanding of the contemporary political apology neither as a category mistake nor as a regression to a less rational or sophisticated understanding of causality and agency. On the contrary, when we let the sharp dichotomization that so often dictates our understanding of what occurs in the spheres of modern secular politics and religion recede, we begin to see that the collective apology, in both spheres, represents our attempt to draw the collective back into the story of responsibility in a manner fully compatible with individual blame. This attempt, I would note in conclusion, is not only important from the point of view of theoretically consistency or rendering compatible practices that offend our theoretical principles. Its real importance lies in the potential that this more capacious understanding of responsibility and of the range of practices that are available to acknowledge responsibility offer to the project of addressing the systematic violations that have characterised the last century. Undoubtedly, the establishment of new institutions, such as the International Criminal Court, represent an important contribution to the project, in so far as they offer the prospect of ending the impunity that individual perpetrators of the worst crimes have enjoyed. At the same time, at the end of a century where whole societies have remained largely silent if not complicit to the systematic murder or impoverishment of women, indigenous peoples, blacks, members of a particular ethnic, cultural or religious minority, people with disabilities and other denigrated groups, we cannot delude ourselves that the future will be any different, if our impunity does not also come to an end.

Notes

[1] The literature on apology and forgiveness is certainly too vast to cover in a footnote. See for example, Elazar Barkan and Alexander Karn (eds.), *Taking Wrongs Seriously: Apologies and Reconciliation*, Stanford: Stanford University Press, 2006, Mark Gibney, Rhoda E. Howard-Hassmann, Jean-Marc Coicaud, and Niklaus Steiner (eds.), *The Age of Apology: Facing Up to the Past*, Philadelphia: University of Pennsylvania Press, 2008; Don Shriver, *An ethic For Enemies: Forgiveness in Politics*, New York: Oxford University Press, 1995; Martha Minnow, *Between Vengeance and Forgiveness: Facing History After Genocide and Mass Violence*, Boston, Mass: Beacon Press, 1998.

[2] See in particular Minnow, *Between Vengeance and Forgiveness*.

[3] See for example M S Rye, K I Pargament, M A Ali, G L Beck, E Dorff, C Hallisey, V Narayan, J Williams, 'Religious perspectives on forgiveness' in

M McCulloch, K Pargament, and C Thoreson, *Forgiveness: Theory Research and Practice*, New York: Guilford Press, 2000.

[4] See for example Stephen Holmes, *Passion and Constraint*, Chicago: University of Chicago Press, 1995.

[5] W Benjamin, *The Arcades Project*, trans. H Eiland and K McLaughlin, prepared on the basis of the German volume edited by Rolf Tiedemann, Cambridge, Mass.: Belknap Press, 1999.

[6] In her introduction to Benjamin's Illuminations, Arendt quotes from Shakespeare's The Tempest (2,1) to convey Benjamin's notion of the relationship between modernity and tradition. See Hannah Arendt, introduction to *Illuminations*, by Walter Benjamin, New York: Schocken Books, 1969, 38.

[7] For a comprehensive list and discussion of contemporary political apologies see Danielle Celermajer, *Sins of the Nation and the Ritual of Apology*, New York: Cambridge University Press, 2009.

[8] Human rights and Equal Opportunity Commission, *Bring them Home; The Report of the National Inquiry Into Aboriginal and Torres Strait Islander Children From their Families*. Sydney: AGPS, 1997. Available at http://www.humanrights.gov.au/social_justice/bth_report/report/index.html

[9] Specifically, recommendations 5 and 6 provided that recommended that all Australian parliaments, as well as police forces and the churches and other non-Government organizations that played a role in removal, should officially acknowledge responsibility of their predecessors, and that they should negotiate an appropriate form of words for public apologies to Indigenous individuals, families and communities.

[10] Commonwealth, *Parliamentary Debates*, House of Representatives, 26 August 1999, 9206-9207 (the Hon. John Howard, MP).

[11] Equally interesting was the response of the President of the Federation of Ethnic Communities Councils, who issued a formal apology, adding that 'we are part of the current society and society is a continuum.' *The Sydney Morning Herald*, 'It Hurts Us, Unapologetic PM Admits,' 13 December 1997.

[12] The Senate Legal and Constitutional Committee, *HEALING: A Legacy of Generations, The Report of the Inquiry into the Federal Government's Implementation of the Recommendations Made by the Human Rights and Equal Opportunity Commission in Bringing Them Home* (Canberra, November 2000), 115. Available online at http://www.aph.gov.au/SENATE/COMMITTEE/legcon_ctte/completed_inquiries/199902/stolen/report/contents.htm , p. 12

[13] In a letter to *The Australian* written in response to an editorial criticizing the apology on precisely this point Sir Ronald Wilson wrote: 'I hope that

your readers will not understand the plea for an apology that comes the Stolen Children Report to be a plea for that kind of apology.' *The Australian*, 10 November 1997. One might ask whether the fact that Wilson had himself been involved with Sister Kate's, one of the religious institutions that held removed children, did not colour his views on responsibility.

[14] Drusilla Modjeska, 'A Bitter Wind Beyond the Treeline,' address at the 1997 NSW Premier's Literary Awards, excerpt published in *The Sydney Morning Herald*, 18 September 1997.

[15] Robert Manne,'Forget the Guilt, Remember the Shame.' *The Australian*, 8 July, 1996.

[16] On Rudd's apology and the popular response, see Danielle Celermajer and Dirk Moses, 'Australian apology and global memory' in Aleida Assmann and Sebastian Conrad, eds., *Memory in a Global Age: Discourses, Practices, and Trajectories*, Routledge 2010.

[17] See however D Celermajer, *Sins of the Nation*, chapter 7.

[18] In the background is Durkheim's concept of the collective conscience and his attempt to articulate social facts in a manner that mediates between external influence and subjective agency. See the preface to the Second Edition of 1901 in Emile Durkheim, *The Rules of Sociological Method*, trans. W. D. Halls, New York: Free Press, 1982.

[19] This example comes under what Joel Feinberg calls 'contributory group fault, collective and distributive.' See Joel Feinberg, 'Collective Responsibility,' in *Doing and Deserving: Essays in the Theory of Responsibility*, Princeton: Princeton University Press, 1970, 247.

[20] Larry May, *Sharing Responsibility*, Chicago: University of Chicago, 1996, 46. May stresses that the attitudes relevant for a story about responsibility are not theoretical, or '*mere* thoughts,' but rather affective states in which people are moved to *act* in certain ways.

[21] Miller, 'Holding Nations responsible,' *Ethics*, 114 (January 2004), 240-268, at 253-254.

[22] Iris Marion Young, 'Responsibility and Global Labor Justice,' *Journal of Political Philosophy*, 12 (2004), 365-388. Young deals more squarely with distributive justice, although her attention to issues like sweat shop conditions entails consideration of wrongful acts.

[23]The full RCIADIC report is available on-line at www.austlii.edu.au/au/special/rsjproject/rsjlibrary/rciadic/

[24] See in particular Dallen, James. *The Reconciling Community: The Rite of Penance.* New York: Pueblo Publishing Company, 1986.

[25] The term 'Israel' does not refer to the modern state or land but to the Jewish people.

[26] Repentance can occur throughout the year, but the most important time of repentance is between *Rosh Hashanah*, or New Year, and *Yom Kippur*, or the Day of Atonement, which occurs ten days later.

[27] This shift is as much about a move to modernity's self-professed rationalism, as it is about a distinction from religion *per se,* as is evident if one thinks of the starkness of Lutheran churches and the elaborate ritual of certain secular political regimes. On the historical changes in performance in politics see Jurgen Habermas, *The Structural Transformation of the Public Sphere*, trans. Thomas Burger, MIT Press, Mass., 1991.

[28] Attributed to Rabbi Shimon bar Yochai, Vayikra Rabbah (Margaliot*)*, 4.

[29] This notion was beautifully expressed by the literary character of Sir Thomas More in *A Man for All Seasons*: 'And when the last law was down, and the Devil turned round on you, where would you hide...the laws all being flat? This country's planted thick with laws from coast to coast...and if you cut them down...d'you really think you could stand upright in the winds that would blow then?' Robert Bolt, *A Man for All Seasons*, Vintage Books, New York, 1960, p. 66.

[30] Gerhard Von Rad, *Old Testament Theology*, translated by D. M. G. Stalker, Harper, San Francisco, 1967, p.263.

[31] Karl Jaspers, *The Question of German Guilt*, Translated by E.B. Ashton, New York: Fordham University Press, 2001.

[32] Ibid., p. 34.

[33] Ibid., p. 118.

Bibliography

Arendt, H., '*Introduction I to Illuminations*, Walter Benjamin, New York: Schocken Books, 1969.

Barkan, E., and Karn A., (eds.), *Taking Wrongs Seriously: Apologies and Reconciliation,* Stanford University Press, Stanford, 2006.

Benjamin, W., *The Arcades Project,* trans. H. Eiland and K. McLaughlin, prepared on the basis of the German volume edited by Rolf Tiedemann, Belknap Press, Cambridge, Mass., 1999.

Bolt, R., *A Man for All Seasons,* Vintage Books, New York, 1960.

Celermajer, D., *Sins of the Nation and the Ritual of Apology*, Cambridge University Press, New York, 2009.

Celermajer, D., and Moses, D., 'Australian apology and global memory' in Assmann, A., and Conrad, S., eds., *Memory in a Global Age: Discourses, Practices, and Trajectories,* Routledge 2010.

Dallen, J., *The Reconciling Community: The Rite of Penance*, Pueblo Publishing Company, New York, 1986.

Durkheim, E., *The Rules of Sociological Method*, trans. Halls, W.D., Free Press, New York, 1982.

Feinberg, J., *Doing and Deserving: Essays in the Theory of Responsibility,* Princeton University Press, Princeton, 1970.

Gibney, M., Howard-Hassmann, R. E., Coicaud, J.-M., and Steiner N., (eds.), *The Age of Apology: Facing Up to the Past*, University of Pennsylvania Press, Philadelphia, 2008.

Habermas, J., *The Structural Transformation of the Public Sphere*, trans. Burger, T., MIT Press, Mass., 1991.

Holmes, S., *Passion and Constraint,* University of Chicago Press, Chicago, 1995.

Human rights and Equal Opportunity Commission, Bring them Home; The Report of the National Inquiry Into Aboriginal and Torres Strait Islander Children From their Families. AGPS, Sydney, 1997.

Jaspers, K., *The Question of German Guilt*. Translated by Ashton, E.B., Fordham University Press, New York, 2001.

Manne, R.,'Forget the Guilt, Remember the Shame.' *The Australian,* 8 July, 1996.

May, L., *Sharing Responsibility*, University of Chicago, Chicago, 1996.
McCulloch, M., Pargament, K. and Thoreson, C., *Forgiveness: Theory Research and Practice*, Guilford Press, New York, 2000.

Miller, D., 'Holding Nations responsible' *Ethics*, 114 (January 2004), 240-268.

Minnow, M., *Between Vengeance and Forgiveness: Facing History After Genocide and Mass Violence,* Beacon Press, Boston, 1998.

Modjeska, D., 'A Bitter Wind Beyond the Treeline,' address at the 1997 NSW Premier's Literary Awards, excerpt published in *The Sydney Morning Herald*, 18 September 1997.

Senate Legal and Constitutional Committee, HEALING: A Legacy of Generations, The Report of the Inquiry into the Federal Government's Implementation of the Recommendations Made by the Human Rights and Equal Opportunity Commission in Bringing Them Home (Canberra, November 2000), 115. Available online at http://www.aph.gov.au/SENATE/COMMITTEE/legcon_ctte/completed_inquiries/199902/stolen/report/contents.htm

Shriver, D., *An ethic For Enemies: Forgiveness in Politics*, Oxford University Press, New York, 1995.

Von Rad, G., *Old Testament Theology*, translated by D. M. G. Stalker, Harper, San Francisco, 1967.

Young, I. M., 'Responsibility and Global Labor Justice,' *Journal of Political Philosophy*, 12 (2004), 365-388.

Danielle Celermajer is currently the director of the Asia Pacific Masters of Human Rights and Democratisation, a European Union funded project establishing networked postgraduate human rights education across the Asia Pacific Region. Her primary areas of research are human rights and political theory. She has held teaching positions at the University of Sydney and Columbia University and received her Ph.D. in political theory (*summa cum laudae*) from Columbia University. Prior to entering academia, she was Director of Policy at the Australian Human Rights Commission, where she authored numerous reports on Indigenous human rights and was principal speechwriter to the Aboriginal and Torres Strait Islander Social Justice Commissioner. Her book, Sins of the Nation and the Ritual of Apology, was published by Cambridge University Press in 2009 and she is editor of a forthcoming collection on Hannah Arendt, Power, Judgment and Political Evil, to be published by Ashgate in 2010.

In Search of Forgiveness: Men and Abortion in Post-Catholic Ireland

Fergus Hogan

Abstract

Catholic Ireland, if not dead and gone, has changed dramatically in the last twenty-five years. Sin and guilt are words or ideas that are heard less and less as fewer and fewer attend the sacrament of confession. Forgiveness as a concept stills holds place though now more so in private relationships or in therapeutic and restorative justice contexts. This paper attempts to hold together three tangentially related concerns. It begins with an overview of the shifting sociological landscape of religion in modern Ireland. The secularisation of society and the privatisation of Irish people's religiosity is explored as a background for the second concern of the paper which explores the meaning that Irish people now attach to considerations such sin, guilt and forgiveness. The concluding section of the paper draws from my recent qualitative study of men's experiences of unplanned and crisis pregnancies[1]; specifically, eight men's stories of abortion experiences are shared in an exploration of how sin and guilt are carried differently and how the search and process of forgiveness is still important in modern times.

Key Words: Catholic Ireland, sin, guilt, forgiveness, men, abortion, confession, sacrament.

*****

Was it Blake I wondered who had said that the difference between Jesus and Socrates was that Jesus could say, your sins are forgiven you.
-   John Moriarty[2]

It is not in the literal past, the facts of history that shape us but images of the past embodied in language.
-   Brian Friel[3]

1.   Introduction: Towards a Post-Institutional Catholic Ireland

Traditionally, Irish society – often referred to as 'Catholic Ireland' – was understood as being held together by the Church through priests who controlled social order by way of their moral authority.[4] Personhood, in this Irish context was very definitely governed by strict adherence to Catholic dogma and teaching. To a large degree, an Irish person's subject, self and soul were a 'holy trinity' that co-emerged in growing up, unquestioningly following the teaching of the Catholic Church. To be born Irish meant in the vast majority of cases being born Catholic. To be a person of any standing was dependent on being a good Catholic; good Catholics not only lived by the rules of the church and were publicly seen to, but more so good Irish Catholics did not question the teachings of their church.[5] The past twenty-five years, however, have seen rapid changes in Irish society, evidenced in part through the liberalisation of social and family mores. Contraception, cohabitation, pregnancies and births outside marriage and homosexual relationships may all be read as evidence of the declining power and influence of the Catholic Church in Ireland and a growing liberalism of individual personhood. Parallel to these social changes has been the rapid change in the position of the Catholic Church in Ireland evidenced in part through the decreasing numbers of regular mass attendees or those who go to confession and the dramatic fall in vocations to the priesthood. While some attribute the crisis in vocations in the Catholic Irish Church to the recent clerical sexual abuse scandals, the crisis in vocations is reflected to different degrees globally[6] and may be better understood as being part of broader social movements from traditional religiosity towards modernism, individualism and secularism.[7]

Grace Davie, in her book *Europe: The Exceptional Case*, argues that patterns of 'secularisation' are different across Europe and the world and that how modernisation and religion interface in Europe is not a measure of similar patterns throughout the world.[8] Discussing the secularisation thesis in an Irish context shows that Ireland has traditionally been recognised as a country with exceptionally high religiosity.[9] The early 1990's, however, brought social change that may, according to the core secularisation thesis, dramatically change the levels of religiosity and secularism in Ireland – the crisis in the Catholic Church exemplified in child abuse and celibacy scandals[10] and the rapid economic developments and modernisation. Tony Fahey reviews figures from the European Values Survey to explore the specific position of Ireland (north and south) in relation to modern Irish attitudes and behaviour to religion and the secularisation theory:

> ...reported weekly church attendance was extraordinary high in the early 1970s, at over 90 per cent, and was still just above 80 per cent by 1990. Thenceforth, it began to shift consistently downwards, falling to below 60 per cent in 1999-2000 and to 50 per cent in 2003.[11]

However they clarify that 'the main movement, therefore was from very frequent to less frequent attendance rather than to no attendance at all,'[12] where in comparison to Europe weekly church attendance in the Republic is 'exceeded only by Malta and is matched only by Poland.'[13] Thus Fahey et al., conclude that the Irish experience of religion and modernism is not so much one of secularisation but, as Bellah puts it, one of 'privatisation of religious faith' [14] or, as Davie phrases it, 'believing without belonging.' [15]

The 'God Survey',[16] a recent survey carried out for the Irish Examiner, a National news paper, interviewed 1,000 adults and found as recently as last year that 84% of Irish adults still believed in God, 78% professed a belief in Heaven, and while 75% believed in Sin only 53% of the Irish believed in Hell.

With regard to attendance at Mass 45% of those surveyed said they went to mass weekly while only 4% said they went to mass daily. 11% said they went to mass monthly yet 30% said they go a few times each year.

Over three-quarters (78%) felt mass attendance should be a personal choice with no pressure put on children or individuals. The various reasons given for *not* going to church were: too time consuming (18%), irrelevant to my life (18%), lost faith with church (16%), don't believe in God/religion (9%), boring (8%), don't feel I need to go to church to pray or believe (6%), just don't go (6%), too busy (4%), lazy/ can't be bothered (3%), don't have the same beliefs (3%), refused to answer (4%), don't know (9%).

Thus the landscape of Catholic Ireland has changed dramatically. Ireland has moved from being a traditional Catholic country to now being one of private faith and individual, personal relationships with God(s). Yet given this post-Catholic institutional context individuals can and still do struggle to construct and ethical sense of personhood. Thus, the central question addressed in this paper – given the privatisation of individual faith, in the once strongly Catholic Ireland – is how or if Irish persons now manage their sense of sin, guilt and forgiveness in any post-Institutional Catholic way?

2.   Stories from Confessional Spaces

Given the traditional Catholic context, Irish people's sense of self, self-confidence to face the world and self-esteem were governed by strict adherence to the teachings of the Catholic Church. Fear of an external, all-powerful and punishing God was the locus of people's internal control and constraint.[17] Where fear of meeting one's maker on the day of judgement was carried as a constant guilt, shame drove Catholic Irish to confession where sins were scaled against a system of penitence.[18] Guilt, shame and sin were a central part of the Irish psyche. Confession, penance and mortification were the means of absolution. For Irish Catholics, self and soul were in a constant state of flux as people moved from the privatised space of confession and 'pure white Souls' back in to the public world, filled as it was, with temptation, occasion for sin and sullied Souls.

Like many, the Irish author Frank O'Connor remembers being 'scared to death of confession':

> Nora's turn came, and I heard the sound of something slamming, and then her voice as if butter wouldn't melt in her mouth, and then another slam, and out she came. God, the hypocrisy of women! Her eyes were lowered, her head was bowed, and her hands were joined very low down on her stomach, and she walked up the aisle to the side altar looking like a saint. You never saw such an exhibition of devotion; and I remembered the devilish malice with which she had tormented me all the way from our door [down to the church] and I wondered were all religious people like that, really. It was my turn now. With the fear of damnation in my soul I went in, and the confessional door closed itself behind me. It was pitch-dark and I couldn't see priest or anything else. Then I really began to be frightened. In the darkness it was a matter between God and me, and He had all the odds. He knew what my intentions were before I even started; I had no chance. All I had ever been told about confession got mixed up in my mind, and I knelt to one wall and said: 'Bless me father, for I have sinned; this is my first confession.' I waited for a few minutes, but nothing happened, so I tried it on the other wall. Nothing happened there either. He had spotted me all right.[19]

3.   Sin, Guilt and Forgiveness

This story attempts to honour the childhood innocence and mystery of what happens to sin and guilt in confession to bring about forgiveness. Recognition of what Mary Anne Coate recognises as:

> The stupendous authority to forgive another's sins in the name of God – muted in Anglican practice, by a request by the priest for prayer in recognition that the person who absolves is also a sinner; the confidence and assurance that something objective has happened – sin has been put away, and the sinner can depart in peace; these are hallmarks of the church's ministry of forgiveness.[20]

For Coate, sin is, by definition, a religious and theological term. 'By itself it [sin] has no meaning. It needs the Other, the sense of God to give it meaning. So sin roots itself firmly within the theological story.'[21] The seven deadly sins comprise: pride, lust, avarice, anger, envy, sloth, and gluttony.

However, sin as a concept seems to have little modern currency, replaced by talk of ethics, laws and crimes. FMacE says:

> It is hard to speak about Pope Benedict's review of sin or of Christ dying for our sins in a climate that has little or no sense of sin. In church, and in the wider society, we seem to have descended into using the word to describe God's reaction to crimes. For the majority of us, murder is a crime and sin is not spoken of. Cheating on your spouse is not a crime, it is not against any state law, and so a lot of us can simply justify it or dismiss it as normal and commonplace. Mention that adultery is contrary to the teachings of the church and you are more likely to be met with scorn. And there are many who believe the church is hardly in a position to preach on moral issues.[22]

The fall from grace of the Catholic Church and the collapse of its moral monopoly can be read as foreshadowing the loss of ability to speak of sin in any public way. Sin as a reference point has become lost in the fluidity of post-modern Ireland. Yet a central question in this paper is how – given the shift away from external forces of control and judgement towards a more fluid and relative post-modern analysis of good and evil, sin and forgiveness – do Irish people now construct or make sense of and ascribe meaning to their inner sense of sin and guilt? What processes or rituals are available in the search for forgiveness and redemption?

Whether we reference God or Religion as sources of Belief and Faith many people recognise times when they feel burdened, weighed down, oppressed with a foreboding sense of wrongdoing associated with their behaviour; consequent, maybe of not showing love to another, or of not living up to a dignified effort to live a good life. It seems to be a human condition to 'get things off our chest', whether we see this as a religious or psychological need is open to debate while the burden of guilt seems something that most of us can nod towards knowing first hand.

In terms of Catholic Theology, Karl Rahner makes the point that the experience of Guilt too is evidence enough of God. Rahner defines guilt as the refusal, from the beginning of human history until now, to accept God's offer of self. For Rahner, guilt is not just a feeling of remorse about this or that sinful act; rather, at its foundation it is a rejection of God. Thus we can never fully extradite ourselves form the feeling of guilt, the guilty situation, of having refused God's gift of self. Thus he argues that without God we cannot even recognise guilt for what it is.[23]

While sin and guilt have lost parlance or the ability to be spoken of in the face of the fall of the church, forgiveness has, in modern times, gained much public attention. Public and political apologies from abuses in children's homes to peace and reconciliation processes all place forgiveness as the central process of moving on – forgiving and forgetting. Similarly, private pains and trauma within relationships, marriages, parenting and work colleagues all place pressures on the place of forgiveness as a modern way of being together.

Yet, forgiving is a complex process. According to Kurtz and Ketcham, forcing forgiveness only gets in the way of the process.[24] Forgiveness, for them, is Spiritual: it is one of the realities that cannot be willed into being. That is to say, the harder one tries to force forgiveness, the harder it becomes to reach. Or as the Irish Family Therapist Jim Sheehan puts it: 'Forgiveness becomes possible only when it is replaced by willingness; it results less from effort than from openness.'[25]

Paul Ricoeur also cautions against too summary a belief in the power of human agency with regard to the difficult task of forgiveness.[26] For Ricoeur, our difficulties with forgiveness arise from five key sources:

1.   Our difficulty at times to reconcile the past as really past, thus, leaving our present open to an ongoing haunting of the past.
2.   Victims, in making acceptable narratives of injuries received, forget certain more positive qualities of the other who has transgressed.
3.   Too strict a demand for justice tends to inhibit forgiveness.
4.   Forgiveness can seem forever deferred due to the fact that memories of historical violence and hatred last a long time.
5.   Forgiveness is most seriously challenged by the fact that some injuries are seen as unforgivable.

The track of forgiveness for Ricoeur is a journey from 'memory to forgetting to forgiving.'[27] In this journey of the healing through forgiveness the process of storytelling becomes central. How we narrate a story of self, from fracture to coherence, is the challenge. The resurrection of hope occurs when sin, which has fractured one's sense of self and is carried as the burden of guilt, is taken away at a time when a new story is told where a forgiven future is possible. Or as Ben Okri puts it:

> There are two essential joys in story-telling. The joy of the telling, which is to say of the artistic discovery. And the joy of the listening, which is to say the imaginative identification. Both joys are magical and important. The first involves exploration and suffering and love. The second involves silence and openness and thought. The first

is the joy of giving. The second is the joy of receiving...of the two joys, the first teaches us humility, while the second deepens our humanity.[28]

Likewise, Derrida sees the concept of forgiveness as needing to be rescued from all attempts to rush closure in order to keep open to the spiritual, divine and mysterious character of genuine forgiveness.[29] Derrida sees forgiveness as being present only in the company of the unforgivable; 'there is only forgiveness, if there is any, where there is the unforgivable.'[30] Rather than being a conscious will, forced as it were, forgiveness, for Derrida, happens, 'it should exceed the order of presence...and happen in the night. The night is its element.'[31] In this regard, forgiveness is something that creeps up upon someone, when their conscious thought is taking a rest. To that degree, forgiveness of our selves or others comes as grace, when, as Paul Tillich would have it, we are accepted:

> Grace strikes us when we are in great pain and restlessness. It strikes us when we walk through the dark valley of a meaningless and empty life. It strikes us when we feel that our separation is deeper than usual, because we have violated another life, a life that we loved, or from which we were estranged. It strikes us when our disgust for our own being, our indifference, our weakness, our hostility and our lack of direction and composure has become intolerable to us. It strikes us when, year after year, the longed-for perfection of life does not appear, when the old compulsions reign within us as they have for decades, when despair destroys all joy and courage. Sometimes at that moment a wave breaks into our darkness, and it is as though a voice were saying: 'you are accepted. You are accepted, accepted by that which is greater than you, and the name of which you do not know. Do not try to do anything now; perhaps later you will do much. Do not seek for anything; do not perform anything; do not intend anything. Simply accept the fact that you are accepted!' If that happens to us, we experience grace. After such an experience we may not be better than before, and we may not believe more than before. But everything is transformed. In that moment, grace conquers sin, and reconciliation bridges the gulf of estrangement. And nothing is demanded of this experience, no religious or moral or intellectual presupposition, nothing but acceptance.[32]

4.   Fracture and Forgiveness: Some Men's Stories of Abortion

Sin and Guilt are concepts deeply rooted in the biblical stories. Since the book of Genesis and the fall from grace, the eating of the apple and Adam's temptation by Eve, sin in a religious sense has become synonymous with sins of the flesh and sex. Made in the likeness of God man can almost experience himself as a god in the creation of life through the act of sex.

The point is that sin for so long has been associated with sins of the flesh, and the guilt associated with enjoyment of sex. Tom Inglis the leading Irish sociologist of religion and sexuality has argued that:

> for generations [the Irish] were devoted to the Catholic Church. This devotion revolved around practices of self-denial and self sacrifice particularly in relation to pleasures and desires, especially in relation to sex.[33]

Sex and sexuality are, therefore, key markers in the decline of Institutional Catholic influence in the personal lives of people. Thus an analysis of changes at the micro level of individual intimacy and sexuality can be considered to be reflective, in some broader ways, of shifts in macro social influences, including a decline in influence and control of the Catholic Church. In choosing to reflect on changing patterns of sexual attitudes and practices in this proposed post-catholic institutional Ireland, this paper draws on an analysis and re-reading of some qualitative, in-depth interviews with eight Irish men of various ages who had experience of abortion.

As part of a larger scale qualitative study of 45 Irish men's experiences of sex, sexuality, unplanned and crisis pregnancies Harry Ferguson and I interviewed eight men, who had experienced ten abortions (two men had gone through two abortions each).[34] The men in this study were self selecting in that they responded to a newspaper article in a national paper asking for men with experiences of abortion to come forward to be part of the study. The length of time between the abortion experience and the research interview ranged from six months to 34 years. In six of the eight men's experiences, the abortion happened with the man's knowledge and some kind of involvement in the decision. Two men were told about the abortion after the fact. Thus six of the men felt they had at least some involvement in the decision to terminate the pregnancy. This varied from men who felt consulted but essentially 'blocked' out by the woman who had already decided to have the abortion, to those who felt intensely involved in negotiations with the woman.

For one man, however, his sin and guilt were, he believed, un-forgivable – the negative effect of the abortion on his life had not 'faded,' even after 34 years. A 57-year-old man, here called Joseph, felt that his experience of an abortion had had such an impact that it had ruined his life.

His girlfriend travelled to England 34 years ago when he 'made her pregnant outside of wedlock.' The context was one where dating meant going to a dance at the age of 18: 'you'd meet someone you liked and you would talk with them for an hour or two and then say goodnight, the most you would do is give them a kiss goodnight.' He felt he acquired the facts of life as a teenager from growing up on a farm, and understood what his father meant when he would tell him 'not to interfere with a girl.'

Part of the 'sadness of it all' for him was that he made his girlfriend pregnant after having what he called 'half sex,' the first time ever they 'fooled around.' Then, after three or four weeks she told him she was pregnant.

> At first all I wanted to do was to run away with her so we could keep the baby. I had seen other girls disappear to Dublin or London and they just never came back. We wanted to keep the baby but we couldn't we weren't married and I couldn't just run away and leave the farm and my [elderly] parents, I was the only son.[35]

With respect to decision-making about the abortion, he remembered that 'they sort of decided together, but she did really.' His girlfriend told her friend in Dublin, who helped her to arrange her trip to England for the abortion. Joseph spoke with or told no one at the time. He met her on the day of her return from the abortion and they announced their engagement. They were married later that year, but did not sleep together on the first night of their marriage:

> We both knew we done wrong, that what we had done was a sin, so on our wedding night we didn't do it [make love] as a way of punishing ourselves....
> ...I'm not proud of myself, I know I did wrong, what I did was a sin and I'm ashamed of myself for having done it first [getting her pregnant] and then for the abortion too.[36]

During the first three years of their marriage, his wife had a number of miscarriages that they both felt were as a result of the abortion, the first in a long line of ailments, 'our punishment for what we had done.' Throughout his marriage he has refused to talk about the abortion, even with his wife. During this time his physical health has rapidly declined. Yet he refused to seek medical attention, believing that he had cancer and that he deserved to die. The combination of not talking with his wife, not caring for his health and, consequently, not being able to play a part in the care of his three young children meant that their relationship became poor. He remembered refusing to do anything with their first child, believing that he himself would soon be dead. Regarding his and his wife's responsibility for the abortion, he feared their children would be 'cursed for their sin.'

Joseph and his wife went to confession, to the same priest, who was really very hard on his wife, but not too hard on him at all. Not talking together has remained a difficulty in their relationship. They have not had any sexual intimacy in seven years, sleeping in different parts of the house. The farm in fact has served to keep them together, needing both of them to work it at times when the other was sick.

His wife has been going to counsellors about the abortion for the past two years. He went with her twice, but has refused to go since. His wife always asks him to talk about how he feels, but he refuses to engage because he does not want to upset her; he feels it is best if they do not mention the abortion at all. It is because he does not like to upset her that when she asked him to come for the research interview (which she heard about in the media) he agreed. He also wondered if it might help some other man in the same circumstances, but he could not see how as he felt another man in the circumstances would never read a book about abortions.

> It does no good for me whatsoever talking about it; it won't take it away will it? And when [wife's name] wants to talk about it I don't coz it will only hurt her feelings reminding her of it, so I keeps it to myself...Usually I just think about the abortion two or three times a day.[37]

When asked, Joseph said he did not find anything easy or helpful about the research interview (which was in contrast to the majority of men in the study). His advice to others was 'do not have an abortion.'

Roy was 35 at the time of the interview and recounted his abortion experience from ten years ago. It was the third 'serious' sexual relationship he had since his first experience of sexual intercourse at 19. He could remember the exact date when the abortion occurred and what he was doing and feeling at the time. He believed it was the right decision at a difficult time, but he left Ireland soon after to get away from the 'traditional conservative culture.'

> I mean we talk about how compassionate we are in this country but Jesus I don't think we are, we're not very compassionate at all. The very reason that there is a stigma associated with unwanted pregnancies is testament to the fact that there is a lack of tolerance of, a lack of compassion in society. There was a big difference between carrying it [the experience of an abortion] in Ireland and

carrying it abroad, do you know, because you don't have,
you're not subjected to the Ann Lovett interview [on the
radio] or the, the abortion referendum, or the referenda in
the media and the hysteria surrounding it and the right to
life campaigns and all this kind of thing, because if you
work abroad there's not this type of hysteria surrounding
the whole situation, there is a very mature, reasoned, frank
discussion in different countries in Europe, for example,
you know, very compassionate...[38]

For some of the men, their guilt and shame over the abortion were
directly related by them to internalisation of Catholic social teaching on sin
and sexuality and what they perceived to be a judgmental society. It took Roy
seven more years before he reached some sort of 'forgiveness' for himself,
when, by chance, he found himself outside a priest's confession box.

Ah sure look, I mean the thing about it is, I know for
somebody who hasn't talked about it I probably seem well
able to talk about it now, I'm well able to talk about it
because I don't, I don't feel the shame or the guilt
associated with it, it's taken a long number of years to cope
with that and it's taken an awful lot of growing up. I mean
one of the legacies, I haven't gone out with, I haven't had a
sexual relationship with anybody since that girl, for
example...

...Would you believe it, I did confess it at confession with a
great priest actually, a very nice priest I had no intention of
going up [for confession] but for some reason I just said,
feck it. I mean it wasn't a case of you know, confessing and
asking the priest or God for forgiveness, you know, it
wasn't a case of that, I actually said to him, you know, and
this was only two or three years ago... I said, this happened
you know, six, seven odd years ago and I said, the only
reason I'm here is that I've just realised sitting down in the
seat that it may be time to forgive myself, do you know, for
what happened...[39]

Nigel was a younger man, but like the other men in this study of
Irish men's experiences of sexuality and crisis pregnancy he had also grown
up influenced by the *habitus* of Catholic Ireland. Like many Irish men of his
age he had served as an altar boy and sung in the folk group at mass. Though

like so many of the younger men in our study he felt no obligation to live by the stricter rules of the Catholic Church. He practiced sex outside of marriage and in general used contraception, however, he too had experienced a number of pregnancy scares and two unplanned pregnancies that both resulted in an abortion.

Nigel's narrative referenced the Catholic Church and the traditional container of ritual forgiveness that confession was in Ireland it also foreshadowed the emerging new narratives of individual and private spirituality and his ongoing search for self-forgiveness. He explained in some detail the synchronicity of his spirituality and self-forgiveness:

> I wouldn't say I was overly religious or anything, but I did have a sense of spirituality. Then one time, it was probably a couple of years after [the abortion], one November, I was saying to myself I have to make some sort of recognition or something even if it's my own personal, because certainly you don't get it from the established, say religious context, so you kind of make your own personal or I made my own personal decision to make my peace or, in some way with God. I found myself going up to the local church where I had grown up in, where I'd played the guitar and sang in and when I went up, you're not going to believe this, I went up and hadn't got a clue hadn't been up there at all and I went up on a Wednesday night, in the middle of the week, half seven mass or whatever, stayed there for the mass and the end the priest turned around and went 'as well as that I'd like to remind you for those that are interested after this mass, there'll a ceremony for children who died within the womb.' I hadn't shared it with anybody, I was still alone in that sense like, and on that particular night I had made a decision because I thought it was the anniversary. I remember shaking like a leaf going, oh my God, so I walked outside and I had a cigarette and I decided to go back in...
>
> ...They had started the ceremony for children who died in the womb and I mean there was a few there and they all had their own different stories whether it was still births or you know, and then there was a ceremony where they'd sign a book and light a candle. Now I was, part of me was there going, ok, but if I even attempted to stand up my legs were shaking like a leaf and I didn't, I didn't take it any

further I just stayed in my seat. And, that was, a watershed moment...

... about two and a half years ago I did have a point where I went, right, I took it a step further and got in touch with, my local parish priest, and went through some sort of a confession aspect of it with him. I don't know how much I got out of, and as far as, with the current kind of, say religious kind of Catholicism in Ireland and what's going on ...

...So I went up to see a parish priest and went through a confession, or what's the word, I'm actually a musician as well, so I went up on, I think it was Easter a couple of years ago, and I did a few songs for one of the ceremonies kind of, and again maybe that's, that's part of the spiritual kind of side of me. I'll always have moments of spirituality it's kind of the great unknown you know...

...I don't know. I don't know, I don't know how to, I don't really know if I can sum up...I don't think you can sum up, you can never sum up. You only get stories, you only get pieces of stories...

5.   Conclusion: Towards a Sacramental Forgiveness
A life is mostly remembered in bursts of short stories
Beautifully interwoven with people, places, and events
A word, a picture, a smell can set it all in motion
And you can close your eyes and see it clearly
As if it happened only yesterday
-      Robert Trammell[40]

For many, forgiveness is a grace and a sacrament. The Irish Mystic John Moriarty (1938-2007)[41] remembers having the good grace to fall back into the sacraments:

During the previous few years I would often be aware of a big but inert sense of sin having its source in the permissively practical attitude I had to abortion earlier in my life. More than once there were times of anxious waiting with one or another of my girlfriends. In the event of conception I would at the very least have suggested a journey to London... All of this I confessed to Fr Norbert, he sitting at his table with only a crucifix on it, I sitting slightly sideways towards him. As I talked, he listened to me as I had never before been listened to, I was aware and he was that we were disposed to each other in the way that we were not just within a cell but within a sacrament. I sensed that already there was healing in his sacramental listening... Quietly, he told me I had made a good confession and then, raising his right hand, he turned towards the crucifix on his table and said, 'In virtue of the power invested in me at my ordination I absolve you of your sin.' Then, turning towards me, he made the sign of the cross upon me saying, 'In the name of the Father, Son and Holy Spirit. Go in peace.' I did go in peace, closing his cell door with as much monastic quiet as he himself would, behind me... Had it been to a psychiatrist or analyst or counsellor or therapist of some sort or other I had gone they would very likely have helped me but the thing I would have most wanted them to do for me they couldn't have done for me, they couldn't have absolved me.[42]

Sin, Guilt and Shame seem to punctuate and fracture our previous narratives of self; we seem to carry the burden in our bodies and on our lands. The search for self forgiveness and reconciliation seem to strive to re-order the narrative and story we tell of ourselves and to others. Ireland seems to be facing a tipping point in turning away from organised religion towards a private, individualised spirituality and relationship with God or gods. The need for a ritual container that holds together the fractured strands of our stories seems to remain a necessary space, sacred and forgiving in the face of a harsh and judgemental world.

Notes

[1] H Ferguson, & F Hogan, *Men, Sex and Crisis Pregnancy: A Qualitative Study*. Dublin, Crisis Pregnancy Agency, Department of Health and Children., 2007
[2] J Moriarty, *Serious Sounds,* Dublin, The Lilliput Press, 2007
[3] B Friel, Translations, London and Boston, Faber and Faber, 1981, p. 66
[4] T Inglis, *Moral Monopoly*, Dublin, UCD Press, 1998
[5] Ibid.,
[6] D Hoge, *The Current State of the Priesthood: Sociological Research.* Boston College, 2005

[7] See P Berger, *The Desecularization of the World: Resurgent Religion and World Politics.*, Grand Rapids MI, Eerdmans Publishing Co, 1999

[8] G Davie, *Europe: The Exceptional Case, Parameters of Faith in the Modern World*, London, Darton, Longman and Todd Ltd., 2002

[9] See M Fogarty, *Irish Values and Attitudes. Report on the European Values Study.*, Dublin, Dominican Publications, 1984 and Hornsby –Smith, M.P. and Whelan, C.T., 'Religion and Moral Values', in *Values and Social Change in Ireland*, Whelan, C. T. (ed), Dublin, Gill and MacMillan, 1994

[10] L Fuller, *Irish Catholicism since 1950. The Undoing of a Culture.*, Dublin, Gill and MacMillan, 2002

[11] T Fahey, B C Hayes, & R Sinnott, *Conflict and Consensus: A Study of Values and Attitudes in the Republic of Ireland and Northern Ireland*, Dublin, Institute of Public Administration., 2005, p. 41

[12] Ibid., p. 43

[13] Ibid., p. 45

[14] R N Bellah, *The Broken Covenant*, Chicago, University of Chicago Press, 1975

[15] G Davie, 'State of the Field: Christianity Moving into The Future', 2004, pp. 217-223

[16] 'God Survey' RedC Poll for *Irish Examiner,* 20 March, 2008

[17] R Kearney, *Strangers, Gods and Monsters*, London, Routledge, 2003

[18] T Inglis, *Moral Monopoly*, Dublin, UCD Press, 1998

[19] F O'Connor, 'First Confession' in O'Connor, F, *My Oedipus Complex and Other Stories*, London, Penguin Books, 1963, pp. 46-47

[20] M A Coate, *Sin, Guilt and Forgiveness: The Hidden Dimensions of a Pastoral Process*, London, SPCK, 1994, p. 22

[21] Ibid., p. 30

[22] FMacE, *Irish Times*, 5th April 2008

[23] M F Fisher, *The Foundations of Karl Rahner,* US, Crossroad Pub, Co, 2005

[24] E Kurtz and K Ketcham, *The Spirituality of Imperfection: Story Telling and the Journey to Wholeness.* Nashville, TN, Abingdon, 1992

[25] J Sheehan, 'Forgiveness and the unforgivable: the resurrection of hope in family therapy', in *Hope and Despair in Narrative and Family Therapy: Adversity, Forgiveness and Reconciliation*, Flaskas, C., McCarthy, I., and Sheehan, J (eds), London and New York, Routledge, 2007, p.163

[26] P Ricoeur, 'Can forgiveness heal?, in *The Foundation and Application of Moral Philosophy: Ricoeur's Ethical Order*, Opedbeeeck, H.J, (ed), Louvain, Peeters, 2000

[27] Ibid., p33

[28] B Okri, *A Way of Being Free*, London, Phoenix, 1997, p.48

[29] J Derrida, *On Cosmopolitanism and Forgiveness*, trans. Dooley, M and Hughes, M. London, Routledge, 2002

[30] Ibid., p. 32

[31] J Derrida, 'On Forgiveness: A Roundtable Discussion with Jacques Derrida', in *Questioning God*, Caputo, J.D. and Scanlon, M.J, (eds), Bloomington, Indiana University Press, 2001, p.53

[32] P Tillich, 'You Are Accepted', cited in, Moore, T, (ed), *The Education of the Heart*, Australia and New Zealand, A Hodder and Stoughton Book, 1996, p. 254

[33] T Inglis, *Global Ireland*. New York and London, Routledge, 2008, p. 156

[34] H Ferguson, & F Hogan, *Men, Sex and Crisis Pregnancy: A Qualitative Study*. Dublin, Crisis Pregnancy Agency, Department of Health and Children., 2007

[35] Ibid., p.100

[36] Ibid., p.100

[37] Ibid., p.101

[38] Ibid., p.98

[39] Ibid., p.99

[40] R Trammell, 'Dreaming', cited in Moore, T, *A Life at Work: The Joy of Discovering What You Were Born to Do*, London, Piatkus Books, 2008, p. 135

[41] www.johnmoriarty.info

[42] J Moriarty, *Serious Sounds,* Dublin, The Lilliput Press, 2007, pp. 19-22

Bibliography

Bellah, R. N., *The Broken Covenant*. University of Chicago Press, Chicago, 1975.

Berger, P., *The Desecularization of the World: Resurgent Religion and World Politics*. Grand Rapids MI, Eerdmans Publishing Co., Grand Rapids, 1999.

Coate, M.A, *Sin, Guilt and Forgiveness: The Hidden Dimensions of a Pastoral Process*. SPCK, London, 1994.

Davie, G., *Europe: The Exceptional Case, Parameters of Faith in the Modern World*. Darton, Longman and Todd Ltd, London, 2002.

———, 'State of the Field: Christianity Moving into The Future'. 217-223, 2004.

Derrida, J., *On Cosmopolitanism and Forgiveness* trans. Dooley, M and Hughes, M., Routledge, London, 2002.

———, 'On Forgiveness: A Roundtable Discussion with Jacques Derrida', in *Questioning God*. Caputo, J.D., and Scanlon, M.J., (eds), Indiana University Press, Bloomington, 2001.

Fahey, T., Hayes, B. C. & Sinnott, R., *Conflict and Consensus: A Study of Values and Attitudes in the Republic of Ireland and Northern Ireland.* Institute of Public Administration, Dublin, 2005.

Ferguson, H. & Hogan, F., *Men, Sex and Crisis Pregnancy: A Qualitative Study.* Crisis Pregnancy Agency, Department of Health and Children, Dublin, 2007.

Fisher, M.F., *The Foundations of Karl Rahner*. US, Crossroad Pub, Co, 2005.

Flaskas, C., McCarthy, I., and Sheehan, J (eds), *Hope and Despair in Narrative and Family Therapy: Adversity, Forgiveness and Reconciliation.* Routledge, London and New York, 2007.

FMacE, Irish Times 5th April 2008.

Fogarty, M., *Irish Values and Attitudes. Report on the European Values Study.* Dominican Publications, Dublin, 1984.

Friel, B., *Translations*. Faber & Faber, London and Boston, 1981.

Fuller, L., *Irish Catholicism since 1950. The Undoing of a Culture.* Gill and MacMillan, Dublin, 2002.

'God Survey' RedC Poll for *Irish Examiner*. 20 March, 2008.

Hoge, D., *The Current State of the Priesthood: Sociological Research.* Boston College, 1995.

Hornsby –Smith, M.P. and Whelan, C.T., 'Religion and Moral Values' in Whelan, C. T. (Ed.) *Values and Social Change in Ireland*. Gill and MacMillan, Dublin, 1994.

Inglis, T., *Moral Monopoly*. UCD Press, Dublin, 1998.

——, *Global Ireland*. New York and London, Routledge, 2008.

Kearney, R., *Strangers, Gods and Monsters*. London, Routledge, 2003.

Kurtz, E., and Ketcham, K., *The Spirituality of Imperfection: Story Telling and the Journey to Wholeness*. Nashville, TN, Abingdon, 1992.

Moore, T., *A Life at Work: The Joy of Discovering What You Were Born to Do*. London, Piatkus Books, 2008.

——, (ed), *The Education of the Heart*. Australia and New Zealand, A Hodder and Stoughton Book, 1996.

Moriarty, J., *Serious Sounds*. Dublin, The Lilliput Press, 2007

O'Connor, F., 'First Confession' in O'Connor, F., *My Oedipus Complex and Other Stories*. London, Penguin Books, 1963.

Okri, B., *A Way of Being Free*. London, Phoenix, 1997.

Ricoeur, P., 'Can Forgiveness Heal?' in *The Foundation and Application of Moral Philosophy: Riccour's Ethical Order*. Opedbeeeck, H.J, (ed), Louvain, Peeters, 2000.

Sheehan, J., 'Forgiveness and the Unforgivable: The Resurrection of Hope in Family Therapy', in *Hope and Despair in Narrative and Family Therapy: Adversity, Forgiveness and Reconciliation*. Flaskas, C., McCarthy, I., and Sheehan, J (eds), London and New York, Routledge, 2007.

Tillich, P., 'You Are Accepted' in Moore, T., (ed), *The Education of the Heart*. Australia and New Zealand, A Hodder and Stoughton Book, 1996.

Trammell, R., 'Dreaming', in Moore, T., *A Life at Work: The Joy of Discovering What You Were Born to Do*. London, Piatkus Books, 2008.

Fergus Hogan is co-ordinator of the Centre for Social and Family Research Waterford Institute of Technology. He is a qualified social worker and family therapist. His research interests include the study of families, men's lives, masculinities and fatherhood. His recently published research projects include: *Re-integration – Life after prison* (Irish Prison Service, Department of Justice, 2008, with Jonathan Culleton); *Men, Sexuality and Crisis*

Pregnancy (Crisis Pregnancy Agency, Department of Health and Children, 2007) and *Strengthening Families through Fathers* (Family Support Agency, Department of Social, Community and Family Affairs, 2004) (both with Professor Harry Ferguson); and, *Listening to Children: Children's Stories of Domestic Violence* (Office of the Minister for Children, Department of Health and Children, 2007, with Máire O'Reilly) (see, www.wit.ie/csfr). He serves on the editorial board of the International Sage Journal, *Men and Masculinities* and the *Irish Journal of Applied Social Studies*. He has been appointed to the International Associate board of Men and Masculinities Research Centre at Bradford University, UK.

PART IV

Narratives of Forgiveness

Reconciling Irreconcilable Differences Through Forgiveness

Carla S. Ross

Abstract

Miscommunication is often listed as one of the top three reasons for separation and divorce and 'irreconcilable differences' in marriage. As an interpersonal communication scholar, I study how the skills of listening, creating empathy, and conflict management and resolution strategies can help troubled couples maintain relational satisfaction and longevity. While most marriage therapy is dedicated to teaching active listening skills and conflict resolution skills to marriage partners, Gottman reports that the national results of marital therapy indicate a relapse rate of 30 to 50 percent and do ot benefit the majority of couples.[1] It appears that even armed with good communication skills, many couples cannot resolve their differences. Brehm distinguishes the difference between a skill deficit and a performance deficit.[2] For instance, a person can know how to communicate clearly but not choose to do so with a particular partner. In this case, it is a performance issue rather than a skill issue. So, even armed with good listening or conflict management skills, some couples refuse to engage in them that indicates an internal barrier. One such barrier may be the ability and/or willingness to forgive. This is an exploratory study of three couples that have married, divorced, and remarried the same partner. Participants completed a demographic questionnaire, the 60-item Enright Forgiveness Inventory (EFI) and the Spanier Dyadic Adjustment Scale (DAS) and answered several open ended questions about how they define marital satisfaction and forgiveness, what their motivations to forgive were, and how they navigated the forgiveness process. These initial results indicate that forgiveness is a primary factor that indicates high marital satisfaction and differentiates couples who choose to reconcile following separation or divorce and those who do not reconcile.

Key Words: Marital forgiveness, marital reconciliation, marital Satisfaction, marital communication skills.

*****

Forgiveness is love practiced among people who love poorly.'
Henri Nouwen [3]

It is unfortunate that we often hurt the ones we love the most. It is the nature of intimacy, self disclosure, and conflict that we can't experience deep intimacy without also experiencing deep vulnerability. When interpersonal conflict occurs, it elicits many strong negative emotions, such as betrayal and disappointment that have a high potential of disrupting any relationship. Nowhere is this truer than in marital relationships. Ongoing United States statistics of divorce maintaining a 50% - 67% rate bear this out.[4] In addition, couples who separate face a daunting 75% probability of divorcing.[5] Approximately only 10 % of married couples in the U.S. have separated and reconciled.[6] And sadly, the divorce rate for second marriages is about 10% higher than for first marriages and 20% higher for 3rd marriage attempts.[7]

Miscommunication is often listed as one of the top three reasons for claiming 'irreconcilable differences' when filing for separation or divorce. Learning the skills of listening, creating empathy, and conflict management and resolution strategies can help troubled couples maintain relational satisfaction and longevity. Gottman, a prolific scholar who has studied marital communication for 30 years, can watch and listen to a couple interacting for 5 minutes and determine with 91% accuracy whether the couple will stay together or divorce one another.[8] While most marriage therapy is dedicated to teaching active listening and conflict resolution skills to marriage partners, Gottman reports that the national results of marital therapy indicate a relapse rate of 30 to 50 % and do not benefit the majority of couples.   It appears that even armed with good communication skills; many couples cannot resolve their differences.

Brehm distinguishes the difference between a skill deficit and a performance deficit.[9] For instance, a person can know how to communicate clearly but not choose to do so with a particular partner. In this case, it is a performance issue rather than a skill issue. So, even armed with good listening or conflict management skills, some couples refuse to engage in them that indicates an internal barrier. One such barrier may be the ability and/or willingness to forgive. Spouses have reported that seeking and granting forgiveness is one of the most important characteristics for marital longevity and satisfaction.[10] In addition, Worthington and Wade suggest that forgiveness has significant implications for marriage conflict resolution and marital longevity.[11] And finally, Worthington and DiBlasio found that forgiveness can restore broken relationships.[12]

The purpose of this exploratory study is to examine whether couples that consider themselves to be highly satisfied in their marriage also rate high in forgiveness. The intention of this study is to find appropriate couples who can speak to the necessity and success of forgiving in marital relationships, as well as provide subjective information about couple partner's definitions, motivations, and processes of forgiveness.

1.   Review of the Literature

Happy marriages are often measured by how satisfied each partner feels in the relationship, which is based on how well each partner perceives that their needs are being met. Marital dissatisfaction is often related to the negative experiences that come from couples that do not handle conflict satisfactorily. Factors such as: ability to give and receive positive support, use of blame, and anger and rejection in conflict resolution were found to be influences on marital satisfaction.[13] Injured partners have great difficulty putting the hurt aside and concentrating on problem solving skills. Often, when partners feel hurt, self-protective acts such as retaliatory or estrangement behaviours are more likely to occur, which further deteriorate the relationship.[14]

Husbands often cite that their marital satisfaction is linked to how their wives resolve conflict.[15] Unhappily married women say that their husbands are too withdrawn in conflict, while husbands say their wives are too conflict engaging.[16] Gottman and Krokoff conducted two longitudinal studies of marital interaction and concluded that disagreements and anger exchanges that involve defensiveness, stubbornness, and withdrawal from interaction strongly correlate with the deterioration of happiness and satisfaction.[17]

For both husbands and wives, conflict resolution style becomes more influential as years pass in predicting marital satisfaction.[18] Factors such as the ability to give and receive positive support, the use of blame, and anger and rejection in conflict resolution were found to be influences on marital satisfaction.[19] Fincham, Beach, & Davila found that the level of satisfaction with the relationship for both marital partners was most affected by the ability to forgive one's spouse in times of conflict.[20] And interestingly, Fenell found that forgiveness was identified by husbands as an even more important characteristic of long term marriages than by wives.[21]

Scholarly definitions of forgiveness identify several different constructs involved in the process. Enright and Coyle defined forgiveness as inherently involving a consciousness by the spouse of having been intentionally or negligently injured or wronged by the other partner.[22] Without this consciousness of wrongdoing, there is nothing to forgive. In addition, the injured spouse has the understanding that he/she has a right to feel negatively toward his/her partner.[23]

Most forgiveness scholars (e.g., Enright & Coyle; Kaminer, Stein, Mbanga, & Zungu-Dirwayi; North) identify ' a lesser motivation to seek revenge' towards the transgressor as the core characteristic that distinguishes forgiveness from other constructs such as condoning (removing the offence) or reconciliation (the dyadic decision to restore a relationship).[24] McCullough, Rachel, Sandage, Worthington, Brown, & Hight take this one step further and identify decreased negative motivations as the basic factor in forgiveness.[25] In addition, some scholars find that 'an attitude of real goodwill towards the offender as a person' indicates the full process of forgiveness.[26]

Enright and Rique developed an operational and psychological definition of forgiveness to aid in the scientific inquiry of forgiveness that includes all of the aforementioned components: 'Forgiveness is a willingness to abandon one's right to resentment, negative judgment, and indifferent behaviour toward one who unjustly injured us, while fostering the undeserved qualities of compassion, generosity and even love toward him or her'.[27] And recently, communication scholars, Waldron and Kelley constructed their own definition in attempt to address the many complex constructs involved in interpersonal forgiving: 'Forgiveness is a relational process whereby harmful conduct is acknowledged by one or both partners; the harmed partner extends undeserved mercy to the perceived transgressor; one or both partners experience a transformation from negative to positive psychological states, and the meaning of the relationship is renegotiated, with the possibility of reconciliation'.[28]

Fenell conducted a study of 147 couples who had been married for 20 years or longer to determine the 10 most important characteristics that most aided long term satisfactory marriages.   Satisfied couples identified forgiveness as one of the factors that is most important for successful, long-term marriage.[29] McCullough, et.al. found that couples in romantic relationships who reported higher levels of forgiveness also reported higher levels of relational satisfaction with and commitment to the relationship.[30] In addition, according to McCullough, Worthington, and Rachel, when people in interpersonal relationships forgive, their motivation to avoid or seek revenge subsides and motivation toward benevolence and goodwill increase.[31]

In terms of communication, forgiveness would represent a willingness to stop potential cycles of negative interactions. For example, couples that engage in conflict avoidance or retaliation (the most damaging styles according to Gottman, McCullough, Worthington, & Rachel) would potentially benefit the most by overcoming unforgiveness.[32] Most marriages experience severe problems at some time in their marriage and if forgiveness is not available, the tension and guilt can damage the marriage beyond repair. However, if couples can discuss the issues and determine what it would take to forgive, they can move on to more productive discussions and strategies to improve their marriage.   In other words, forgiveness may stop ineffective conflict strategies that arise from unresolved anger, resentment and defensiveness and lead to more successful conflict resolution, and thus longer and more satisfying marriages. McCullough, et. al, concluded that forgiving takes place far more often in the context of happy, satisfied, and committed close relationships.   In addition, forgiveness is also highly associated with restored relational closeness after interpersonal transgressions.[33]

Based on the review of literature, forgiveness is shown to be a necessity for marriages to be satisfactory and to succeed long-term. For the purposes of this exploratory study, couples that have married, divorced, and remarried the same partner will be investigated to determine how they deal with forgiveness in their marriages. Based on the previous research findings and suggestions, this study will use survey responses and open-ended responses to test the following hypothesis: H1 – Couples who report higher levels of satisfaction also report a higher propensity for forgiveness.

2.   Method

The present exploratory study examines three heterosexual couples that have married, divorced, and remarried the same partner. These couples were considered 'experts' because of their previous experience of making the painful decision to end a marriage and then obviously finding the wherewithal that enabled them to reunite and remarry the same partner despite earlier grievances that tore them apart. Couples were recruited by word of mouth to fit the purpose of the study and were asked to participate in a study about communication in remarriages. All participants were Caucasian and reported a Christian religious affiliation. The wives ranged in age from 46 to 68 ($M = 56$) and the husbands from 48 to 71 ($M = 58.3$). Education ranged from 'some college' to masters degree. The mean age that the couples were first married was $M = 19.6$ for the wives and $M = 21.6$ for the husbands. The average number of years for the first marriages was 15.6 years and the average number of years of the second marriages was 10 years. The average number of years that all the couples were separated and divorced was 3 years. The average number of children between all couples was 2.66 and their ages ranged from 7 to 48 years old.

The major criteria being examined were levels of forgiveness and ratings of martial satisfaction. Participants first completed the 60-item Enright Forgiveness Inventory (EFI) which indicated a reliability ranging from .67 - .91 in previous samples.[34] The EFI uses 6-point Likert-type scales to measure both positive and negative affect, behaviour, and cognition toward the spouse. The EFI also contains a final single item that asks the individual to indicate to what extent he/she has forgiven the partner. A total score is obtained by computing a mean score for all 60 items. The higher the score in a range of 0 – 360 indicates the higher the level of forgiveness.

To measure quality of adjustment and satisfaction in marriage, the Spanier Dyadic Adjustment Scale (DAS) was administered next.[35] This more recently developed scale correlates highly (.86) with the standard scale developed by Locke-Wallace and has a reliability of .96.[36] Spanier used 11 items from the Locke and Wallace scale in the new DAS. The DAS includes 32-items that that are self-administered. The instrument has 4 subscales using 5-point Likert scales and a total global score. The four subscales measure dyadic satisfaction, cohesion, consensus, and affectional expression.

The higher the total global score on a range of 0 – 151 reflects a greater level of adjustment in marriage.

The participating couples were asked to answer their questionnaires individually and to not discuss responses until each partner completed the full survey. Each spouse then completed packets that contained the consent forms and the questionnaire measures described above and were instructed to individually answer several written open-ended questions about how they define marital satisfaction and forgiveness, what their motivations to forgive were, and how they navigated the forgiveness process.

3.   Results

The results from this study indicated that forgiveness is correlated with marital satisfaction. The mean scores for the DAS administered to the long-term satisfied marriage partners in Fenell's landmark study was 115 for wives and 116 for husbands out of the possible 151 points.[37] The corresponding overall average of dyadic adjustment in the couples of this pilot study was 117.6 for the wives and 111.6 for the husbands. However, one couple admitted to being 'a little unhappy' which brought the mean score down. In terms of the subscale of satisfaction specifically, the wives reported a score of 40.6 out of 50 points which reflects 81.3% of the possible score and husbands reported a score of 39.3 out of 50 points that reflects 78.6% of the possible score.

In terms of forgiveness, participants could reach the highest score of 360 points on the Enright Inventory. The higher the score, the higher the level of forgiveness. The mean score for both husbands and wives was 349 out of 360, which is an average of 96.9% of the possible score. This is an extraordinarily high forgiveness average, which may indicate that forgiveness is higher in couples who have reconciled. In addition, couples with the higher forgiveness score also reported higher levels of adjustment and satisfaction. While, a much larger population is needed to find and support these correlations, this appears to be a promising start.

Open ended questions that addressed couple's definitions of marital satisfaction, forgiveness, and motivations and processes of forgiving were also examined and provided some valuable subjective data. These responses will be examined in the next section.

4.   Discussion

Forgiveness may prove to be one of the most important elements in marital transactions because in the absence of forgiveness, the desire to resolve marital problems is lessened, destructive interactional processes are increased, and dissolving the relationship becomes a more likely outcome.

Perhaps the most revealing data from this study were the open-ended answers to questions about how and why these 'experienced' couples chose to forgive and reconcile. This information offers a more thorough understanding of the motives and processes couple's enact to promote forgiveness of partner transgressions that later enable reconciliation or make it more likely.

The participants were asked to briefly describe what happened when their partner hurt them and the transgression that led to the divorce. The answers ranged from an affair, to not feeling valued or loved by the partner, to being so overly controlled that they had to 'get away', to sexual addiction, to feeling unloved when self disclosing past sexual abuse, and to not giving the spouse a chance to help. More research conducted to examine the type of transgressions committed in broken marriages and identify if certain transgressions are more apt to be forgiven than others would be beneficial. Are there unforgivable or irreconcilable transgressions? Some former research has examined this and found that the 'most unforgivable transgressions' identified by married couples involved physical violence, drug abuse, and neglectful parenting.[38] Other research also shows that abuse has one of the lowest levels of forgiveness and reconciliation.[39]

Participants were also asked what makes them most satisfied with their marriage relationship. The wives said that respect, gladness to be together, ability to talk about deep issues, friendship and acceptance were most important to them. Husbands said the ability to know one another, the total family experience, communication, deep love and affection, fun and laughter, common philosophies about finances and children, and encouragement to become what they were meant to be were most important. Research should be continued to determine if satisfaction means different things to husbands and wives.

Participants were also asked how they would define forgiveness. The answers in the words of the participants were:

- Acceptance of our human frailties.
- Turning the negative loose – verbalizing it.
- Remembering that it is not a license to offend again, letting go of the incident so that you can be free to experience life as God intended it without bitterness or hatred.
- Once we forgive we don't hold anything over the other person's head. It frees us to love again.
- Not having anger or resentment towards others when thinking of a wrong that was done to me.
- The ability to accept 'I'm sorry' from your partner and go on to grow the relationship.

The motives that led to forgiveness were also investigated. Several participants said that 'love' and 'commitment' were the main motivators. In addition, belief in God and His forgiveness for both self and spouse was also mentioned numerous times. McCullough et. al., identified variables such as satisfaction, commitment and closeness as being high predictors of forgiveness of transgressions in interpersonal relationships.[40] These answers support their findings.

Each partner was also asked what processes they went through to forgive their spouse. Answers included identifying the emotions (anger and hurt) the transgression evoked, talking about what happened, why it happened, and what their needs were in resolving the occurrence, and letting it go. Also, multiple spouses mentioned realizing their part in the cause. Empathy, prayer, and taking the appropriate or proper time to process the transgression were also stated. This raises an interesting question about the length of the process of forgiveness and if it could differ significantly for partners based on type of transgression, and who the initial perpetrator was. Communication and talking was most mentioned. This answer is reminiscent of research by Fincham, Beach, and Davila who concluded that couples who learn better conflict resolution skills are more likely to forgive.[41]

The final question asked was, 'What changes took place that enabled you to remarry your spouse?' Some answers focused on how much they were loved by God and how He wanted good things for them. Other answers had to do with something the partner did and included communication, changing behaviours, and true heart repentance. However, most answers were self and relationally focused. The realization of the importance of their relationship over any issues was mentioned often:

> How important is the issue as compared to the value of our relationship? What is more important, the situation or the relationship? I realized that our relationship had more going for it, than against it. We grew to a place that our love for each other overcame our issues.

And importantly, self-knowledge and growth were also frequently mentioned:

- I grew up – gained more confidence. I learned that most of the pain had been caused by my 'reactions' rather than him.
- Realization of my role and many mistakes, changing my behaviours developing close friendships, serving in church, basically working on myself.

- I needed to understand that some of my past issues that were trigger issues between us were the hurt really came from (family of origin issues).
- We both learned about ourselves.

5.   Conclusion

The data and answers given by reconciled couples have wide implications in terms of directly and positively impacting current and future marriages.   The identified strategies could provide insight into ways to improve current marriages and provide training for couples contemplating marriage in preparing more adequately for a more satisfactory and long-term marriage.

Current counselling and reconciliation rates are abysmally low. Seventy-five percent of couples that separate file for divorce. Of those who receive counselling, 30-50% relapse into the same unhealthy patterns. Several studies have already identified forgiveness strategies in counselling and how they can aid clients in overcoming the control that past events have exerted over them and the tendency to project angry feelings onto partners in relationships,[42] and claim that forgiveness can assist in restoring broken relationships.[43] Wade, Bailey, and Shaffer found that 75% of clients in counselling indicated a desire to forgive their offender and to continue the relationship.[44]

Couples who have overcome major transgressions in marriage that initially tore them asunder and have found a way to reconcile and create highly satisfactory marriages have much to share with others. However, this is a difficult population to find. From an examination of census records and several state records, it appears that less than 6% of Americans have remarried the same partner. However, marriages are recorded differently in each state and while second and third marriages are tracked, remarriage to the same initial partner is often not identified. Further research with this population would be extremely valuable.

Education, support groups, workshops, etc. on what it means to forgive and how to truly 'let go' of resentments could be designed for couples contemplating marriage to improve their satisfaction, odds of success, and longevity. For marriages in distress, education about forgiveness could create more options and strategies for success than past experiences dictate and increase chances of reconciliation after transgressions. Forgiveness seminars also would be helpful for couples going through divorce to increase the odds that future marriages will be more healthy and satisfactory and enable divorced couples with children to forgive and promote healthier family dynamics. Healthier family dynamics will be perpetuated for generations.

Notes

[1]J M Gottman, *What predicts divorce?   The relationship between Marital processes and marital outcomes,* Hillsdale, NJ: Lawrence Erlbaum Associates, 1994.

[2]S S Brehm, *Intimate relationships*, (2nd Ed.), New York, NY: McGraw Hill, 1985.

[3]According to the Henri Nouwen Society, this quote was first published in a magazine entitled, *Weavings*. It was also quoted in the *Yaya Sisterhood*. A more accurate and fuller text of the quote is as follows: 'It is the greatest step a human being can take. It is the step of forgiveness. Forgiveness is the name of love practiced among people who love poorly. The hard truth is that all of us love poorly. We do not even know what we are doing when we hurt others.   We need to forgive and be forgiven every day, every hour -- unceasingly. That is the great work of love among the fellowship of the weak that is the human family.'

[4]A Cherlin, *Marriage, divorce, remarriage,* Cambridge, MA: Harvard University Press, 1981. T.C. Martin, & L. Bumpass, Recent trends in marital disruption. *Demography,* vol. 26, 1989, pp. 37-51.

[5]B Bloom, W.F. Hodges, R.A. Caldwell, L. Systra, & A.R. Cedrone,
Marital separation: A community survey. *Journal of Divorce,* vol. 1, 1977, pp. 7-19.

[6]Wineberg & McCarthy, Separation and reconciliation in American marriages. *Journal of Divorce and Remarriage,* vol. 29, 1993, pp. 131-146.

[7]P C Glick, How American families are changing. *American Demographics,* vol. 6, 1984, pp. 20-27.

[8]J M Gottman, *What predicts divorce?   The relationship between Marital processes and marital outcomes,* Hillsdale, NJ: Lawrence Erlbaum Associates, 1994.

[9]S S Brehm, *Intimate relationships*, (2nd Ed.), New York, NY: McGraw Hill, 1985.

[10]D Fenell, Characteristics of long-term first marriages. *Journal of Mental Health Counseling*, vol. 15, 1993, pp. 446-460.

[11]E L Worthington, Jr., & N G Wade, The psychology of unforgiveness and forgiveness and implications for clinical practice. *Journal of Social and Clinical Psychology,* vol. 18, 1999, pp. 385-418.

[12]E L Worthington, Jr., & F A DiBlasio, Promoting mutual forgiveness within the fractured relationship. *Psychotherapy,* vol. 27, 1990, pp. 219-223.

[13]L A Pasch, & T N Bradbury, Social support, conflict, and the development of marital dysfunction. *Journal of Consulting and Clinical Psychology,* vol. 66, 1998, pp. 219-230.

[14]M E McCullough, E L Worthington, & K C Rachel, Interpersonal forgiving in close relationship. *Journal of Personality and Social Psychology*, vol. 73, 1997, pp. 321-336.

[15]L A Kurdek, Predicting change in marital satisfaction from husbands' and wives' conflict resolution styles. *The Journal of Marriage and the Family*, vol. 57, Feb. 1995, pp. 153-164.

[16]H J Locke, *Predicting adjustment in marriage: A comparison of a divorced and a happily married group*, New York, NY: Henry Holt and Company, 1951. L M Terman, *Psychological factors in marital happiness*, New York, NY: McGraw-Hill, 1938. J M Gottman, and L J Krokoff, Marital interaction and satisfaction: A longitudinal view. *Journal of Consulting and Clinical Psychology*, vol. 57, (1), 1989, pp. 47-52.

[17]J M Gottman, and L J Krokoff, Marital interaction and satisfaction: A longitudinal view. *Journal of Consulting and Clinical Psychology*, vol. 57, (1), 1989, pp. 47-52.

[18]K A Schneewind, & A K Gerhard, Relationship personality, conflict resolution, and marital satisfaction in the first five years of marriage. *Family Relations*, vol. 51, (1), 2002, pp. 63-71.

[19]L A Pasch, & T N Bradbury, Social support, conflict, and the development of marital dysfunction. *Journal of Consulting and Clinical Psychology*, vol. 66, 1998, pp. 219-230.

[20]F D Fincham, S R H Beach, & J Davila, Forgiveness and conflict resolution in marriage. *Journal of Family Psychology*, vol. 18, (1), 2004, pp. 72-81.

[21]D Fenell, Characteristics of long-term first marriages. *Journal of Mental Health Counseling*, vol. 15, 1993, pp. 446-460.

[22]R D Enright, & C T Coyle, Researching the process model of forgiveness within psychological interventions, In E L Worthington (Ed.), *Dimensions of forgiveness: Psychological research and theological perspectives* (pp. 139-161), Philadelphia: Templeton Press, 1998.

[23]J North, The 'ideal' of forgiveness: A philosopher's exploration, In R D Enright & J North (Eds.), *Exploring forgiveness* (pp. 15-45), Madison, WI: University of Wisconsin Press, 1998.

[24]R D Enright, & C T Coyle, Researching the process model of forgiveness within psychological interventions, In E L Worthington (Ed.), *Dimensions of forgiveness: Psychological research and theological perspectives* (pp. 139-161), Philadelphia: Templeton Press, 1998. D Kaminer, D J Stein, I Mbanga, & N Zungu-Dirwayi, Forgiveness: Toward an integration of theoretical models. *Psychiatry*, vol. 63, 2000, pp. 344-357. J North, The 'ideal' of forgiveness: A philosopher's exploration, In R D Enright & J North (Eds.), *Exploring forgiveness* (pp. 15-45), Madison, WI: University of Wisconsin Press, 1998.

[25]M E McCullough, K C Rachel, S J Sandage, E L Worthington, Jr., S W Brown, & T L Hight, Interpersonal forgiving in close relationships: II. Theoretical elaboration and measurement. *Journal of Personality and Social Psychology,* vol. 75, (6), 1998, pp. 1586-1603.

[26]M R Holmgren, Forgiveness and the intrinsic value of persons. *American Philosophical Quarterly,* vol. 30, 1993, pp. 342-352.

[27]R D Enright, & J Rique, *The Enright forgiveness inventory,* Madison, WI: Mind Garden, Inc., 2004, p. 1.

[28]V R Waldron, & D L Kelley, *Communicating Forgiveness,* Los Angeles, CA: Sage Publications, Inc., 2008, p. 5.

[29]D Fenell, Characteristics of long-term first marriages. *Journal of Mental Health Counseling,* vol. 15, 1993, pp. 446-460.

[30]M E McCullough, K C Rachel, S J Sandage, E L Worthington, Jr., S W Brown, & T L Hight, Interpersonal forgiving in close relationships: II. Theoretical elaboration and measurement. *Journal of Personality and Social Psychology,* vol. 75, (6), 1998, pp. 1586-1603.

[31]M E McCullough, E L Worthington, & K C Rachel, Interpersonal forgiving in close relationship. *Journal of Personality and Social Psychology*, vol. 73, 1997, pp. 321-336.

[32]J M Gottman, *What predicts divorce? The relationship between Marital processes and marital outcomes,* Hillsdale, NJ: Lawrence Erlbaum Associates, 1994. M E McCullough, E L Worthington, & K C Rachel, Interpersonal forgiving in close relationship. *Journal of Personality and Social Psychology*, vol. 73, 1997, pp. 321-336.

[33]M E McCullough, K C Rachel, S J Sandage, E L Worthington, Jr. S W Brown, & T L Hight, Interpersonal forgiving in close relationships: II. Theoretical elaboration and measurement. *Journal of Personality and Social Psychology,* vol. 75, (6), 1998, pp. 1586-1603.

[34]R D Enright, & J Rique, *The Enright forgiveness inventory,* Madison, WI: Mind Garden, Inc., 2004.

[35]G Spanier, Measuring dyadic adjustment: New scales for assessing the quality of marriage and similar dyads. *Journal of Marriage and the Family,* vol. 38, 1976, pp. 15-28.

[36]H J Locke, & K M Wallace, Short marital adjustment and prediction Tests: Their reliability and validity. *Marriage and Family Living,* vol. 21, 1959, pp. 251-255.

[37]D Fenell, Characteristics of long-term first marriages. *Journal of Mental Health Counseling*, vol. 15, 1993, pp. 446-460.

[38]Waldron,V R & Kelley, D L, *Communicating Forgiveness.* Los Angeles, CA: Sage Publications, Inc., 2008.

[39]N G Wade, D C Bailey, & P Shaffer, Helping clients heal: Does forgiveness make a difference? *Professional Psychology: Research and Practice,* vol. 36, No. 6, 2005, pp. 634-641.

[40]M E McCullough, K C Rachel, S J Sandage, E.L.Worthington, Jr., S W Brown, & T L Hight, Interpersonal forgiving in close relationships: II. Theoretical elaboration and measurement. *Journal of Personality and Social Psychology,* vol. 75, (6), 1998, pp. 1586-1603.

[41]F D Fincham, S R H Beach, & J Davila, Forgiveness and conflict resolution in marriage. *Journal of Family Psychology,* vol. 18, (1), 2004, pp. 72-81.

[42]R P Fitzgibbons, The cognitive and emotive uses of forgiveness in the treatment of anger. *Psychotherapy,* vol. 23, 1986, pp. 629-633.

[43]E L Worthington Jr., & F A DiBlasio, Promoting mutual forgiveness within the fractured relationship. *Psychotherapy,* vol. 27, 1990, pp. 219-223.

[44]N G Wade, D C Bailey, & P Shaffer, Helping clients heal: Does forgiveness make a difference? *Professional Psychology: Research and Practice,* vol. 36, No. 6, 2005, pp. 634-641.

Bibliography

Bloom, B., Hodges, W. F., Caldwell, R. A., Systra, L., & Cedrone A. R., 'Marital separation: A community survey'. *Journal of Divorce,* vol. 1, 1977, pp. 7-19.

Brehm, S. S., *Intimate relationships,* (2nd Ed.), McGraw Hill, New York, 1985.

Cherlin, A., *Marriage, divorce, remarriage.* Harvard University Press, Cambridge, 1981.

Enright, R. D. & Coyle, C. T., 'Researching the process model of forgiveness within psychological interventions'. In E.L. Worthington (Ed.), *Dimensions of Forgiveness: Psychological Research and Theological Perspectives* (pp. 139-161) Templeton Press, Philadelphia, 1998.

——, & Rique, J., *The Enright forgiveness inventory.* Mind Garden, Inc., Madison, 2004.

Fenell, D., Characteristics of long-term first marriages. *Journal of Mental Health Counseling,* vol. 15, 1993, pp. 446-460.

Fincham, F.D., Beach, S. R. H. & Davila, J., Forgiveness and conflict resolution in marriage. *Journal of Family Psychology,* vol. 18, (1), 2004, pp. 72-81.

Fitzgibbons, R. P., 'The cognitive and emotive uses of forgiveness in the treatment of anger'. *Psychotherapy,* vol. 23, 1986, pp. 629-633.

Glick, P. C., 'How American families are changing'. *American Demographics,* vol. 6, 1984, pp. 20-27.

Gottman, J.M. and Krokoff, L.J., 'Marital interaction and satisfaction: A longitudinal view'. *Journal of Consulting and Clinical Psychology,* vol. 57, (1), 1989, pp. 47-52.

——, *What predicts divorce?   The relationship between Marital processes and marital outcomes.* Lawrence Erlbaum Associates, Hillsdale, 1994.

——, & Silver, N., *The seven principles for making marriage work.* Three Rivers Press, New York, 2007.

Holmgren, M. R., 'Forgiveness and the intrinsic value of persons'. *American Philosophical Quarterly*, vol. 30, 1993, pp. 342-352.

Kaminer, D., Stein, D. J., Mbanga, I., & Zungu-Dirwayi, N., 'Forgiveness: Toward an integration of theoretical models'. *Psychiatry,* vol. 63, 2000, pp. 344-357.

Kurdek, L.A., 'Predicting change in marital satisfaction from husbands' and wives' conflict resolution styles'. *The Journal of Marriage and the Family,* vol. 57, Feb. 1995, pp. 153-164.

Locke, H. J., *Predicting adjustment in marriage: A comparison of a divorced and a happily married group.* Henry Holt and Company, New York, 1951.

——, & Wallace, K. M., 'Short marital adjustment and prediction Tests: Their reliability and validity'. *Marriage and Family Living,* vol. 21, 1959, pp. 251-255.

Martin, T. C., & Bumpass, L., 'Recent trends in marital disruption'. *Demography,* vol. 26, 1989, pp. 37-51.

McCullough, M.E., Worthington, E.L., & Rachel, K.C., 'Interpersonal forgiving in close relationship'. *Journal of Personality and Social Psychology*, vol. 73, 1997, pp. 321-336.

———, Rachel, K. C., Sandage, S. J., Worthington, Jr. E. L., Brown, S. W., & Hight, T. L., 'Interpersonal forgiving in close relationships: II. Theoretical elaboration and measurement'. *Journal of Personality and Social Psychology*, vol. 75, (6), 1998, pp. 1586-1603.

North, J., 'The 'ideal' of forgiveness: A philosopher's exploration'. In R.D. Enright & J. North (Eds.), *Exploring forgiveness* (pp. 15-45), University of Wisconsin Press, Madison, 1998.

Pasch, L.A. & Bradbury, T. N., 'Social support, conflict, and the development of marital dysfunction'. *Journal of Consulting and Clinical Psychology*, vol. 66, 1998, pp. 219-230.

Schneewind, K.A. & Gerhard, A.K., 'Relationship personality, conflict resolution, and marital satisfaction in the first five years of marriage'. *Family Relations*, vol. 51, (1), 2002, pp. 63-71.

Spanier, G., 'Measuring dyadic adjustment: New scales for assessing the quality of marriage and similar dyads'. *Journal of Marriage and the Family*, vol. 38, 1976, pp. 15-28.

Terman, L. M., *Psychological factors in marital happiness.* McGraw-Hill, New York, 1938.

Wade, N. G., Bailey, D. C., & Shaffer, P., 'Helping clients heal: Does forgiveness make a difference?' *Professional Psychology: Research and Practice*, vol. 36, No. 6, 2005, pp. 634-641.

Waldron,V.R. & Kelley, D.L., *Communicating Forgiveness.* Sage Publications, Inc., Los Angeles, 2008.

Wineberg & McCarthy, 'Separation and reconciliation in American marriages'. *Journal of Divorce and Remarriage*, vol. 29, 1993, pp. 131-146.

Worthington, E. L., Jr. & DiBlasio, F. A., 'Promoting mutual forgiveness within the fractured relationship'. *Psychotherapy*, vol. 27, 1990, pp. 219-223.

Worthington, E. L., Jr., & Wade, N. G., 'The psychology of unforgiveness and forgiveness and implications for clinical practice'. *Journal of Social and Clinical Psychology,* vol. 18, 1999, pp. 385-418.

Carla S. Ross, PhD. is an Associate Professor of Communication at Meredith College in Raleigh, North Carolina.   She teaches Interpersonal Communication, Relational Communication, Nonverbal Communication and Forgiveness and Communication.   Her current research and writing is devoted to unveiling the importance of forgiveness in interpersonal relationships.

Prisoners and Forgiveness

Marieke Smit

Abstract
In my work as a prison chaplain, I ask prisoners how they feel and think about the subject of forgiveness. The group-work I do with them gives an inside look into their beliefs and interest in the subject. The main subjects in the group meetings are the definition of forgiveness, the feelings connected to forgiveness, and their own need for forgiveness or their need to forgive others. The meaning of 'self-forgiveness' seems to be especially important to the participants. The participants are different in many ways, including age, crime, relationships, and detention time. The results of the series of five meetings about forgiveness are that the participants are thinking about their own responsibility, their own guilt, and that they start thinking about the possibilities and boundaries of forgiveness in their personal situation. Many feel like talking further after we end the series of meetings.

Key Words: Forgiveness, prisoners, group meetings, moral guilt, prison chaplaincy.

*****

1.   The Setting

In the summer of 2008 in a Dutch prison, I held a first series of group meetings with prisoners.[1] These meetings were about the theme of forgiveness. During the last meeting the participants filled in a questionnaire about guilt, forgiveness, and detention.[2] In this article, I will regularly refer to the answers they gave in the questionnaire. I led these meeting in the position of a prison chaplain. Within the Dutch system, the position of chaplains from different denominations is governed by law. Prisoners have conversations with chaplains on a basis of secrecy. The statements of prisoners in this article are, for that reason, anonymous. (For the participants this is more difficult because only the chaplain has this secrecy. The participants have to trust each other on no other basis than the agreements we make with one another towards secrecy. It is always possible that participants do not keep these agreements and tell others about what has been talked about.)

The men with whom I held these meetings are all sentenced for juridical reasons by a Dutch judge. In the questionnaire they indicate that they understand why they are being punished. At the same time, 50% of the participants hold that their punishment isn't correct or justifiable. Most of them, on the contrary, have confessed in court and say that they didn't say sorry to influence their case in a positive way. Most participants acknowledge their juridical and moral guilt. The moral acknowledgement of guilt is a difficult concept. The word 'moral' leads to a wide range of different reactions – some say it has to do with themselves, others say that it has something to do with their conscience.

The philosopher Margaret Walker rightly mentions 'not all juridical guilt leads to a conviction. Often things happen that are someone's fault in a moral way. Not all offences are being punished.'[3] This difference is made by the participants, if they say that they have broken certain values. We can conclude that an examination of the conscience has taken place if they say they are conscious of their guilt. The theologian Roger Burggraeve calls this 'an introspective exploration of their own inner life.'[4] In the meetings, we talk about the background of their guilt and the way they experience their guilt. The reason why we do this comes from their answers to the question about the justifiability of their punishment. Prison minister Pieter Lootsma poses that 'fear is a major reason for prisoners not to talk about their guilt. It makes a person vulnerable, therefore it asks for courage and trust.'[5] He defines guilt as the failure towards the value system they were raised in or that they have made their own. It is important to get an idea about the content of these systems if you want to achieve change.

2.   Moral Community

The circumstances in the lives of these men have changed dramatically since their conviction to detention. Their freedom has been taken away from them and their freedom of movement and living space is limited. Together with others (first unknown) they form a community. The rules that are operative in this community are set by personnel and management of the institution. These rules are governed by law and have to submit to international laws as well. Prisons can be seen as subcultures. Goffmann calls this a total institution.[6] In a total institution, certain rules and laws are determined by the totality of the institution. It concerns a total institution when sleeping, working, and free time takes place in the same living situation and under the same authority. This gives prisoners a way to survive detention time. Goffmann shows us that there are different ways of dealing with this situation. He calls it 'mortification' of the ego when an individual becomes simply a number or object and the system seems to forget that they are human beings. Goffmann speaks of different ways of fitting in the system and, as a prisoner, trying to survive detention. It can lead to withdrawing from the system into one's own small world and showing no interest in others whatsoever. Others will confront the system; the institution is confronted by refusing to cooperate with the management or other personnel. There is also the possibility that prisoners colonise with the institution; the prisoner feels at home and leads a relatively satisfied life by making use of the supplies that the institution provides. Another tactic is when a prisoner tries to look good in the eyes of the staff and tries to play the perfect prisoner – so-called conversion. The last tactic can be called 'playing it cool'. Everything is done to avoid problems to make sure that the time in detention can be sat out rather quietly.

We see that certain manners of dealing with the situation of detention occur in different stages of the detention. In the middle phase, the culture of the prison will provide a clear guideline. In the beginning and at the end, there is more need for the orientation outwards, to the social values and standards society claims. Especially for long time serving prisoners, this orientation towards society at the end of their time causes a difficulty because, for a long time, only the norms of the prison were important.

In the situation of detention the feeling of not being free is the basis of the experiences of these men. We can speak of a reversed world. The same goes for trust. In prison, distrust comes first. This is important to remember for the treatment of prisoners, the building of a connection will take more time and effort. Despite the fact that the reason for the detention lies in the guilt of causing the harm, the circumstances of the detention make it easy to ignore or rationalize the crime. This frees the prisoner from feelings of guilt and makes the life in a total institution bearable.

The participants of the meetings say that they talk about their punishment and guilt with personnel and other prisoners. It is worthy to note that conversations about punishment are more common than conversations about guilt. The experiences of these men differ much as they are being asked if they talk about guilt inside the prison. They agree on the fact that being in prison is not about living but about survival. However, that doesn't mean that prisoners have no influence in this community. Even though the rules are set by others, the atmosphere and the way rules are interpreted depend both on personnel and inmates. In this way they form a moral community. Within this community, the chaplain has its own place. Due to their education and background, spiritual caregivers should be able to give a substantiated opinion of good and bad. In the reality of detention they're 'justified' to give a moral judgment about the (past) actions of prisoners. Such a moral judgment consists of a well-based opinion of the crimes committed. This justification makes that prisoners come to them and ask for their opinion. In a strange way, people have a need for the recognition of their actions – even if it concerns negative deeds. Beyond this opinion, the pastoral caregiver will provide him with the necessary care and will not only hold on to the conviction.

Within a moral community, participants develop their own ideas about right and wrong.[7] Besides that, the confrontation with other opinions provides a way to develop and to test your own behaviour. This can take place in a safe situation in which people can ask each other what they think, like in a group meeting where people can trust each other and are prepared to listen to other opinions. Interpreting the situation of detention as a moral community is a valuable contribution to the development of the moral awareness of prisoners.

For the participants, the group meetings are a place where they can reflect on the values that are legitimate in the system in which they live. But, if we change certain ideas about how much influence they have, the system has to go along with it. The position of personnel is not to be underestimated in this: a positive as well as a negative approach will have its influence. The idea of a moral community gives responsibility back to members of the community. They can be more easily addressed as to their behaviour than in a situation where others determine everything and have a right to do so.

If personnel respond very normally towards certain positive ways of approaching people, then there is a fair chance that prisoners will follow this behaviour. Prisoners are then able to recognize and practice stipulated moral competences. It isn't always clear to the participants in the group meetings why personnel are interested in their stories. Some people suggest that it is merely a fascination for the exciting story and not a sincere interest in the inmate. One participant of the meetings tells us that he has been asked several times about his former life as a drug dealer, not about his newborn baby.

3.   About Forgiveness in Detention

In a situation of detention, forgiveness is a subject that is not very common. The mutual stories of prisoners are about how to 'crack the next crib,' about others at the department, and what they have done wrong. It is not about feelings like anger or sadness, about personal matters, or about their own feelings of guilt. In the research that was done in Dutch prisons, an outcome was that prisoners feel a need for contact with pastoral (spiritual) caregivers.[8] The subjects of the conversations differ a lot. 29% of Dutch prisoners have talked in individual conversations with pastoral caregivers about 'regret and forgiveness', 20% talked about 'guilt and punishment', and 16% say that they talked about 'the crime and the victim(s)'. In the group meetings prisoners had with pastoral caregivers, the subject of 'regret and forgiveness' was mentioned as a theme in 37% of the cases. 'Guilt and punishment' was mentioned as a subject in group meetings in 21% of the cases. In other research, we see that, according to representatives of the management and psychologists, it is expected that pastoral caregivers speak about guilt and forgiveness.[9] 'Promoting the processing of guilt is seen by representatives of the management as an important function that, within the whole of detention, contributes to a meaningful use of time during punishment.'[10] But this happens a lot less than can be expected.

Society expects prisoners to undergo some sort of re-socialisation. They expect that punishment helps in avoiding recidivism. But if nothing happens in prison to stimulate change, the recidivism figures will not diminish. A past that has been processed can be interpreted as a moral transformation and can benefit to a successful re-entry in society. A moral transformation is the change in the moral argumentation that has been followed so far. This moral argumentation is a line of thinking that is learned by parents or has been adjusted by peers, but in many cases it is a line of thinking in which negative behaviour is not considered negative. A change in the line of thinking about the reasons for their negative behaviour will have an effect on their behaviour. But, to be able to talk about moral transformation, a prisoner has to be willing to speak about himself. He has to be open to change or has to experience slowly that change is needed.

In the questionnaire, the majority of the participants indicate that they think about motives or reasons why others have hurt them. If you are able to recognize that others have hurt you, the next step is to acknowledge that you may have hurt others as well and that forgiveness is something that you can ask for, but also something you can offer to the ones that have hurt you in the past.

Such a moral transformation can be achieved by giving prisoners a chance to reflect on the subject of forgiveness and guilt. The recognition of their own responsibility can be an important step towards the realisation of their own guilt and, from that point on, can be followed by repentance. For most of the prisoners, it is a new situation when they talk about guilt. It is very personal and makes a person very vulnerable. Therefore, it demands the necessary confidence in the people with whom they talk. As Achiel Neys, the Belgian prison chaplain, writes in an article in *Metanoia*: 'important others with whom one feels existentially linked/connected are obviously the entrance to the notion of good and evil, even with a poor conscience. The need for warmth and security and the emotions that come with that, the notion of being dependent on family too is a bed for exploring a moral notion.'[11]

But in most cases, it isn't fair to look at only one side of the guilt. This is the case because there are different people and circumstances that play a part in a human life. A reflection with others on the way one responds to guilt and forgiveness can lead to a moral transformation. It is not a matter of abdicating the guilt or to hold others responsible for the crimes committed, but it is important that a reframing take place. 'Reframing' is the change in the way they look towards the situation afterwards. One of the participants of the group indicated that he now realises that he was wrong just because his girlfriend tells him that certain things are not self-evident.

Often this argumentation can be reduced to finding arguments that fit their situation that have nothing to do with legislation, laws, and rules and are rather often based on self-interest and one's own justice. While listening to stories of others that are based on the same argumentation, but for that reason are clearly not valid, people see the failure in their own argumentation.

4.   Religious Vision on Forgiveness

The meetings began from a Christian-inspired ethical point of view. Forgiveness like Jesus Christ has lived it. A lot of literature about forgiveness is written from a psychological background, and this kind of research has shown that forgiveness has a positive effect on people who forgive others. People who feel a strong connection with one another especially find a benefit in forgiving.[12] For the participants of the group meetings, it is not evident that they had a strong connection with their victims, for instance, a love relationship or a parent-child relationship. Forgiveness is, in these cases, not merely about forgiving by victims. There can also be a need to be forgiven by important close ones, like partners or parents. This need can develop itself. In the series of meetings I had with the participants, my starting-point is not to achieve a psychological change, but rather I choose to aim for a moral or spiritual change to develop itself further. In the core of the matter, my main concern is 'reframing'. Of course, I do not want to deny the importance of psychological models, but my goal does not lies there. Regarding my task as a prison-chaplain, my main concern is to make them think about guilt and forgiveness. Unconditional forgiveness is, for human beings, quite difficult, but it is always good to compare your own argumentation for your actions with other opinions. For me, it is a major question whether God is the only one who will forgive everyone. I use a definition of forgiveness as follows: 'Forgiveness is the motivation – based on cognitive, affective, and spiritual arguments – and the competence of a person to leave behind feelings of anger and thoughts about revenge and retribution in order to arrive at an experience of peace with the situation.'

The theologian Monbourquette poses that forgiveness has to do with love and spiritual quality. 'The spirituality of forgiveness places us opposite to a person and not under the obligation of law. Jesus didn't make a law for it, but a commandment, with the conditions of your own obedience.'[13] The Belgian theologian Pollefeyt adds to this that 'punishment is a crucial condition for forgiveness but punishment can never lead to the earning of forgiveness. Forgiveness is not a moral obligation. A perpetrator can create conditions in his own life which can lead to a situation where there is a structural possibility of receiving forgiveness.'[14]

Most important is the realisation that forgiveness is about relationships between people and the realisation that guilt has been acknowledged. The questionnaires show that participants find forgiveness important, because God will forgive them eventually. One of them says that the use of the word 'will' suggests that God's forgiveness is conditional, but in his own experience that is not right. God always forgives him.

5.   Forgiveness According to Participants

The participants don't use forgiveness as a way of having power over others – at least they say so. Denying someone forgiveness or promising someone forgiveness would be an inappropriate way of pressuring people. Most participants say that they find forgiveness important because there is no other way to live together and it gives us a way to restore relationships. They are prepared to forgive the other person when he admits his wrongdoing. Also in the literature we recognize this idea. It seems very obvious that one first has to acknowledge his mistakes and crimes before an answer to the question of forgiveness can be expected. Taking revenge is not an option for most participants. Some say that they don't even take the trouble because the other person will do enough for his own ruination, you don't have to help them with it. The participants answer in the affirmative when asked whether they are mentally strong if they are able to forgive someone.

Walker poses that forgiveness is not only about the past, but also has to do with the future. She gives an interpretation of Hannah Arendt's vision of forgiveness, where Arendt says that forgiveness is a unique remedy of the irreversibility of human action. Forgiving isn't simply about settling the past, but looks hopefully towards an uncertain future. Forgiving, Walker says, is something morally valuable and even admirable.[15]

6.   The Participants of the Group Meetings

The six participants of the first series of group meetings are all convicted. There are no participants who deny their crime, although some put different accents in their criminal case than the public prosecutor. The length of their punishment varies and so does the duration of it. Some are waiting for the next phase of their punishment; others have to stay in prison for several years more. The men vary in age from the mid-twenties to the mid-forties. Some are in a relationship and have children that vary in age from baby to teenager and even older.

Others have no relationship. The contact prisoners have with their families varies depending on the prisoner. Some of them decided that during their detention they don't want to have any contact with family members, others have intensified their contact and have improved it. The prisoners stay in different departments of the institution and four of them are regular visitors of the church services. One of the other two came every week up to six months before the start and the other never visited the church services.

The prisoners are being punished for different kind of crimes, diverging from life crimes, sexual crimes, violence, possession of weapons, and theft. I had personal conversations with five of them before the meetings began, so I am familiar with their stories and personal backgrounds. The way they deal with their punishment naturally differs from person to person, but they all acknowledge having made mistakes in their life. They are capable of introspection that is very important in the conversation. Furthermore, they are prepared to listen to each other and to answer questions of the other participants. This is an important condition to participate to the meetings. Especially considering the heat of the discussions, it is important that they can put up with that, and are prepared to listen to another story even though it is totally different than their own opinion.

The four participants of the second series of group meetings stay in a department where their addiction is in the centre. They receive help to get over their addiction. Their personal characteristics are quite equal to the first group. This second group is conducted by my colleague. I was there as a participating observant.

7.   Form of the Group Meetings

The five group meetings are centred on the theme of forgiveness. For several reasons, I have chosen to have group meetings. First of all, it is one of my tasks as a prison chaplain in a detention institution. Moreover, a group meeting gives the possibility of hearing and sharing stories and experiences of others. Also, these stories and experiences can lead to a situation where participants start thinking in a different way than they are used to do. Another reason is that group meetings create a certain security that one-on-one conversations do not. A person can choose to listen to the others and not put himself in the middle. Obviously, there are also disadvantages in the group setting. The earlier mentioned idea of security is hard to impose or to enforce. The feeling of security has to develop itself. The participants have to produce a certain degree of faith to be able to start with the meetings. Secondly, it is of major importance that the discussion leader knows the participants. It concerns mainly the stories of the crime that can make a person vulnerable and can cause unexpected emotions and reactions of the person himself as with others. If the story is known, the discussion leader can take the attention away at difficult times during the meeting. The discussion leader can redirect the conversation.   In this situation, the safety of the participants can be assured better. An example of a sexual crime prisoner can clarify this. I knew his background story and knew that he did not want to speak about his crime and certain details of his life. At the point that he was being asked difficult questions, I was able to redirect the attention for his story away from him and I asked someone else what he would do in a same situation. The conversation ended up at a more abstract level and turned away from the story of this one participant.

The participants have voluntarily subscribed to these meetings. The first meeting revolves around two questions: what are your thoughts on the subject of forgiveness? Which value belongs to forgiveness in your opinion? The participants can use the paperboard cards that have values printed on them.

This first meeting is a general exploration of the theme of forgiveness. I start from a definition of forgiveness as follows:

> Forgiveness is the motivation –based on cognitive, affective, and spiritual arguments – and the competence of a person to leave behind feelings of anger and thoughts about revenge and retribution in order to arrive at an experience of peace with the situation.

This definition functions as background information and will not be shared explicitly with the participants.

Another goal of this meeting is that participants get to know each other and each other's stories. Obviously, the first thing that was agreed upon is the way we deal with each other. One of the most important agreements is about trust, which means that what we talk about stays inside the group and is not to be shared with third parties.

The second meeting revolves around the difference between victims and perpetrators. I talk about the fact that participants are seen as perpetrators by the outside world. That doesn't mean that they agree with that view. We use a text written by a prisoner in a Dutch prison, so that we can take a little distance from our own stories, and look from a distance to his role as a criminal. The man describes his background and tells us that he sees a future for himself, where there is a place for people whom he can trust and where there is no place for drugs. He is writing a book about his life. He advises others to talk about themselves and their crimes and to write it down. It is a short, but intense, story.[16]

The second part of the meeting is spent on the way victims lead their lives after the crime. The story of a victim is read to the participants and a question is asked as to which way the participants look at their victims. The goal is to let the participants look at the world from a different point of view. In their present detention, they are not confronted with their victims or with victims in general (as far as that is possible). To them the story of their being an offender is the only story they hear around them.

During the third meeting we look at a part of the movie called 'The Mission,' where there is a clear link between guilt, punishment, and forgiveness.[17] I show approximately 45 minutes of the movie, the beginning where Rodrigo Mendoza kills his brother in a duel because he is cheating with Rodrigo's wife. Without many words the situation is clear, the subtitles aren't necessary.[18]

Mendoza locks himself up in the local mission house. He stays there for six months until the priest from the mission house above the waterfalls comes to talk to him. He asks the man if he dares to choose his own punishment or penance. The man answers with a counter-question: is the priest willing to stay with him when he fails? He chooses to go with the priest to the mission house above the waterfalls, so he has to travel a long road up the waterfalls. He drags along with him a load of belongings acquired over several years. Before the duel he lived as a hireling and hunted for the Indians, who, as we find out, are now being converted by the priest.

The part we see ends as the man – after a physically and mentally heavy expedition – is released from his load by one of the Indians, who first puts a knife to his throat. Mendoza probably killed some of his villagers. The word isn't mentioned, but it's clear to all of us that this is about forgiveness. The way Mendoza deals with his guilt is confronting. First, he locks himself up, like many prisoners at first do, but then he looks for his punishment and starts confronting himself with his crimes.

This is a step which not all prisoners take. After watching the movie I ask a general question about what they think of the movie and what they think Mendoza is carrying with him. At the end of the meeting the participants are given six questions to fill in later.

During the fourth meeting, we discuss the movie and the homework questions. Some have chosen to answer the questions referring to the movie; others choose to refer to their own lives. The meeting is continued with the question: what kinds of feelings are connected to forgiveness? We use pre-printed cards with all kind of feelings written on them. The last question we deal with is one about what advice to give to others concerning forgiveness.

During the fifth and last meeting, I give the participants a questionnaire to fill out, consisting of three parts: part one is about forgiveness, the second part is about guilt, and the third part is about detention and how to deal with that.

8.   The Content of the Meetings

The participants mention different values when asked which values, in their opinion, belong to forgiveness: responsibility, personal development, tolerance, love, acknowledgement/appreciation, peace, commitment, independency, honesty, clarity, security, equality, freedom, gratitude. These values are all mentioned in literature about forgiveness, but noteworthy is the twice-mentioned personal development. This usually isn't very explicitly mentioned in literature and also refers to a personal benefit. Furthermore, it's interesting to see that most participants choose different values. The philosopher Charles Griswold poses that forgiveness isn't merely psychologically a valuable step, but that forgiveness in itself has value.[19] If a perpetrator has set all the necessary steps to return to society, this society should give him a chance. Apparently, the value of forgiveness is very personal to the participants. We can conclude that the moral value of forgiveness is clear to them.

8.1. Perpetrators and Victims

One of the participants clearly states his opinion about the story from the 'criminal'. Jonathan calls it a standard story. The argument the man uses to defend his choices in life is not accepted by Jonathan. He thinks it is a worthless argument to use your background as a reason for criminal behaviour. It is your own responsibility to decide which choices you make in life. There's no excuse for you to go excusing yourself afterwards with these kinds of arguments. Jonathan mentions two kinds of stories. First, a story based on arguments from ones background, addiction, or family. Second, the story which you can write books about, a romanticized story which makes it looks very nice altogether.

Why did he make those bad choices himself? Jonathan answers: 'I thought it was normal, not such a bad thing. Women behind windows (in prostitution), well, they were making enough money as it was.' And so did he.

Only later, older and wiser, Jonathan realised that it wasn't that normal. He tells us about his wife. She points it out to him that he still follows strange reasoning, and she makes him aware of that. Some things are not normal, but because he has lived in this kind of environment for so long he doesn't see that anymore. So he needs another person to show him. He has often used the status that came with this world. 'Now I see through that, it gave me nothing.'

The question is raised whether this 'criminal' confesses his guilt. Opinions vary on this question. A participant calls it a mental note, a promise not to do it again. But the man is not a victim of circumstances, the participants agree on that statement. The plain fact that you are addicted doesn't make you a victim.

Having heard the story of the 'criminal', one of the participants tells us that he was only able to identify with his victims at the moment he had to deal with the same thing. Then he also felt angry and sad. The feeling of fear raises two types of reactions. If you are feeling anxious it makes you alert, which is not such a bad thing. But if other people are afraid, you can use that for your own benefit, which is wrong. Most participants agree that they were mad with the one that had hurt them, but almost all of them felt sad about what had happened.

Through sharing a different way of looking at situations the participants develop a new view on the relationship between victims and perpetrators and their own role in this. A number of participants are convicted for violent crimes. Together we conclude that acknowledging the value of persons is not something one does when one is able to hurt and even kill another person. That deepens the realisation that being accepted as a person oneself is very special.

Why are people who surround you capable of valuing and acknowledging you as a person, even though you might not feel like you're worth it? The thesis 'I am worthy to receive forgiveness' is affirmatively answered by a majority of the participants. A lot of discussion follows. One of the participants says that it is very difficult to call yourself a valuable person. In theory, he finds all people worthy as a person and worth forgiving, so that would apply for him as well. But is a lack of self-confidence, self-respect/self-esteem and self-love a major reason to question this? In the first series of conversations, I ask the six participants if they love themselves, five of them answer in the negative.

8.2.   The Mission

The discussion as a result of watching the movie shows us that a certain level of intelligence is important for the development of the group. The first group is capable of reaching a higher level of abstraction watching the movie than the second group is. For the second group we use the pre-printed cards with the names of feelings written on them so that the participants don't have to think about the feelings themselves. Instead, they can just choose one of the cards. This helps move the conversation in the right direction and places them in the position of Mendoza. The first group is able to do that without help from the cards. They look from a distance to the position Mendoza is in.

The movie evokes a lot of emotions. If we compare the lives of the characters in the movie to the detention life participants are in, we see parallels. Some recognize themselves in the reaction of Mendoza to his guilt. They also have withdrawn themselves into their cells, becoming depressed and crying for nights in a row on their own. The question 'what is it that he is carrying?' is answered differently. His burden is a burden from years and years, but it is also everything he has, his past, everything he is. 'Insight will not arise because of punishment but because of the ongoing time' is a conclusion of one of the participants.

Another participant points out that Mendoza needed his fellow men to get to this stage, he couldn't have done it on his own. Forgiveness is, in the eyes of the participants, only possible between people, so-called 'interpersonal forgiveness.' People can forgive each other. For some participants, God has a role to play in this; they say that people need Him to forgive others. Some think that only God can forgive in the end. The participants do not agree on this.

One conclusion can be that the participants seem likely to accept the concept of reframing. Reframing is the process that leads to a different view on the same situation, because of a new or different input. From watching the movie they see that things, opinions, and situations can change in a human life and that is also true for their own life, situation, and position.

There are things you can feel responsible for (afterwards) and you can be open-minded to different voices and opinions about your own behaviour. The wrongdoing will always be there, it will not disappear and the responsibility will stay as well. But the way you look at it can change.

The participants' answers to the thesis that 'they only forgive if someone asks for it' are mostly negative. For them, it is not necessary that the perpetrator is punished before they could come to forgiveness. Also, the offer of an excuse is not a determining action. But they respond very differently to the question as to whether or not they're open to forgiveness if the perpetrator admits his wrongdoing and shows insight of his guilt. Some say that they are willing to forgive a person who asks for it and confesses his guilt; others clearly say that they will not forgive the person(s) who have harmed them.

How do these men deal with their own guilt? In the questionnaire, they say that they pray for forgiveness. Praying for their victims is a less familiar thing to do. One of them tells us that he finds it difficult to pray for his victim, because he doesn't have the words for a prayer especially for her, although she deserves it. (The chaplain who conducted this meeting helped him with this during the meeting. He gave a simple example of a prayer to show him that it is possible to pray and find the words which could say what he wants to say.) Participants offer their apologies, make up with others, talk about problems, and ask others for advice about how to deal with what has happened. This could be evaluated as open-mindedness towards moral transformation in which their value system is open to questioning. On the question of letting their victims, or the victims' families, know whether they were sorry for what they have done, 8 participants answer that they would apologize to their victims, 4 say they would not. One of the participants tells us that there is no actual possibility to get into contact because there is no family left. Another one tells us that he has written a letter, and he finds it difficult to wait for a response.

The priest plays a big part in the life of Mendoza. We discuss the role of bystanders. One of the men reveals that he receives comments on his participation in the group. It is expected for prisoners to show off like a 'macho' and not to show your emotions. (There is, of course, the challenge of motivating those who are suspicious of the meetings and getting them to join anyway in a later series of meetings.)

So, it takes a lot of courage to join a group like this and tell about yourself and share your feelings. One of the participants describes this by saying: 'At some point I thought about Mendoza as a sissy, because he starts crying when the Indian withdraws his knife and uses it to let him get rid of his burden.'

We ask the question 'how can you tell if you can be trustworthy?' and 'how can you trust another person?', because people are able to commit crimes. How can one tell if contrition is sincere? The sociologist Tavuchis (cf. Smith[20]) talks about the paradox of an apology. 'An apology, no matter how sincere or effective, does and cannot *undo* what has been done. And yet, in a mysterious way and according to its own logic, this is precisely what it manages to do.'[21] The participants seem to realise how true that is. It may lead to people getting cynical and losing faith in their moral connections with others. What is the use in offering apologies if that does not change the situation? Walker poses that we are capable of leaving this cynical thinking behind us.[22] People are capable of leaving the pain of their past behind them and forgiving others. That realisation is based on trust and hope. During the meetings, the discussion on the value of people leads to a typical statement: 'If you are capable of saying sorry, then you are able to look at the people around you, and to your victims as valuable persons.'

After the meetings the participants evaluated the meetings as valuable. They say it has provided them with a different way of looking at their lives and got them out of the daily routine in the institution. Besides, the confrontation with others is clarifying. When listening to the flaws in the reasoning of others, you can see more easily that your own reasoning makes the same odd moves. The participants are vulnerable talking about themselves, but sometimes they choose to tell about themselves without making clear that it was their own story.

8.3.   End

These conversations aren't based on the idea of restorative justice. They are concentrated around the position and situation of perpetrators. There is no benefit for them if they show contrition and say that they feel sorry. The contrition they show and the improved insight in their behaviour and value system are only beneficial to their own personal development. Reframing and moral transformation are, in my opinion, two necessary steps towards a successful re-entry into society. Forgiveness plays an important part in all of this. It appeals to the moral competence to 'imagine oneself in another situation or in another person's shoes' and it appeals to their moral and affective communication skills. Mostly these men aren't raised in communities where communicating about your feelings and moral responsibility has been taught.[23] These group meetings have helped to improve these competences.

According to Dickey, an American professor of law: 'If restorative thinking and forgiveness are becoming a part of the judicial system then participation of the community is necessary.'[24] The conversations challenge the judicial system to formulate their view on restorative justice and the meaning of forgiveness in all of this. We conclude that the participants of these meetings started thinking about their own responsibility and the meaning of forgiveness in their own lives. They were unanimously positive about the contents of the conversations.

Notes

[1] In December 2008 two more followed.

[2] Statements like this refer to the outcomes of the questionnaire. For more information about the questionnaire you may contact the author.

[3] M Walker, *Moral repair*. New York, Cambridge, 2006, pp. 153-154.

[4] R Burggraeve, *Van de meerzinnige betekenis van fout en schuld naar de paradoxale rijkdom van betekenis en vergeving*. In: Zand erover? Vereffenen, vergeven, verzoenen. Davidsfonds, Leuven, 2000, pp. 205-245.

[5] P Lootsma, *Schuld, een eigentijds taboe*. In: Over schuld en schaamte. KSGV, Tilburg, The Netherlands, 2005 (2-67) pp. 30-31.

[6] Goffmann, *Totale instituties*. Universitaire Pers Rotterdam, Rotterdam, 1975, pp. 14-15.

[7] In most prisons, a hierarchy of crimes is accepted which means that a sexual crime is considered worse than murdering another person.

[8] Spruit, L., Bernts, T., Woldringh, C., *Geestelijke verzorging in justitiele inrichtingen*. Kaski Rapport, ITS, Nijmegen, 2003, pp. 59/ 73-74

[9] F Flierman, *De kwaliteit van het justitiepastoraat*, Niset Nijmegen, 2000, pp. 50-52, 69.

[10] F Flierman, *De kwaliteit van het justitie pastoraat*. Niset, Nijmegen, 2000, pp. 57

[11] A Neys, In: Metanoia, 2001, p. 98.

[12] J Karremans, *Forgiveness. Examining its consequences*. Ridderprint, Ridderkerk, 2002, pp. 9-10.

[13] J Monbourquette, *Integrale vergeving*. In: Hoe vergeven? Vergeven om te genezen, genezen om te vergeven. Uitgeverij Averbode, Averbode, 2001, pp. 49-82.

[14] D Pollefeyt, *Vergeving: valkuil of springplank naar een betere samenleving? Op zoek naar een nieuw begin voor daders en slachtoffers*. In: Vergeven, vereffenen, verzoenen. Davidsfonds, Leuven, 2000, pp. 143-170.

[15] M Walker, 2006, pp. 152-153.

[16] This is an anonymous story which a colleague gave me to use.

[17] *The Mission*, directed by Roland Joffé, 1986.

[18] This is an important detail in a situation where functional illiteracy is common.

[19] C Griswold, *Forgiveness. A philosophical exploration*. Cambridge University Press, New York, 2007, pp. 69-70.

[20] N Smith, *I was wrong. The meanings of apology*. Cambridge University Press, New York, 2008.

[21] N Tavuchis, *Mea Culpa. A sociology of apology and reconciliation.* Stanford University Press, 1991, pp. 5.
[22] M Walker, *Moral repair,* New York, Cambridge, 2006, pp.162.
[23] B Stokkom, van, *Vergeving en verzoening in herstelrecht.* In: Tijdschrift voor Herstelrecht, 2008 (4) pp.7-19.
[24] W Dickey, *Forgiveness and crime. The possibilities of Restoratative Justice.* In: Exploring forgiveness. Enright, R., North, J., (ed.) University of Wisconsin Press, Madison,1998, pp. 106-120.

Bibliography

Burggraeve, R., 'Van de meerzinnige betekenis van fout en schuld naar de paradoxale rijkdom van betekenis en vergeving'. in *Zand erover? Vereffenen, vergeven, verzoenen.* Davidsfonds, Leuven, 2000, pp. 205-245.

Dickey, W., 'Forgiveness and crime. The Possibilities of Restorative Justice' in *Exploring Forgiveness.* Enright, Robert D., and North, Joanna, ed. University of Wisconsin Press, Madison, 1998, pp. 106-120.

Flierman, F., *De kwaliteit van het justitie pastoraat.* Niset, Nijmegen, 2000.

Goffmann, E., *Totale instituties.* Universitaire Pers Rotterdam, Rotterdam, 1975.

Griswold, C., *Forgiveness. A philosophical exploration.* Cambridge University Press, New York, 2007.

Karremans, J., *Forgiveness. Examining its consequences.* Ridderprint, Ridderkerk, 2002.

Lootsma, P., 'Schuld, een eigentijds taboe' in *Over schuld en schaamte.* KSGV, Tilburg, 2005 (2-67) pp. 30-31.

Monbourquette, J., 'Integrale vergeving'. in *Hoe vergeven? Vergeven om te genezen, genezen om te vergeven.* Uitgeverij Averbode, Averbode, 2001, pp. 49-82.

Pollefeyt, D., 'Vergeving: valkuil of springplank naar een betere samenleving? Op zoek naar een nieuw begin voor daders en slachtoffers' in *Vergeven, vereffenen, verzoenen.* Davidsfonds, Leuven, 2000, pp. 143-170.

Smith, N., *I was wrong. The meanings of apology.* Cambridge University Press, New York, 2008.

Stokkom, van B., 'Vergeving en verzoening in herstelrecht' in *Tijdschrift voor Herstelrecht*, 2008 (4).

Tavuchis, N., *Mea Culpa. A sociology of apology and reconciliation.* Stanford University Press, 1991.

Walker, M., *Moral repair.* New York, Cambridge, 2006.

Marieke Smit is a Ph.D. student at the Faculty of Catholic Theology at Tilburg University, The Netherlands and she is working as a prison chaplain in a Dutch prison. E-mail: mariekesmit1@gmail.com

The Community Response To Violence: Do Rituals Of Healing Support Forgiveness?

Barbara Flood and Christina Tomacic-Niaros

Abstract
In previous research, we have discovered that individuals who have lost a loved one in a senseless random act of violence report that forgiveness is most successful when they are assured that the community in which they live supports and acknowledges their pain and loss. But it is clear that it is not just the immediate family that is affected when a crime occurs in a public venue such as the federal building in Oklahoma City, the twin towers in New York City and academic institutions across the United States. These violent events are shared globally through mass media that personalize the impact they have, or potentially can have, on each of our lives. We are therefore challenged to reconsider our definitions of community to include an extended circle of observers emotionally connected to the tragedy they are witnessing. Research on vicarious trauma indicates that those observing can be as affected as the victims themselves. *What kind of rituals impact and support the community in a process of forgiveness? Does the repeated ritualistic act of remembering delay the forgiveness process or encourage it?* Our interest here is to investigate the ways in which communities demonstrate their support immediately after the event and on subsequent anniversaries of the event. Are these rituals memorialising the initial tragedy intended to simply show solidarity for the victim and their families and friends or are they an expression of a greater need for the entire community to restore a sense of balance, safety and unity? Communities are united in tragedy through ritual; they are the voice of the victims. Rituals of loss, especially traumatic losses have similar trends and expressions. We are interested in rituals that also encompass strategies for forgiveness. The question of how one defines community informs the method and context of healing modalities and intervention that will allow for true internal resolution of these unthinkable crimes. Looking at both urban and rural communities, clearly defined and in the global context, we will investigate what supported forgiveness and what may have impeded the process. Finally we will suggest treatment intervention based on the data, both for individuals and for the larger communities.

Key Words: Forgiveness, violent crime, spirituality, communities.

*****

'All sorrows can be borne if you put them into a story or tell a story about them. The story reveals the meaning of what otherwise would remain an unbearable sequence of happenings.'
- Hannah Arendt

In previous research, we have discovered that individuals who have lost a loved one in a senseless random act of violence report that forgiveness is most successful when they are assured that the community in which they live supports and acknowledges their pain and loss. But it is clear that it is not just the immediate family that is affected when a crime occurs in a public venue such as the federal building in Oklahoma City, the twin towers in New York City and academic institutions across the United States. These violent events are shared globally through mass media that personalise the impact they have, or potentially can have, on each of our lives. We are therefore challenged to reconsider our definitions of community to include an extended circle of observers emotionally connected to the tragedy they are witnessing. Research on vicarious trauma indicates that those observing can be as affected as the victims themselves. What kind of rituals impact and support the community in a process of forgiveness? Does the repeated ritualistic act of remembering delay the forgiveness process or encourage it?

When Mayor George Moscone and Harvey Milk, the first openly gay person elected to political office, were assassinated on November 27, 1978, a powerful memorial ritual/service was quickly and spontaneously organized for the grieving community of San Francisco. The line of mourners was overwhelming. Gay and straight persons came together in this momentous occasion of honouring not only two loved leaders, but also the movement toward gay rights and equality that Harvey Milk had championed. The crowd of thousands stretched from one end of the city to another and was strikingly quiet and subdued. They carried candles and walked in silence. This was a gentle remembrance. It had the appearance of one without any need for retribution or retaliation. Perhaps this was the mood because the reasonable expectation was that the perpetrator, Dan White, a fellow city supervisor, had been arrested and was clearly going to be convicted and held accountable.

Mr. White's trial was short and weeks later, when he was granted a sentence of 5 years for a conviction of involuntary manslaughter based on the 'Twinkie' defence, riots broke out throughout the city. The overwhelming need for retribution and justice, thwarted by this conviction, rippled through the community and the possibility of forgiveness was lost to vengeance.

Communities can be united in tragedy through ritual; they are the voice of the victims. Rituals of loss, especially traumatic loss, have similar trends and expressions, yet the community may refuse to acknowledge space for forgiveness. Our interest here is to investigate the ways in which communities demonstrate their support immediately after a violent event and on subsequent anniversaries of the event. Are these rituals memorialising the initial tragedy intended to simply show solidarity for the victim and their families and friends or are they an expression of a greater need for the larger community to restore a sense of balance and safety and unity? We will investigate the various rituals communities engage in and compare and contrast the impact of these rituals on the communities' process of forgiveness. We are also interested in rituals that encompass strategies for forgiveness.

In previous work we have outlined two such examples: the Amish children at the Nickel Mines School in Pennsylvania where 5 were killed and 5 more seriously injured in October of 2006 and the tragic shooting at Platte Canyon High School in Colorado where a gunman took 7 students hostage and shot Emily Keyes, one of the students. Both of these were small rural communities that embraced forgiveness as part of their healing process.

In Bailey, Colorado, Emily Keyes' family, when asked how the community could support them in their grief, requested the creation of a ritual of offering random acts of kindness in Emily's name. I would walk into area businesses and see the pink ribbon with the invitation to 'offer random acts of kindness for Emily' and my heart would melt in utter amazement that this community, that had suffered so deeply, could find such a compassionate and kind expression for their grief, filled with such forgiveness.

This decision appeared too altruistic and supportive of the community being able to forgive the perpetrator, the man who killed their daughter, Emily, at Platte Canyon High School. In an interview with Ellen and John Michael Keyes, it was discovered that in fact the decision to offer random acts of kindness had little to do with forgiveness. In fact, Ellen found it difficult to consider forgiveness. As has been the case with others we have surveyed, Ellen put forth the question: how could she forgive someone she has never met; someone who is dead? For her, forgiveness was difficult to separate from condoning, or allowing the wrong to be normalized, without the necessary atonement or retribution. Forgiveness in this case remained theoretical; justice, on the other hand, was more tangible and necessary. Ellen concluded that perhaps forgiveness, if it were at all appropriate to the situation, would be more a matter of acceptance. Acceptance, as painful as it has been to endure the grief and loss, would mean coming to the end of a long hard road of difficult emotions. Ellen and John Michael have not come to that place in their personal healing process. It is something for further inquiry and exploration.

What they have done, which resonates with other victims of heinous crimes, is to establish the 'I Luv U Guys Foundation', named after the last texting words of their daughter before her death. Their mission is to bring training to schools so they will be prepared for incidents such as what happened at Platte Canyon High School, in hopes that other children will be protected from the violence that their daughter fell victim to.

In contrast, in *Amish Grace*, Kraybill, Nolt and Weaver-Zercher tell us that although the Amish do believe that crime should carry consequences, they hold forgiveness as a high virtue and one to rely on in all matters of conflict. Kraybill, Nolt and Weaver-Zercher cite numerous examples of tragic loss where the Amish people embraced the offender with a multitude of acts of forgiveness.

But not all communities are so clear about the place of forgiveness in their memorials. Do the participants of memorial rituals establish unity through a shared need for justice and retribution? The impact of memorial rituals cannot be trivialized for it is clear they satisfy a need we have as human beings to honour the one who has died with remembrances of shared moments of great joy and great sorrow. We have developed detailed rites or ceremonies to mark these passages in time. But perhaps there is another purpose or opportunity for such rituals. Is it possible for these markers to facilitate the transformation of grief from anger to acceptance, retribution to forgiveness? Further, we will suggest that, outside of specific sub-cultural norms that specify forgiveness as a pre-determined way of life, forgiveness is not common to our cultural conversation within communities. We propose that developing and including forgiveness rituals may promote a larger social transformation from revenge and retribution as empowerment to forgiveness as true power and reconciliation.

The Encyclopaedia of Social Work defines homicide as the 'wilful killing of one human being by another.' Current statistics released by the Chicago Police Department have seen a 14.6% increase in homicides in 2008. The City of Chicago reported 510 homicides in 2008, compared to 445 in 2007. On October 18, 2008, 520 people attended the 14th Annual Memorial for Victims of Homicide in Chicago, IL. This memorial is the primary avenue of remembrance for those who have lost their loved one through homicide. There is a sense of shared purpose and intent. Friends and neighbours gather and together they grieve.

The questions surrounding community and forgiveness rituals inspired a survey that 87 participants agreed to answer. We will review the findings of this survey and suggest that in fact memorial rituals that do not specify forgiveness as one of the stated intentions only marginally encourage the process of forgiveness for those participating. Many stated a desire to forgive but were unsure of what avenues were available to them to explore forgiveness.

1.　　Defining Rituals of Mourning and Forgiveness

Robert Grimes, in his book, Rite of Place; Ritual, Media and the Arts, defines ritual as 'actions characterized by a certain 'family' of qualities, for instance, that are performed, formalized, patterned, condensed, and so on.' He goes on to define ritualisation as 'activities not normally viewed as rites but treated as if they were or might be, for instance, giving birth, house cleaning... have been regarded as ritual.' He states that ritualisation is the 'act of deliberately cultivating or constructing a new rite.'

The Annual Memorial for Victims of Homicide in Chicago, although clearly a ritual, is not necessarily focused on forgiveness. The memorial has structural elements of a ritual. It occurs at roughly the same time every year. The group shares a common purpose and experience. The participants are regional; they live in the same geographical community of Cook County, IL. The recitation of victim's names and the display of photos are necessary elements to this ritual. They construct a memorial book filled with graphics and letters that the family has offered to the loved one lost to the homicide.

Of the 87 participants of the survey, the demographics were equally divided by gender. Their ages ranged from adolescence to senior citizens. The group majority claimed a Christian background. It was not surprising that 94.9% of the respondents indicated prayer as the ritual of their faith that was practiced regularly. Is the 'power of prayer' the ritual that promotes forgiveness or is the recitation of the prayer within the context of communal rituals the act that can approach forgiveness?

The emotional effects of victimization are far-reaching. Violence not only assaults/destroys the intended victim(s), it also destroys families, loved ones and communities. Our cultural choices in response to violence, with rare exception, are twofold: we are either limited to countering the emotional and psychological devastation by continuing to be victimized or we can become the perpetrator in the name of revenge or justice. New research suggests that practicing rituals of forgiveness can be a third alternative. One can be empowered without becoming the aggressor, as Alexandra Asseily, a proponent of forgiveness in Beirut Lebanon, states in *The Power of Forgiveness: A Documentary*. She states: 'Forgiveness lets us let go of the pain in the memory so the memory no longer controls us.' She says that forgiveness is 'the road to peace,' that we need to 'take the bridge to forgiveness.' Victimization, on the other hand, continues when the rage against the perpetrator is unresolved and the grief of loss is subdued and left unresolved. Alexandra has been supporting a community project in Beirut creating a garden for Christians, Muslims, and Jews to share, a place for each person to reflect on forgiveness.

Elisabeth Kubler-Ross, in her many years of working with dying patients, described five stages of grief: denial, anger, bargaining, depression, and acceptance. Acceptance is perhaps where forgiveness lies, if at all, as evidenced by the grieving process of Ellen Keyes. One typically moves from denial ('that can't have happened') to acceptance ('I am ready to accept this in my life') not in a linear fashion but like a series of spirals that circle inward to redefine our sense of what is real in our world. This movement into one's sense of reality is described very simply in Dr. Roberta Temes's book, *Living with an Empty Chair: A Guide through Grief*. She suggests three stages: numbness (mechanical functioning and social insulation), disorganization (intensely painful feelings of loss), and reorganization (re-entry into a more 'normal' social life).

Traditionally, our community memorial rituals are designed to support the early stages of grief, particularly the second stage of anger ('why is this happening to me?') in an attempt to avert the cycling of depression and despair that can come with a tragic loss. Our resources for answering this fundamental question, – 'why is this happening to me?' – are limited. Miriam Greenspan, in *Healing through the Dark Emotions*, says that we have a 'widespread ignorance about how to tolerate painful emotional energies.' She goes on to say that we need to 'honour three basic emotions that are an inevitable part of every life: grief, fear, and despair.' Anger allows for action; an opportunity, as Temes's suggests, reorganising our lives around a new purpose, revenge or retaliation.

Rituals of mourning are necessary for healing. When that grief is shared collectively through memorial ritual and prayer, the emotional isolation that the bereaved often find themselves in is now validated by the collective experience. Grief is experienced individually. Yet, it can be a group experience. With such tragic loss, there is naturally a feeling of having lost the focus of one's daily routine and purpose. It is in this sense of purposelessness that anger arises.

It is here, when the anger threatens to engulf a community as it did in San Francisco that night in 1978, that forgiveness is most needed. It is true that forgiveness is a very personal and individual experience, yet groups can validate or condemn the individual's struggle with forgiving the perpetrators of heinous crimes. Our research supports this. Of those surveyed, 91% have supported attending memorial rituals, claiming that such rituals have helped them through the grief process, through the shock and the denial and the anger.

In his book, *The Work of Mourning*, Jacques Derrida recalls the memory of his friend, author and philosopher Jean-Marie Benoist (1942-1990). Benoist stated that one must not 'drink the tear and wonder about the strangeness of its taste compared to one's own.' Derrida comments in his eulogy that '[o]ne should not develop a taste for mourning, and yet mourn we *must*. We *must*, but we must not like it – mourning, that is, mourning *itself*, if such a thing exists: not to like or love through one's own tear but only through the other, and every tear is from the other, the friend, the living, as long as we ourselves are living, reminding us, in holding life, to hold on to it.'

Stages of grief are likely to occur whether or not we develop memorial rituals or rituals of forgiveness.   But, in the constructing of community forgiveness rituals, we may be able to impact the level of personal and community distress.   Greenspan and others make a case for community rituals of forgiveness.   Greenspan suggests that we look at the possibility of community responses to public events.   She says: 'our age asks us to reevaluate the accepted notion that individual healing takes place in a social vacuum.'   Grimes notes that 'we don't have any ritual resources with which to handle traumatic public events.' This may be true for the community that comes to support the grieving family, but is it true for the closest relatives?   In some cases, it may in fact stimulate cycles of trauma and grief, leaving the family feeling as vulnerable and raw as when the incident initially occurred.

In our survey of the participants in the memorial service in Chicago, 88.6% of the respondents agree that participating in a community ritual impacted them in a positive ways.   Those surveyed described ritual as:

- an act performed on a regular basis with a defined purpose
- something practiced on a regular basis with conviction, purpose and meaning
- like an act of prayer
- a ceremony held in honour of a loved one that you have lost to show them that they are not forgotten and will be remembered through the many memories you have of them.

Ritual is a repeated act that is engaged in with mindful intent. Can cultivating forgiveness as a ritual become a successful practice in communities permeated by violence?   In *Mental Health Response to Mass Violence and Terrorism: A Training Manual* (U.S. Dept. of Health and Human Services), it is suggested that community-based rituals may 'reinforce community strengths and promote community recovery.'   Community leaders can 'foster understanding, tolerance, and forgiveness across groups through public ceremonies.'

We have seen this fostering of tolerance and forgiveness in the Amish community of Nickel Mines, Pennsylvania. Having lost 5 children in an execution-style murder by the hand of Charles Roberts in the Nickel Mines School, the community entered the grieving process free of the burden of having to seek revenge.   Forgiveness allows them the ability to absorb a wide range of possibilities in life without becoming angry with God or mired in the disappointments and sorrows of life. The community had already embraced a ritual of forgiveness that they relied upon to restore balance and unity with both small and large grievances.

Although we have limited our investigation of forgiveness rituals in communities to recent violent crimes in U.S. history, one clear example of a forgiveness ritual can be found in the Acholi tribe of Uganda. The 'Mato Oput' ceremony is conducted specifically in cases of homicide. Mato Oput involves making a bitter tea from the fruit of the oput tree. Clans of the victim and perpetrator sip the drink in a symbolic expression of reconciliation and forgiveness. An article published by the Institute of War and Peace Reporting explained how the Mato Oput ceremony has been adapted to address victims of the rebel war raged by the Lord's Resistance Army (LRA). Former rebels are able to use the ceremony as a truth-telling event combined with offers of compensation to then be able to ask for forgiveness from the victimized clan.

Greenspan suggests that we consider a new focus that in fact includes a larger community. She says: 'When we psychologise human suffering, we narrow our focus to the individual – perhaps in order to be less overwhelmed by the sheer enormity of human suffering, which, in the modern era, has reached a crescendo of atrocity.' She goes on to suggest that embracing our larger cultural grief will allow for movement through these dark emotions. Perhaps the limitation of community memorial rituals as we have known them is this focus on the healing of the individual, rather than a larger global community. Joseph Campbell, in *The Hero with a Thousand Faces*, reminds us that, in looking at great civilizations from the past, 'it becomes apparent that the purpose and actual effect of these was to conduct people across those difficult thresholds of transformation...'

Our research supports Greenspan's observation of the yearning people have for community. Of those surveyed at the Annual Memorial for Victims of Homicide in Chicago, IL. 'Community' was defined, in their open-ended responses, as:

- people reaching out and supporting and helping one another
- people you feel comfortable with and know you personally
- the place where you are accepted by everyone
- a group of people such as my neighbourhood, church or organization

The social transformative aspect of ritual can be seen when we look at the initiative to create 'Gardens of Forgiveness' at the ground zero site of the fall of the twin towers on September 11, 2001. Several of the family members who lost a loved one there have been advocating for movement to a new focus, from justice to forgiveness. They are clear that they value justice being served and, like the Amish, do not see forgiveness as an 'either/or' proposition. Yet they have come to the understanding that their individual healing process entwined with the larger global community needs to move toward forgiveness. They suggest that we decide internationally to opt out of violence and revenge. Although some victims and some communities have directly embraced forgiveness as an essential element of their healing process, others have not. Perhaps it is this tension between solidarity and unity, as an attempt to re-order life, that prevents a more active embrace of forgiveness rituals.

Grimes identifies several mourning rituals that have evolved to honour 9/11:

> The roles assigned to ritual were of wrapping victims in a blanket of comfort and of replacing factionalism with solidarity.... The terrorist attack was ritualised. In the newspaper we read translated excerpts from the preparation manual. It was a liturgical text prescribing the men's activities: Shave closely. Polish your shoes. Wear tight fitting clothes. Chant verses. Visualise your goal. Anticipate your rewards.

And finally there were the flags, as Grimes described it: 'Flags, flags, flags. Prayer flags – not Tibetan, not Zuni, but pure, 'good old' American flags.'

Yet with all of these mourning rituals none have moved us toward forgiveness. Those supporting the creation of the 'Gardens of Forgiveness' believe the creation of this sacred space would honour those who have died and provide the victims a place to reflect and forgive. Diane Horning, an advocate for the gardens whose son was killed in the attack on the twin towers, said: 'We must have something to symbolize our movement forward' (from the documentary *The Freedom of Forgiveness*).

Dr Everett Worthington is a professor of psychology who has published over 20 books on forgiveness, marriage, and family topics. As a victim of homicide his experience with forgiveness comes not just from study and research. He has had some first-hand experience with forgiveness. One New Year's Eve, his mother was brutally beaten and murdered by intruders who entered her home unaware that she was present. When she fought back, this intruder beat her to death. The perpetrator was arrested and confessed to the murder but was not convicted due to 'some issues with the evidence' taken at the scene. Worthington and his siblings declared that they had forgiven the perpetrator within 6 months of the assault. In his book *Dimensions of Forgiveness*, Worthington says: 'Genuine forgiveness constitutes an internal process that transforms the forgiver and also the one forgiven, if he or she is able to receive the gift of forgiveness.'

In our survey, we found that 49% of the people who answered the survey agree that forgiveness is important in healing from their loss. 48% believe that forgiving benefits the one forgiving and 50% believe that forgiveness is possible over time. This indicates that communities believe in, and are willing to embrace, forgiveness as part of the healing process. Forgiveness as a transforming experience is represented by the 62% who either somewhat or strongly agreed that the tragedy has deepened their understanding of life. This, alongside the stated belief that forgiveness is indeed possible, beneficial, and an important element in their healing, would indicate that forgiveness is transforming for the forgiver.

The Tariq Khamisa Foundation in San Diego was founded to support the transformation of both the one forgiving and the one forgiven. Azim Khamisa lost his son Tariq to a random homicide when he was delivering a pizza to a group of adolescents and was murdered by a 14-year-old boy named Toni Hicks. Tariq's father Azim Khamisa embraced his grief and as part of his grieving process founded the Tariq Khamisa Foundation. He is dedicated to breaking the cycle of youth violence by teaching children alternatives ways to resolve conflict. In short, he teaches forgiveness. He models these concepts in two ways: first, by teaching alongside the grandfather of Toni Hicks and, secondly, by having directly forgiven Toni Hicks who is serving a lengthy sentence for the murder. Toni, who had been abandoned by both of his parents, had been transformed by this act of forgiveness.

The Tariq Khamisa Foundation has expanded the process of forgiveness from a personal response to loss to a broader societal transformational gift. Grimes has considered this larger, global perspective and draws our attention to the work of Victor Turner who has 'articulated a new, or unrecognised, function to ritual's repertoire: social transformation.' Our research suggests that indeed people are open to sharing their grief in community while embracing forgiveness, which in turn creates the possibility of a larger social transformation. Community rituals focused on forgiveness may be the necessary final step in completing the grief process and allowing for the expansion of our choices when confronted with these tragedies. Perhaps, along with spontaneous memorials, candlelight parades, and the waving of flags, we will be simultaneously inspired to ritualise our forgiveness, and move forward reorganizing our lives with a new wisdom and deeper understanding of how to live in unity.

2.   Conclusion

There are many layers of communities affected by violence, from small neighbourhoods to entire countries. The homicide victims of Chicago represent only one such community but our research indicates that their experience is common. There is a strong need for those who have experienced violent crime to come together in community, to memorialise their loss, not in isolation, but in finding solace with others. There is an agreed-upon understanding that violence does not just affect the direct victims and their families, but, in fact, draws the entire community into the grieving process.

We have found that the memorial rituals do not delay the forgiveness process but they also do not endorse it. Forgiveness is not directly mentioned or encouraged. There remains a belief that some acts are simply unforgivable. The tension between solidarity, the joining together against a common enemy, and the internal need to forgive may have prevented communities from including rituals of forgiveness in their memorial services. Yet, forgiveness is a strong component of the healing process for almost 50% of those surveyed. This would suggest that communities are likely to embrace forgiveness rituals if they were given the opportunity. Given the power of ritual, as we have seen in the events following the attacks on the World Trade Centre in New York on September 11, the candlelight ceremony honouring Harvey Milk, and the memorial service in Chicago, it is reasonable to consider that ritual can be a vehicle for social transformation. The question is: are we willing to allow that transformation to occur? Can we move from 'creating a bridge' toward forgiveness and tolerance? The study of grief and the results of our survey would encourage us to embrace this final step in the grieving process and create such community leaders that can 'foster understanding, tolerance, and forgiveness across groups.'

Bibliography

Campbell, J., 'The Hero With A Thousand Faces'. Joseph Campbell Foundation, Novato California, 2008.

Derrida, J., 'Jean-Marie Benoist 1942-1990' in 'The Work of Mourning', University of Chicago Press, Chicago, IL 2001.

Encyclopedia of Social Work, 'Homicide', 19th edition, National Association of Social Workers Press, Washington, D.C. 1995.

Greenspan, M., Healing Through the Dark Emotions Shambala Publications, Inc., Boston Massachusetts, 2003.

Grimes, R., 'Rite of Our Place: Ritual, Media and the Arts'. Oxford University Press, New York 2006, pp.84-85, 163,12.

Kraybill, D., Nolt, S., and Weaver-Zercher, D., *'Amish Grace'*. John Wiley and Sons, Inc. San Fransisco, CA. 2007.

Kubler-Ross, E., *On Death and Dying*. Scribner Press, USA, 1997.

Oketch, B., *'Tribal Justice Takes Root'*. Institute for War and Peace Reporting, www.iwpr.net, November 10, 2008.

Temes, B., *'Living With An Empty Chair: A Guide Through Grief'*. New Horizon Press Publishers, Inc. USA. 1992.

U.S. Department of Health and Human Services, Mental Health Response to Mass Violence and Terrorism. A Training Manual. DHHS Pub. No. SMA 3959. Center for Mental Health Services, Substance Abuse and Mental Health Services Administration, Rockville, 2004.

Worthington, E., *'Dimensions of Forgiveness'*. Templeton Foundation Press, Radnor PA, 1998.

The Power of Forgiveness: A Documentary. A film by Martin Doblmeier, 2007.

The Life and Times of Harvey Milk. A film by Robert Epstein and Richard Schmeichen, 1984.

Barbara Flood, PhD., is an international speaker, award winning author and guest lecturer. She received her Ph.D. in Psychology from the University of Integrated Learning - Southern California, Masters in Social Work from the University of Wisconsin – Milwaukee and her B.A. from the University of Wisconsin – Madison. She is associated with the National Coalition against Domestic Violence. She is presently adjunct faculty in the Department of Psychology at Metropolitan College of Denver, Denver, Colorado. Barbara is a Business and Executive Coach.

Christina Tomacic-Niaros is a licensed clinical social worker residing in Chicago Illinois. She has facilitated a support group for loved ones affected by homicide for several years. Their struggles with the impact of violence in their lives has been a source of sorrow as well as inspiration. She dedicates this article to everyone affected by violent crime; you are not forgotten.